Canvas Craft

The Homesewer's Guide to Creating
Useful and Delightful Objects
From a Noble Cloth

All work, even cotton-spinning, is noble;
work is alone noble.

Thomas Carlyle

Canvas Craft

The Homesewer's Guide to Creating
Useful and Delightful Objects
From a Noble Cloth

written and illustrated by

Susan Dworski

CAPRA PRESS   1979   Santa Barbara

Library of Congress Cataloging in Publication Data

Dworski, Susan.
    Canvas craft.

    1. Textile crafts.   2. Canvas.   I. Title.
TT699.D87   746′.04   78-32138
ISBN 0-88496-090-0

Cover Design by Mary Schlesinger
Camera work by Santa Barbara Photo Engraving

CAPRA PRESS
P.O. Box 2068
Santa Barbara, CA 93120

for Jacob and Amanda

ACKNOWLEDGMENTS

A craft book, perhaps more than any other genre, depends less upon the toil of a lone writer than upon the richly collaborative effort of the many artists, designers and technicians whose personal visions and expertise converge to make the whole. To all of those whose talents have been interwoven with the production of this book, I have especial gratitude. Most particularly, I wish to thank my far-flung collaborators, the artists whose work is included here. Their willingness to share their experiences working with canvas has greatly enriched the text, as it has enriched my own life during the writing of this book.

A few special thanks, however to

Eva Roberts, whose pencils and pens demonstrate that the ordinary is extraordinary

Sarah Dixon, for her unflagging advice and inspiration

Brian McKinney, whose knowledge of silkscreen is exceeded only by his mastery of chess

Wendy Drake for being there at the beginning

Harry Butler for his textile knowledge and technical assistance

Olivia Batchelder for magically appearing on the other side of the mountain

Judy Young, my editor, whose efficient, quiet hand steadied the production throughout.

Mary Schlesinger, the book's designer, whose special talent was to see it beautifully and to see it whole.

Table of Contents

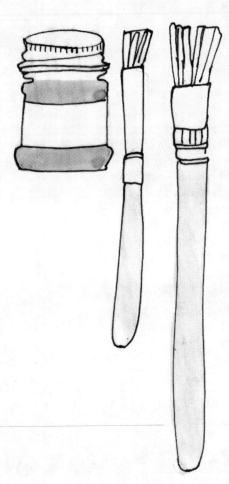

A ship is the noblest of all man's works—a cunning fabric of wood, and iron, and hemp, wonderfully propelled by wings of canvas, and seeming at times to have the very breath of life.

James N. Hall
Charles Wordhoff

A Short
History of Canvas

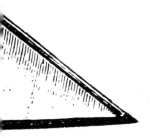

A bivouac of a large train is a very picturesque sight. The white canvas of the wagons and the tents resemble a small village, while the campfires shed their ruddy light on the surrounding darkness with its ever-changing hues, making the increasing darkness more impenetrable.

J. Henry Brown

The history of canvas is as interwoven with man's explorations as are the warp and weft threads of this durable fabric. Without these goods, ships would never have sailed forth —"wonderfully propelled by wings of canvas"—and the entire westering of European man would not have been achieved. As many as 2500 years before the birth of Christ, papyrus boats plied the slow-moving surface of the Nile, thrust down the Red Sea, and along the African coast in search of gold, slaves and ivory. One such voyage carved on an ancient temple wall clearly shows a ship carried by a square sail. Whether this sail was cotton, linen or hemp canvas is not known, but canvas it was.

The earliest history of cotton canvas in Europe is sketchy at best, often hemp and linen were interwoven with the shorter cotton fibers to add strength and durability. It appears that the culture of cotton is very ancient and probably began in the Indus Valley. Alexander the Great carried the knowledge of the cotton plant back with him after his conquests in Asia Minor, and Herodotus makes reference to a "wooly plant." During the time of Mohammed, the Moors brought cotton plants to Spain, where its culture flourished. It was said that the weaving and dyeing of cotton in Spain compared favorably with that of Baghdad and Damascus. Today, cotton grows wild along the busy highways of Spain, competing with billboard advertisements, a poignant memory of a far-off age.

Most of the canvas produced in Spain, Marseilles and Genoa during the 13th through the 17th centuries was destined for sailcloth, and it was much finer in texture than that used by the early Mediterranean sailors. However, it was not more cleverly decorated than that carried by the ancient ships. Early Egyptian sails were often embellished with brilliantly appliqued designs, or dyed deep, majestic colors.

The Athenians dyed their ropes and sails the color of seawater to keep them out of sight of their enemies. They also patched their sails with multitudes of colored canvas, and wove various devices into the rough sailcloth. The emblems of an emperor were displayed in characters of shimmering gold upon the cloth. The Norsemen often striped their sails with blood red dyes to symbolize the destruction they wrought. In later centuries the sails of Spanish galleons carrying gold back from the New World were painted with huge multi-colored portraits of saints. The Portugese ships were known by the gigantic crosses which emblazoned their mainsails.

The mills of southern France and Spain turned day and night spinning and weaving massive lengths of canvas to outfit the adventurous ships that opened up the globe to European influence. It is impossible to gauge the profound influence this sturdy fabric had on world history, for at that time those giant ships could only have been propelled by the force of wind on their sails.

In the 1840s another migration started, this one across the beckoning distance of the American continent. Again, canvas was essential to the trip. Trains of white-topped wagons up to three quarters of a mile long made their way across the Great Plains to a new life in the Far West. The pioneers often found traveling difficult in their Conestoga wagons. Constructed of hardwoods and iron, the wagon's sole concession to comfort was the canvas cover which protected the travelers. Waterproofed with linseed oil, the canvas top often had pockets and slings sewn on its interior by handy wives to provide extra storage space.

Canvas came West with the settlers not only by land but also by sea. During the two decades after the discovery of gold in California, the sea

And when the squall came (for it's squally off there by Patagonia) and all hands—visitors and all—were called to reef topsail, we were so top-heavy that we had to swing each other aloft in the bowlines; and we ignorantly furled the skirts of our jackets into the sails, so that we hung there, reefed fast in the howling gale.

Herman Melville

lanes between Boston and San Francisco saw fierce competition as the big clippers vied to make the best time. The work must have been intolerable for the ships' crews who were forced to spend most of their time aloft on the yardarms, reefing and unfurling the masses of heavy canvas that would give their ship an edge over its hardpressing competitor. Some of the largest ships carried an impressive two acres of canvas aloft.

Canvas stored the westering traveler's goods and provided a shroud for others less fortunate who died en route. It duffled the necessities for thousands of seasick passengers rounding the Horn, and in native villages often provided an uneasy night's rest.

Canvas tents were pitched around newly discovered lodes in the gold country of Colorado and California. Lumber mills were scarce in those days and labor was concentrated in the diggings, so canvas housing was quite common. One traveler even described a hotel whose second story and front were entirely composed of canvas, with the name "The Empire" painted on in huge letters. Imposing as "The Empire" must have been, one wonders how much protection the shifting canvas could have provided against the heavy Sierra storms.

It took Doc Baggs, a master conman operating in Denver during the gold rush, to push this notion of a canvas front one larcenous step further. A circumspect but thorough mountebank, Doc Baggs rigged up an elaborate office, including a fake safe of canvas. The safe was actually a tromp l'oeil painting on canvas glued to thin panels of wood. His customers would make deposits which Doc would place in the fake safe. After the suckers had been fleeced, he'd take the money and the masterfully painted safe, and walk away whistling.

Canvas has long been linked with entertainment, though usually of a

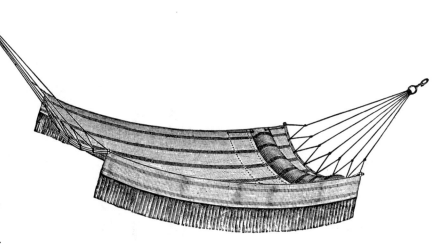

The owner of the hut swung my hammock awhile, and I turned in to secure it for the night. To lie there was one thing, to sleep was another. A dozen natives crowded around the table, drinking aguardiente and disputing vehemently; the cooking fire was on one side of me, and every one who passed to and fro was sure to give me a thump, while my weight swung the hammock so low, that all the dogs on the premises were constantly rubbing their backs under me.

Byard Taylor

more legitimate kind than Doc Baggs provided. Touring dramatic shows were constantly on the move from one western town to another, and a band of notorious women from Lola Montez to Mme. Nellie Melba appeared before the painted canvas backdrops. These portable stages were most elaborately painted and embellished lavishly with gold leaf. It was not much later that traveling circuses began touring the Far West. These were modest affairs and it was not until Barnum and Bailey that they became known as two and three ring circuses, all under the canvas Big Top.

It remained for the United States military to complete the westering begun by the Phoenecians and the Greeks. Not under brilliant canvas wings this time did the armies move, but under countless yards of olive duck. Wherever armies marched there was canvas. Officers and enlisted men alike logged through swamps on gaitered canvas legs and shivered under canvas pup tents during monsoon downpours. They stored their treasured love letters from home in canvas duffles and covered their guns, trucks, jeeps and canteens with it. And, if fate were unlucky, they recuperated in jungle hospitals on canvas cots.

Wherever man has ventured across the globe, canvas has provided him with shelter, transportation and clothing. The same canvas that harnessed the winds for ancient Mediterranean sailors clothed the doughty crew of the Pequod on its search for Moby Dick. The canvas that protected pioneer women and children from the scorching Utah sun later provided a recreational canoe for their great-great-grandsons as they fished in the Russian River. With what beauty, utility and efficiency canvas bends itself to man's devising. As we take this material to hand, as we shape it, stitch it, paint, stuff and design it, we join ourselves to the long line of artisans who have worked with this noble textile.

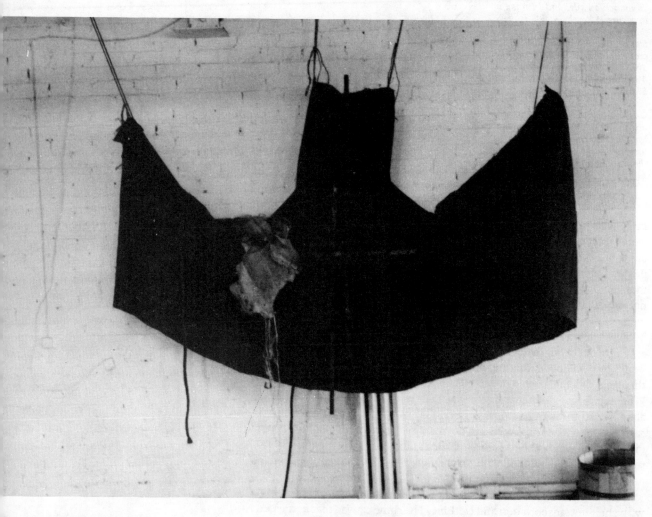

Lorraine Farrow
Fisher of Men
Canvas, sticks, rope, hair, tree mould, cheesecloth, leather

Canvas: What It Is
Where To Buy It
How To Sew It

What Canvas Is

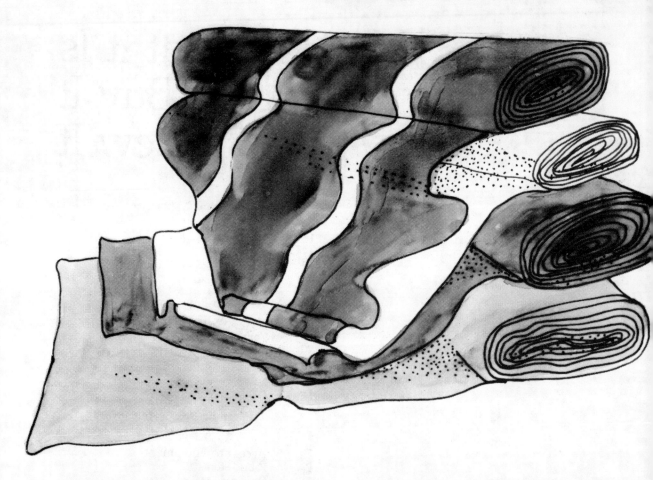

The type of canvas used in this book is made of 100% cotton and is generally referred to in the textile trade as "duck." Duck is a name applied to a broad range of heavy, flat woven fabrics made for uses other than clothing. The name derives from a trademark of a duck stencilled on sailcloth imported to this country from Scotland and England prior to the mid-19th century. "Doeck" is a Dutch word meaning heavy cotton cloth. There are eight basic types of duck used in the United States. Generally speaking, the canvas you will find readily available at awning,

sailmaking or fabric outlets will be one of three kinds: *army duck, ounce duck* or *number duck.*

Although all the different basic types of ducks are now woven in a great variety of widths, they were originally made in just one width. This original width was used as the weight basis for these ducks, therefore, the ounce classification of ducks may not bear any resemblance to their actual weight. If this seems confusing, it is. Peruse any catalog of a major textile supplier and you will find yourself awash in pages of weight-width tables.

Army Duck   Army duck is the cloth used for almost every project in this book. This canvas is known in the trade as "10.10" which means it is 30-31 inches wide and 10.10 ounces per square yard. It has usually been treated to repel water and mildew, and is used most often for awnings, tents, hammocks, wading pools, and coveralls.

Canvas comes in a range of bright colors. An overall list would include the following:

White	Field Green (Billiard)
Dark Green	Black (Indo Carbon)
Chrome Yellow	California Blue (Medium)
Red (Napthol)	Linen (Light Flax)
Royal Blue	Turquoise Blue
Tangerine	Lemon Yellow
Lemon	Earth Brown (Coffee)
Sunset (Brick)	Navy (Midnight Blue)
Corn (Beige)	Maize (Light Cream)

Occasionally available are pink, salmon, powder blue, purple, lilac, olive green, and pearl gray although these are special dye lots and might have to be purchased from bolt ends by your local fabric outlet. Burgundy, pumpkin and sky blue are sometimes available in bolt ends from tennis shoe manufacturers. If you need these colors and cannot find them locally, you can substitute sailcloth. This can be bonded with fusible webbing first to give it the body of canvas, and can be worked into any of the projects with success.

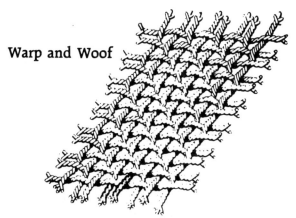

Warp and Woof

Ounce Duck and Number Duck   Ounce duck and number duck are natural, off-white canvas that has been sized lightly. The cloth retains its natural oils (and lovely smell) and is quite naturally water-repellant. Ounce duck goes up to 14.90 ounces per square yard, 8 ounce being the lightest, and 14.90 ounces being quite heavy. 12 ounce duck is the heaviest duck I have found sewable in a home machine. After 14.90 ounces, the nomenclature of canvas changes, and it is called number duck. The numbering now begins to decrease as the weight of the fabric increases. # 12 duck is 11.45 ounces per square yard, #10 duck is 14.73 ounces per square yard, and so forth down to #4 duck which is a hefty 24.54 ounces per yard. Number duck is the heaviest and strongest fabric used today and it is made into mailbags, golf bags, tents, hammocks, sails, and waterbuckets.

Synthetic Canvas   There are several synthetic canvases on the market, you can find them at the manufacturers listed in the back index. They come in colors even brighter than cotton duck, and are often completely fade-resistant. However, the feel and the manueverability of synthetic canvas is inferior to that made of 100% cotton. It has a rubbery feel, seams don't lie flat, and it warps under a hot iron. The natural cotton will do your bidding more readily. If you want to experiment with synthetic canvas, use it for large, flat projects that don't require much shaping. It is fine for applique, too, but don't try to apply paint, inks, or dyes to synthetic canvas. In some cases you may have to substitute acrylic canvas or bonded cotton for duck.

Where to Buy Canvas

Canvas is available at several specialized stores, and some fabric stores. You'll probably find that fabric stores are limited in the weights and colors of canvas that they carry. However, if you are willing to do a little hunting you can find any kind of canvas you need. Look in the yellow pages of the phone book, check for these listings: Awnings, Auto Trim, Boat Covers & Tops, Canvas, Canopies, Tarpaulins, Tent Rental, and Upholstery. Generally speaking, the shops found under these listings will welcome retail yardage trade. They very often buy large shipments of canvas and have short lengths left over from contract jobs. You can even dicker over the price of roll ends if you are inclined towards bargaining.

When you buy canvas yardage, find out if it has been treated in any way. Manufacturers often buy canvas that has been processed to make it water-repellent, mildew-resistant, or flame-retardant. If you intend to embellish the canvas with any paints, dyes, or inks it is best to use UNtreated yardage.

Remember that you may have to search for the specific colors you want. Be prepared to adjust your project to whatever colors are available. In some cases you may have to substitute synthetic canvas or bonded cotton for canvas duck.

How to Sew It

Your Workspace   You will need a large, flat place for laying out your canvas. A smooth work-table is ideal, but a floor will do nicely for cutting and measuring. If you are planning a large project you will want to have a spacious area where you can lay out the pattern pieces and visualize your progress. This is especially important when laying out applique. Clear away enough space so the entire project can be viewed at one time.

When sewing, you will find it *very* helpful if you have another table stretching out to the left of your sewing table. This second table can be anything that is flat and approximately the same height as your sewing table. Large, heavy, obstreperous canvas yardage can then be laid across this table while you are sewing. Otherwise the weight of the goods will drag down onto the floor, pulling your seams crooked and fraying your temper. If you haven't access to a second table of some sort, then you can

19

try sewing large pieces on the floor itself, the way sailmakers work. You will need a foot treadle and not a knee-bar on your machine for this. As you feed the material through the machine, the bulk will Iie flat out to the left of you, neat and unwrinkled. The rest of the canvas must be rolled to slip under the machine arm. Lay a sheet or tarp on the floor before trying this.

Your Sewing Machine   Almost every sewing machine can sew canvas up to 10 ounces per yard. That is the weight of common, vat dyed cotton duck. For heavier canvas, you will want a machine with a powerful motor of relatively recent vintage. Additionally, it is helpful to have a zigzag or satin stitch attachment. Those of you who cherish an old, vintage Singer should not hesitate to sew a project. Just be aware that raw edges which are not zigzagged or overcast will ravel, and ravel! If you are an experienced sewer you will find ways to circumvent this problem by using rolled or felled seams wherever feasible.

Before sewing, you must make sure your machine is in tip-top working order. This is especially important in working with canvas because the machine will inevitably strain from time to time as you stitch through several layers of heavy cloth. Don't make it work harder than it has to. Have the drive belt and the clutch checked. Keep the machine clear of fuzz and threads. Oil it often. Cover it when not in use. Dirt and dust are your machine's greatest enemies. Love your machine and take care of it. It is one of mankind's greatest tools.

Secondly, understand your machine. Study the manufacturer's manual carefully. Learn the names of the parts and what they do. Be aware of what kinds of breakdowns can occur and why. Don't be intimidated by your machine and just sort of hope that it will work. If you have lost the manual, go to a local shop for a new one, or write to the manufacturer. I cannot stress this enough. Familiarize yourself with the potential of your machine and you will enlarge your sewing horizons.

20

Tips for Sewing Canvas

Sewing canvas requires using certain techniques and precautions that are not required when sewing dress fabrics. A few tips will be helpful if you have not worked with it before.

- Use the heaviest needle possible for sewing on canvas. A size 16 or 18 is best. Have plenty on hand. Do not try to get away with a lighter needle, it is guaranteed to break. Remember, too, that you may need to switch to a thinner needle when appliqueing with satin stitching.

- All the seams in this book are ½ inch wide, unless otherwise indicated. This may be hard for a dressmaker to adjust to. An easy way to mark this is by sticking a strip of masking tape along the side of your throat plate. This will keep all your seam allowances even.

- Canvas is stiff and heavy. Its structural—even architectural—qualities will be omnipresent as you work on a large, unwieldy project. As large projects, particularly "enclosed" objects like luggage, near completion they will be bulky and defiant. You will coin new obscenities as you try to sew around one last, recalcitrant corner.

- Canvas ravels. A lot. Before you begin putting together a project, take the time to zigzag the free edges of the pattern pieces. This is tedious, but necessary for a good finish, especially if you intend to wash the item.

- Canvas does not turn inside out easily. Small, pointy enclosed shapes are not particularly well suited to canvas.

- Mark cutting lines and designs with tailor's crayon. You can draw right on the fabric with this yellow or white wax. It irons away easily.

- Bend foldlines, pleats or hems with the flat of your hand. This is very helpful to remember while you work. It is easy to mark a seam line, the center of a bag, or a pleat by folding it and pressing down with your hand. Canvas creases easily.

- Canvas wrinkles very easily too, and the wrinkles can be difficult to iron out. So handle it smoothly.

- Always use high quality threads when working with canvas. Cotton wrapped polyester will work best on these projects, but if it isn't good thread it will split when you zigzag. If you work with any synthetic canvas, use a synthetic thread.

- When sewing, watch out for pins sticking towards you. Canvas has no give, and the pins can drive into the side of your hand while you feed the material through the machine.

Yardages   The project patterns have been designed to maximize the use of canvas yardage for the home sewer, to make it easy to you to cut and understand the logistics of the construction, and to save you money. Unless otherwise stated, the yardages given are based on 30-inch 10 ounce duck. However, you may be able to buy only 48- or 60-inch yardage from your supplier. The table below gives an approximate conversion table to assist you as you shop. But when in doubt, err on the generous side.

Approximate Yardage Conversion Chart

Fabric Width	30-31"	36"	48"	60"
Yardage	$1^7/_8$	$1\frac{3}{4}$	$1\frac{1}{4}$	1
	$2\frac{1}{4}$	2	$1\frac{1}{2}$	$1\frac{1}{4}$
	$2\frac{1}{2}$	$2\frac{1}{4}$	$1^5/_8$	$1^3/_8$
	$2\frac{3}{4}$	$2\frac{1}{2}$	$1\frac{3}{4}$	$1^5/_8$
	$3^1/_8$	$2^7/_8$	2	$1\frac{3}{4}$
	$3^3/_8$	$3^1/_8$	$2\frac{1}{4}$	$1^7/_8$
	$3\frac{3}{4}$	$3^3/_8$	$2^3/_8$	2
	4	$3\frac{3}{4}$	$2^5/_8$	$2\frac{1}{4}$
	$4^3/_8$	$4\frac{1}{4}$	$2\frac{3}{4}$	$2^3/_8$
	$4^5/_8$	$4\frac{1}{2}$	3	$2^5/_8$
	5	$4\frac{3}{4}$	$3\frac{1}{4}$	$2\frac{3}{4}$
	$5\frac{1}{4}$	5	$3^3/_8$	$2^7/_8$

Enlarging Patterns   Each pattern in this book has the scale indicated on it. Usually, 1 square represents 1 inch, making it easy to translate the pattern drawings into fabric. The exact dimensions of the pattern pieces are also given in case you are uncertain. In large projects, the scale changes to 2 or more inches per square. Always check the scale before you cut out. Some of the patterns overlap on the page, but this need not be a problem if you take a little time at first. In many instances you *will not* need to make paper patterns of the pieces, but can cut the canvas out directly. Use a straight edge ruler or T-square and wax tailor's chalk to measure and mark the canvas surface directly. Most of the patterns are on the straight grain of the canvas so you can line up selvages and cut with ease.

When you are working with curved pieces or applique shapes you will have to enlarge the patterns in the book. You can do this on purchased pattern paper (already marked off in ¼-inch increments) or any large sheet of paper. Use brown wrapping paper, tracing paper, newsprint or rolls of shelf paper. On the paper mark off a grid large enough to accomodate the pattern pieces you are enlarging. Make the grid correspond to the scale indicated on the pattern. For instance, if the scale is 2 inches per square, then the squares in your grid would be 2 inches on a side. A 1-inch scale would correspond to 1-inch squares.

Now number and letter the squares in the book and the larger squares on your paper grid. Give each corresponding square the same number-letter. Start with square "1A" and begin drawing on the large square whatever you see in the small square and voila . . . the pattern is enlarged.

Now a word about accuracy: When enlarging pattern pieces it is very important to be accurate. If your pattern pieces aren't measured and reproduced *carefully* then corners won't fit, edges won't match, and you will have a strange object. Accuracy isn't as critical on the applique shapes since they are usually designed to decorate. Usually it is vital only that applique pieces cover one another in a design.

Transferring Designs to Canvas   If you want to transfer a design to canvas before drawing or painting it, use this simple method. First, enlarge the design on a larger sheet of paper. Then, you trace the enlarged design onto tracing paper or thin typing paper with a black, felt tip pen. Place a sheet of dressmaker's carbon between your design and the canvas. Tape it all down with masking tape. Now trace around the design again, this time with a pencil or an empty ball point pen. The carbon will transfer the design onto the canvas.

In most fabric stores, you can buy a transfer pencil to simplify this process. In this case, you would turn over the enlarged design and trace around it on the back of the paper with the transfer pencil. Flip the tracing paper over so the image made with the transfer pencil is face down on the canvas. Iron the paper with a hot iron to imprint the image on the canvas. There are many other methods of transferring a design to fabric, but my experience has shown these to be the least complicated and time consuming.

Sewing Jargon   The sewing projects that follow in this book are generally quite straightforward, requiring little in the way of specialized sewing techniques. You will use only a straight stitch and a zigzag or satin stitch. Here are several terms that will appear again and again in the instructions:

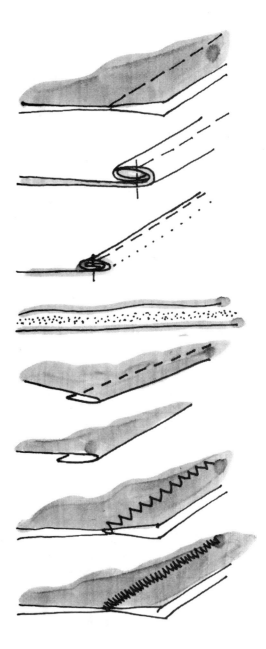

- Plain Seam:
  Place fabric right sides together, edges even. Join edges by a line of even stitching ½ inch from the edge.
- Rolled seam: .
  Place fabric right sides together. Edges are folded under ¼ inch to one side, then folded again ¼ inch more and stitched through center of roll.
- Felled seam:
  Fabric is placed *wrong* sides together, edges even. Sew a plain seam. Trim one seam allowance ¼ inch. Fold the longer edge over the shorter, fold down flat and stitch edge.
- Sandwich:
  A layer of lining fabric, one or two layers of polyester batting, a layer of canvas.
- Topstitch:
  Edge of fabric is rolled to back and stitched ¼ or ½ inch from edge with long stitches. Decorative thread may be used.
- Turn under:
  Turn pre-zigzagged or overcast edge towards inside, or back.
- Zigzag Stitch:
  Since canvas ravels so easily, you should zigzag any edges that will be left exposed on your project. Set your machine for a medium zigzag and go around the raw edges before assembling the pieces. This will make a neat and sturdy edge, one that won't ravel apart.
- Satin Stitch:
  A tight zigzag stitch, often used in machine embroidery and embellishing the projects. When appliqueing, a small satin stitch is best for completely adhering the fabrics together. However, in embroidering and decorating interesting effects can be achieved by varying the size of the satin stitch.

Access To Equipment

The home sewer familiar with dressmaking may not know where to buy some of the equipment needed to make the projects in this book. Everything is readily available if you just know where to look for it. The following lists give you a general idea of where to go for the equipment you will need. Too, become familiar with awning, or sailmaking stores in your area. They can offer much that will work well with canvas. Search your hardware, art, and fabric stores for unusual and beautiful items; the more you experiment with novel equipment the more you will enlarge your sewing repertory. The appendix also includes a list of sources.

Fabric Stores

sharp dressmaker scissors
pointed embroidery scissors
#16 or #18 machine needles
quality threads
clear plastic ruler
compass
tailor's chalk
embroidered ribbons
transfer carbon
glass headed straight pens
tape measurer
straight edge
T-square
gripper snaps
purse handles
brass rings
polyurethane stuffing
   & batting

"D" rings
overall buckles
webbing
Velcro
cording
vinyl
frogs
fringe, braids
bodkin
purse clasps
polyurethane pellets
shredded foam
upholstery cording
grommets and
   setter

Hardware Stores

grommets and setter
snap-shackle
wooden dowels
wood stain
enamel paints
spring-loaded curtain rod
electric drill and bits
quick links
masking tape
varnish or shellac
gram measuring cups
awning snaps
eyebolts with washers & nuts

paintbrushes
"S" hooks
aluminum pipe
wire
wire cutters
wood, lumber
rasp
sandpaper
nylon cord
rope
chain
scale

Art, Craft, or Hobby Stores

acetate
stencil paper
fabric paint
marking pens
stencils
stencil ink
X-acto knife & blades
brushes
watercolor inks
silkscreen inks
silkscreen kits and equipt.

India ink
acrylic paint
lino blocks
lino cutting tools
florist's tape
lino inks
rubber cement
fabric crayons
brayers
fabric dyes

Needlework or Weaving Stores

needlepoint mesh
assorted yarns
needlepoint yarns & needles

silk cording
upholstery cording

Fire-Retardant Canvas   Canvas, being natural cotton, burns easily. A good method of treating canvas to reduce the fire hazard is by spraying or brushing with a solution of:

- ½ cup ammonium phosphate (available at garden supply stores)
- 1 cup ammonium chloride (available at drugstores or chemical supply stores)
- 1 quart water.

Mix together and store in a glass or plastic container. Re-treat canvas if it has been rained upon, the solution is water-soluble. Useful for projects you would place in a child's room; it won't make the canvas fireproof, but rather *fire-retardant*.

If you don't want to mix your own fire-retardant solution you can buy a commercially manufactured one at industrial supply stores, or look under Fire Protection Equipment in the yellow pages.

Embellishing Canvas:
Techniques of
Hand and Heart

Throughout this chapter you will see photos of works contributed by guest artists working in canvas. The wide diversity of vision in these pieces indicates how protean a fabric canvas is. Hopefully, they will stimulate your own experimentation with canvas and lead you to find your own personal aesthetic vision.

Techniques of Embellishment

Cotton canvas is a generic material, in the same sense that clay and glass are generic. Natural, unpretentious and even-textured, canvas has that receptive quality of all great source materials, the ability to be worked and transformed by the hands of each artist, to be the quiet vessel of his or her particular vision. No longer content with merely stretching canvas on wooden bars and painting its surface, artists and craftspeople are wrapping, dyeing, twisting, batiking, embroidering, blueprinting, fringeing, and even burning it. The techniques used to embellish canvas are seemingly limitless, and with a little attention to a few particularities of the fabric, one can create almost any effect. Approaches to the ornamentation of canvas may be as simple and direct as appliqueing bands of color together, or as baroque as the impulse to stud a duck jacket with rivets and colored rhinestones. Whatever the impulse, this integration of beauty and usefulness has always been the task of the handcraftsman. Recent industrial design has attempted to sweep away ornamentation in favor of the efficiency of function, but the urge towards decoration persists. A frieze of silly stencilled rabbits on the hem of a canvas apron, or a plush needlepointed panel on the side of a shopping tote add nothing to the usefulness of the object — nothing, except the vital elements of surprise and delight.

It is basic for the craftsperson to create visual pleasure with his handmade objects. The humble everyday canvas projects in this book — bags, hammocks, toys, backrests, boots — are designed to be used hard and often. They are not meant to last forever but, like quilts, cups, bowls and chairs, baskets, masks and hats, they are meant to be handled, enjoyed, and allowed to age naturally.

The projects that follow employ a variety of embellishment techniques, some familiar from childhood and others more abstruse, like blueprinting. Experienced sewers and textile devotees will no doubt be familiar with most, if not all these processes. But it is hoped that a reiteration of their essentials will provoke those readers to conceiving new combinations of techniques — for instance space dyeing, ripping and then interweaving canvas strips to form the sides of a simple tote — and that the contemplation of new decorative approaches will stimulate even experienced craftspeople afresh.

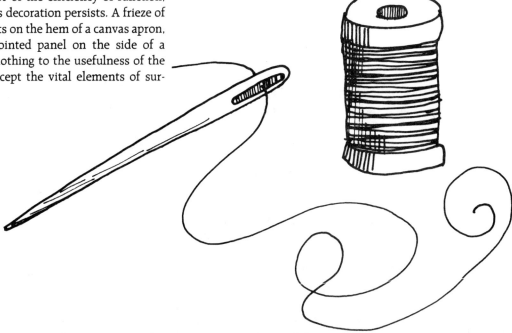

The reader may choose to complete the canvas projects using no embellishment whatsoever. If so, they shall remain strong, utilitarian and pleasing objects. But they may also be looked upon as building blocks of color, upon which you express your own perceptions about the world (by drawing), shout at the world (by lettering), or relax into the world (by stuffing). Because canvas is so receptive, so "docile" and accepting of different modes of ornamentation, it has a universal appeal. A certain day, a certain mood, may propel you into the making of a perfectly plain, abstemiously off-white bag with a dozen pockets for your personal arsenal of junk. Another day might find you willing to spend five hours locked in a dialogue with an 8-inch square of army duck and a rainbow of dye bottles, painting an elaborate paisley design onto the outside of a tiny evening bag. Later you might heartily rip up scraps of canvas to fringe the bottom of a banner for the front porch.

Canvas is capable of withstanding almost infinite forms of torture while still retaining its integrity. In that sense it is similar to its cousin, blue denim, the fabric star of the past decade. During the 1960s denim jeans and jackets underwent extraordinary and surreal transmogrifications at the hands of stitchers, painters, rivetters, furriers and crocheters, resulting in a wholly new concept of personalized, ecologically responsible, grass-roots fashion. The denim craze became a kind of textile-Populism the banner of which was a worn pair of Levis whose ripped and reembroidered buttocks bespoke eloquent human histories.

Like denim, canvas becomes in different hands, variously stark and architectural, faded and friendly, patched and memory-laden, or grandiose and overpowering. When you begin your project lay the cutout pattern pieces on your worktable and study them for awhile, letting your own notions about their embellishment, or non-embellishment take shape. The big canvas sides of the Art Portfolio, for instance, may cry out to you for SUPER graphic stencilled letters. Or they may provoke you into sloshing on wildly original acrylic color washes which you later amplify with delicate drawings in ink. The embellishments within each project are intended merely as suggestions. As you look through the graphed pattern pages you will notice that most of the patterns are flat, making the projects quite simple to construct. Darts and tricky curves have generally been avoided so that the sewer will be able to devote more time to the pleasurable pursuit of hand decoration. It is always astonishing to see how even the most basic tote bag can be completely personalized by the addition of painting, applique, quilting, or printing.

A length of cotton canvas is like a whitewashed wall, fresh, beautifully functional, complete in itself. But who can say that a passer-by might not enjoy the addition of a glossy rainbow arching across the wall's surface, the dusty tattooed pattern of an errant handball, or the surprise of a poetic piece of graffiti to entertain him on his stroll. Embellishment on canvas is like that — a place where you can flaunt your colors, strut your stuff, tell your story in ink, paint, or stitching.

To Wash or Not to Wash

Natural off-white canvas as well as vat dyed canvas of every weight has been treated with sizing to give it body. Sizing is a combination of starch, oils and plastic resins that give the cloth a smooth finish and make it stronger. The sizing makes it difficult for dyes and pigments to penetrate the fabric. The amount of sizing in canvas varies according to the weight and the manufacturer. To test your canvas, drip a small droplet of water on the corner of the fabric. The faster it is absorbed, the less sizing it has in it. Vat dyed canvas duck is additionally treated with a water- and stain-resistant finish which makes it even more difficult — although not impossible — to draw or paint upon.

Obviously, canvas that has had the sizing removed will hold color better than canvas that has not. However, being a natural fiber, cotton canvas has a nasty habit of wrinkling badly when washed. These wrinkles are sometimes nearly impossible to remove. The best results may be had by ironing the canvas with a HOT iron while it is damp, or with a dampened press cloth. Another successful method is to run the fabric through an old-fashioned mangle, the kind that used to be in every home for finishing sheets and pillowcases. Unfortunately, not many of us today have access to a mangle. Therefore you will have to make a decision as you approach printing on the surface of your canvas as to whether you want a crisp, unwrinkled finish on your printed tote, with the risk that much of the color may leach from the fabric, or whether you prefer a colorfast print job on slightly wrinkled goods.

Some projects in the book are clearly not made to be washed, like the Nesting Bubbis whose delicate faces and detailed costumes would be destroyed in the washing machine. Others, like the Baby-All, are printed with fabric paints especially made to be colorfast through many washings and dryings.

31

Washing Canvas Before Applying Color

Generally speaking you will be painting or dyeing natural, off-white canvas, however the washing instructions apply to vat dyed goods as well. In order to remove the oil and starch in the sizing, wash the canvas yardage in detergent and hot water and rinse thoroughly. Canvas shrinks up to 10%, so if you cut out the pattern pieces first and then wash them, cut each pattern *larger* than the actual pattern piece needed. Then, after the canvas has dried and been ironed, you can cut out each piece accurately. To completely remove the sizing with the resins, you need to wash the canvas in a solution of Sal-Soda washing soda and detergent. This washing can be done in a machine or in a bathtub by hand, with a sturdy brush.

The business of wrinkling is perhaps the only disadvantage encountered in painting or printing on prewashed canvas. If true machine-washability is demanded of a canvas item, then it is best to use it plain or appliqued. Otherwise, there is no reason not to forge ahead and experiment with all kinds of surface embellishment. I have a bag silkscreened with white letters on deep green duck which was Scotchguarded after completion, and which has gone for several years without needing to be washed. If a design idea presents itself to you which needs to be executed on crisply finished goods right off the bolt, yet you also want to print or paint on it, by all means prepare to sacrifice practicality and permanence for inspiration.

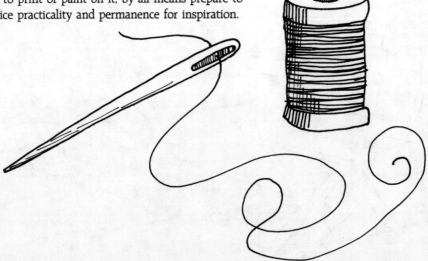

Printing On Canvas

Canvas is a natural for any kind of printing technique. Some of the simplest potato or vegetable prints are often the most effective owing to the felicitous combination of the rough, uneven designs and the rustic associations engendered by the cloth itself. More sophisticated techniques, such as silkscreening and airbrushing are just as successful, and offer intriguing possibilities for the craftsperson wishing to work in multiples, or even in the manufacture of canvas items.

Pigments, Dyes, Inks and Markers

There are many kinds of colors that may be adhered to canvas with varying degrees of success. Among them are:

Artists' oils:
Stiff when dry, these crack with handling.

Household water-base paints:
Not washable and fade rapidly.

Drawing inks: These come in a fine range of colors and are fun to work with. They are not always waterproof (except India ink). Luma Inks are permanent drawing inks that are fast to light but fade in washing. Dr. Martin's Radiant Watercolors offer a brilliant range of aniline dyes which will eventually fade in sunlight and wash out, but which are such fun to work with on canvas that they must be included. They are suitable for detailed items like ethnic bags and for wall hangings which will not be exposed to direct light.

Joanne Hammer
Landscape for a Dream
Canvas, acrylic paint, batting, aluminum

Acrylic paints: Fast to washing but *not* dry cleaning, these come in bright, pre-mixed colors and can be purchased in small amounts. The pigments are powerful and permanent if washed by hand in cold water. They may be thinned with large amounts of water and used in a plastic spray bottle to give an airbrushed effect. They are also good on large areas, like hammocks, when fabric paints would be much too expensive. Experiment with wetting the canvas first, then applying thin washes.

Fabric crayons: Cheap and remarkably effective, crayons work well on canvas, although they work best on synthetics. The image is slightly blurred on canvas, owing to the rough weave. They are not totally fast to washing. Children's drawings transfer well in fabric crayons.

Block printing inks: Oil-based inks work well for lino block or found object prints. They tend to be stiff, though.

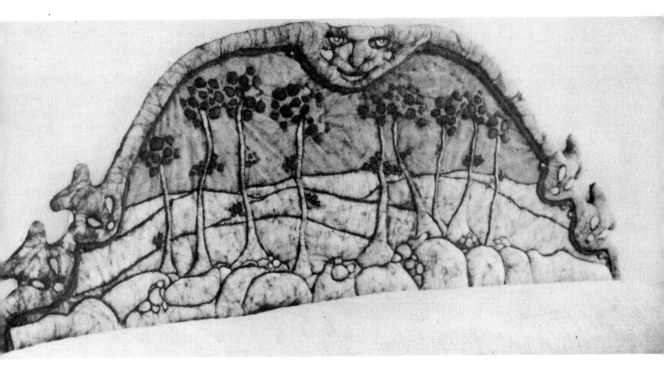

Karin Russo
Headboard
Canvas, batik dyes

Fabric paints:

Designed especially for fabric, these come in water-base or oil-base. Dylon, Versatex and Hot Air are water-base. Prang is oil-base. They have a thick consistency, but may be thinned by using an extender and a binder to hold the color. Made colorfast by heat, these paints are very successful on canvas. They may be applied directly out of the jar, or thinned. Do not buy a kit unless you are completely boggled by mixing colors. With red, yellow, blue and white you can mix up a rainbow.

Silkscreen inks:

Water-base or oil-base, these inks work extremely well on canvas. Your choice would depend upon your silkscreen block-out. If you do not wish to pre-wash the canvas first, use oil-base printing ink.

Marking pens:

Brilliant colors and fun to use, pens come in a wide range of colors and nib widths. Be sure and choose permanent pens for work on items which will be washed. Even then, the colors will fade and run somewhat. Handwash quickly in cold water. Do not hang dripping wet, they will run. Nibs can be sharpened with a razor blade or X-acto knife. Colors are transparent compared to paints. Pens bleed a little in use. Allow for bleed-line by coloring *inside* the outline of your shape.

Batik dyes:

Add thickener to create a dye paste that can be brushed or pounced onto the canvas. Dyes are transparent rather than opaque like fabric paints, and a very different effect is created. Be sure and follow manufacturer's instructions exactly to set the color and remove thickener after application. Procion is the best dye for all-over dyeing, though attempts to dye yardage in general are not too successful and the results are not anywhere near the intensity of vat dyed canvas.

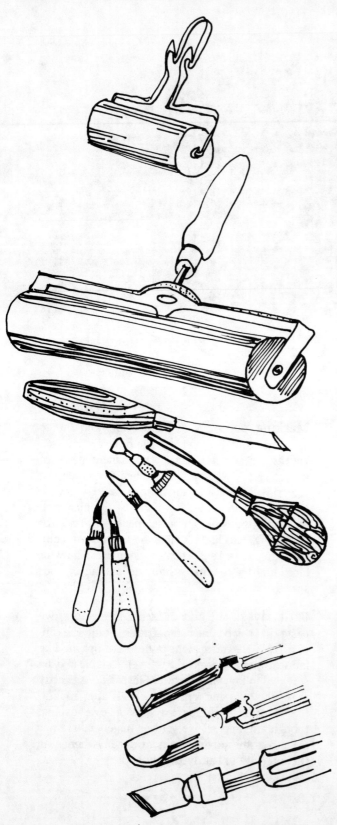

Block Printing

Block printing is one of the oldest methods of embellishing a plain fabric. The block can be anything on which color can be transferred in a patterned shape onto cloth. Hands, feet and fingers were undoubtedly the first blocks and, though primitive, are still effective in creating designs on fabric. A two-year-old will chortle with delight if you dip his feet in paint and let him walk on a length of canvas. The printed textile could then be used for the sides of a baby tote, a poignant reminder of the passage of time.

In block printing, the dyes or paints must be able to stick to the printing block well enough to be transferred to the canvas. And they must have binders or thickeners in them to prevent the complete absorption of the pigment into the fabric, allowing the print to lie on the top of the fabric without bleeding into it. Silkscreen inks, block printing inks, acrylic paints or fabric paints are best for block printing. Before you begin, test a sample on a small square of canvas before printing, both for color and washability.

Although block printing may at first seem to be a rather narrow field in comparison with airbrushing or silkscreen, a little experimenting will quickly disabuse you of that notion. For instance, a band of printed thread spools cruising along the shoulder of a cooking apron and wandering down to disappear into the front pocket is whimsical and unexpected. By varying the printing of this one simple shape, exciting possibilities soon emerge. Relationships among the repetitions of the printed shapes, between the positive and negative spaces created, and even the blotchy texturing of the ink on the woven goods, makes block printing on canvas a challenging endeavor.

Things That Make Great Printing Blocks

Potatoes, turnips and rutabagas: these are cheap and wonderful. They work well with fabric paints and with dyes. They can be used in a myriad of ways: cut into halves as mirror-images, carved into shapes that can be repeated in the same, or other colors, or used as a base for another, more defined image to print over. Dense placement of these potato blocks creates an exciting negative space which stands out clearly as a patterned rhythm develops.

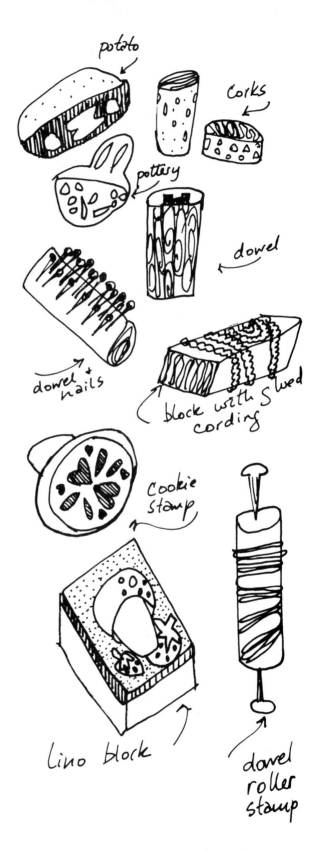

potato

Corks

pottery

dowel

dowel + nails

block with glued cording

cookie stamp

lino block

dowel roller stamp

- Corks:

  Readily available, corks make fine printing blocks. They are difficult to cut, and should be used as is. Make a collection of corks of different sizes and experiment with a modulation of colors and shapes in blocks or diagonals.

- Wood doweling:

  Doweling is great stuff. Take the ends you have left over from some of the projects in the book and experiment with sawing the round, butt ends. Glue these ends onto blocks or boards, and print in multiples. You can modify the curved sides of the doweling with saws, rasps or files. Hammer a nail into each end and then roll the cylinders onto the canvas, making interesting repeat patterns. Wrap the dowels with string or rope glued with white glue and roll these patterns onto the cloth.

- Wood blocks:

  Carve a design into the wood. Hammer a series of nails at the same height into the block in a precise, or random pattern. Or wrap and glue cording, yarn or felt onto the block for fascinating patterns.

- Ceramic stamps:

  You can make your own clay stamps and fire them at 1650 – 1670 degrees F. Punch designs into the block face before firing. Or you might use Scandinavian-style cookie stamps to make repeat patterns.

- Linoleum blocks:

  These are available at any craft or art supply store. Buy an inexpensive set of lino cutters and experiment with carving a design. You can draw your design on the white linoleum directly, or you can transfer it from paper with carbon paper. Remember, whatever you cut *out*, will not print on the canvas. The image comes from that part you have *not* cut out. Lino block printing looks especially good on 12 and 14 ounce heavy natural duck.

Preparing to Print with Blocks

You will need to clear a workspace large enough to accomodate your canvas adequately. A floor or long table will do. Spread a layer of newspaper under the canvas as a pad so that the fabric will give under pressure of the block. Tack or pin canvas down tautly. Cover the area surrounding the yardage with newspapers for easy clean up. You will want to wear a smock and gloves while you work. Line up your tools and equipment to the right of your fabric, if you are right-handed. Otherwise, to the left. The basic materials you will need are:

- a slab of glass to roll out ink (a padded board or cardboard wrapped in aluminum foil works well too)
- brayer—a hard rubber roller to spread the ink on the glass and transfer it smoothly to your block
- small paintbrushes
- fabric paint, lino inks, silkscreen inks or dyes
- water (or solvent for oil-base inks)
- paper towels or newsprint

If you want to truly personalize your canvas project, you can cut out the pattern pieces first, and then tailor the printing of the design specifically for each piece. Remember the seam allowances and other hidden areas and don't work them in your designs.

It is important to keep your printing equipment clean. You can discard vegetables after using them as blocks, but the brayer and the brushes and the glass should be scrupulously clean. You don't want your second printing marred by a smudge of ink from the first printing.

The Actual Printing

There are a few things to remember when printing on fabric, whether you use vegetable, wood or linoleum blocks. First, you must re-ink the block *each time* you make a new impression. This insures a clear, bright print. Too, you must be careful to make sure no ink adheres to the outer edge of the printing block. Make a few trial prints to ensure that no messy ink residue mars the edges of the print; wipe off any excess ink before you print.

For vegetables, it is sufficient to dip the block in a pigment and print. If the design wasn't cut evenly, you can paint the vegetable block with a paintbrush before each printing.

Roll the pigment onto wood or linoleum blocks with a brayer. Squeeze a little ink onto a pallette and work the brayer back and forth until the color is dispersed evenly. Then apply the ink to the block with an even motion of the brayer, make sure all surfaces of the design are covered. Now place the block over the canvas and apply a steady, even pressure to transfer the ink to the fabric. Generally speaking, the heavier the weight of canvas, the heavier the pressure needs to be for a clean print. You can hit the block with a wooden mallet, or step on the block using your whole weight. Use small amounts of ink as you work, it dries quickly on the palette. Replenish your brayer often and develop a rhythm as you go. The actual printing process should be quite pleasant and satisfying, as you watch your designs emerge on the canvas.

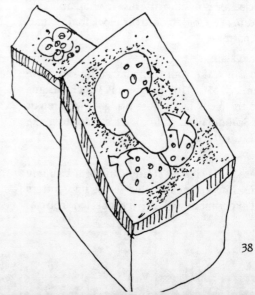

Stencilling on Canvas

Stencils are one of the oldest methods of applying color patterns to fabric, the art having reached its zenith in Japan where the stencil bridges linking the cut out sections were painstakingly made with human hair. Canvas, of course, does not require the same delicacy of design as would a piece of ornamental silk, and the stencils you will use will undoubtedly be larger and more graphic, with strong bridges which are a part of the overall design.

Stencilling color on canvas is simple and satisfying. Precut stencils are readily available at art and craft stores, and inexpensive as well, or you can make your own. They can be used over and over again to create all sorts of designs. Stencilled letters can add interest to the most basic item, like a zippered briefcase. Use bold monogrammed initials to personalize your handmade items.

Designs for Stencilling　　　You can buy precut stencils, but they are fun to make yourself. There are two basic types of stencils: full design stencils and modular stencils. Full design stencils are used for full panels and very large repeats. Modular stencils are much smaller and easier to maneuver, they are used in designs requiring many repeats in the pattern. Experiment with a variety of the simplest modular shapes — stars, hearts, arcs, lines, triangles, etc. With these, you can fashion an endless range of designs from the simplest lines of repeats to complex free-form patterns.

Stencilling Equipment　　　Stencilling on canvas requires a few tools. If you are going to make your own stencils you will need:

- Illustration board
- The stencil material itself
- Tracing paper
- Carbon paper
- Pencils
- Masking tape
- X-acto knife

- Fabric paints, dyes, acrylic paints, watercolor inks, or marking pens
- Stencil brush, or filbert brush
- Plastic spray bottle (optional)
- Small sponge

  There are many kinds of materials that you can cut to make stencils. A few which have proved successful when used on canvas are:

- Acetate:
  Good for many repetitions. Available in art or drafting supply stores. Choose .005 gauge.

- Stencil paper:
  White, waxy paper, slightly transparent. Good for modular stencils because you can see through to the design as you work. Not as durable as acetate but easier to cut.

- Contact paper:
  Buy rolls at the supermarket or art supply store. Contact paper can be used many times and can be washed off with water after use without losing its stickiness. Be sure to press all edges down to adhere contact paper to canvas.

- Auto upholstery vinyl:
  Makes a heavy, durable stencil that can be used indefinitely. Stays down on the fabric fairly well if held with points of fingers.

Stencilling Inspiration　　　Designs for stencilling are all around you. Often the simplest shapes will be the most effective. An after-breakfast table, for instance, is an everyday example. The shapes of mugs and creamers, a basket of fruit, forks, spoons can all be abstracted into powerful graphic designs. When cutting stencils, though, learn to look for the overall outlines, not the tiny details.

Cutting the Stencil　　　When you make your own stencils you must be very aware of the bridges. These are the bits joining one section of the design

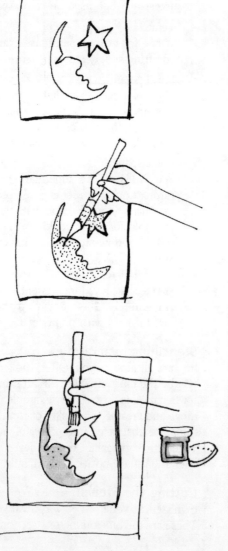

with another so that the center doesn't fall out, and they are an integral part of the design. The bridges hold your stencil together and make it strong enough for repeated usage, correctly placed they enhance the design. Usually, bridges that follow the contour of the object work best.

Trace your design onto tracing paper, then move each line outward about 1/8 inch. These will form the sections you cut out. Plan your bridges carefully and make them of equal size. If a bridge breaks, you can repair it with transparent tape.

If you are cutting your stencil from anything other than contact paper, you will first need to put your design on a sheet of illustration board. You can draw the design on paper then transfer it by carbon onto the illustration board, or you can draw directly onto the board.

Tape your stencil material over your design on the illustration board. The stencil material should be at least 3 inches larger than the design to provide the stencil with a strong margin. Cut the design into the stencil material with an X-acto knife. Hold the knife in an upright position. Use steady, smooth strokes. Don't go over the edges twice, they never look as sharp the second time around. A steel ruler will help you cut straight lines. Curves are a bit harder, and you should practice before you begin.

If you are using contact paper for the stencil, trace your design directly onto the back of the paper. Remember to *reverse* any lettering or numbering since you are drawing on the back, not the front, of your stencil. Cut through the contact paper with the X-acto knife. If you make a mistake and cut through

one unit

four units

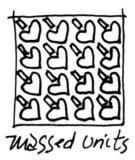
massed units

diagonal units

a bridge, you can correct with a tab of masking tape.

When using contact paper, press the stencil firmly onto the canvas, making sure that all the tiny edges are adhered. The excess pigment can be wiped or hosed off the contact paper after you have peeled it off the canvas. Contact paper stencils can be used for several days, or until the stickiness begins to dry out. Sometimes placing them face up in the sun will increase the tackiness of the backing, allowing you to use them one last time.

Applying the Color   Lay your canvas onto a worktable or the floor, with a pad of newspapers underneath. Using masking tape or push pens, fasten the canvas down so it will not move during the stencilling. Now you will lay the stencils on the cloth. If you are doing repeat patterns with modular stencils, you should lightly indicate with pencil where you want your patterns to go. Remember seam allowances and sections to be covered with pockets, don't include them in your stencilling. Hold your stencil material firmly with your hands, or tape it down with masking tape. Contact paper will adhere by itself.

Dip your brush into color and stroke it on the fabric, work from the edges of the stencil *inwards*. Don't overload your brush. Have some newsprint or a swatch of canvas beside you on which to pounce off the excess color. Besides a brush, you can use a small sponge to apply the color. Dip the sponge in paint, and then squeeze out the excess before painting the stencil. Too much color applied too quickly will creep out of the borders of the stencil. Try to work the color into the very weave of the canvas.

Generally speaking, it is difficult to apply light colors onto dark canvas. If you want a good, bright color on very dark canvas you should first stencil the design in white. Let the paint dry and then restencil the design in your chosen color.

Your stencilled design can have as many colors as you choose, just be sure each color dries thoroughly before applying the next. You can achieve many different results depending upon whether you stencil with paints, dyes, or markers. Paints are more opaque than dyes or watercolor inks, the latter can be thinned until they color the fabric with only a hazy wash. Marking pens will stencil the canvas with strong colors, but they tend to bleed under the edge of the design. Acrylic or fabric paints can be diluted and then sprayed through the stencil with a plant mister to create an airbrushed effect. Spray paint drifts everywhere, however, so you should cover your work area with newspapers first.

Stencilling is easy and you will enjoy experimenting with the various paints and techniques you can use. However, patience is an important part of any project. There is always a great eagerness to lift off the stencil to see how the design looks on the canvas. But that first peek, if you rush it, can ruin your design. Let the canvas dry a bit before removing the stencil, then your edges will stay clean and well defined. You can speed the drying process by blowing over the surface of the canvas with your hair dryer. Do this only if you are coloring with fabric paints or acrylics. Contact paper somewhat reduces your waiting time, because it is easier to color in many design elements at the same time with this stencil material.

41

Silkscreening on Canvas

Silkscreening is similar to stencilling, only much more sophisticated. In silkscreening, pigment is rubbed onto the canvas through a screen mesh. Portions of the screen have been blocked off, so the color is transferred only through the open sections. Great complexities of color and design can be achieved with this process, with the fabric passing under many different screens in succession until an entire polychromatic design is printed. With screen printing extremely fine designs can be executed with comparative ease. However, similar effects may be obtained using fabric paints or marking pens, and silkscreening may well prove too time consuming and costly for use on just one project.

Screen printing is a rewarding and complex art. The discussions below are simplified somewhat for the home craftsperson, and do not give expression to the multifarious ways in which silkscreening may be used. However, these instructions will give you a basis upon which to begin experimenting on your own.

Tools for Silkscreening

Several silkscreen kits are available at art and craft stores. Generally these kits are quite adequate for your first screen printing experiments, and can serve as a sensible, inexpensive introduction to the technique. In order to print large designs, you will need to purchase supplies separately from a silkscreen supply house. If you are intrigued by the process, send for catalogs from several of the supply sources listed in the back index.

Choosing Inks and Dyes

Your choice of pigments for silkscreening will depend upon the method of block-out you use. If you use an oil-base stencil, you will need water-soluble inks. If you choose a water-base block-out, you will need oil-base paints. Both types of colors are suitable for use on canvas, and both can be heat-treated for permanence and washability.

Photo silkscreening is a highly technical process used commonly for T-shirts and other mass produced items where fineness of detail is required. A perusal of silkscreen supply catalogs and instruction books will give you an idea of the virtuosity of this method.

Printing

There are several methods of preparing the silkscreen for printing. All of them serve to block off sections of the screen so paint won't pass through it. Three of the most common methods are discussed below. They use liquid block-out, plastic laquer film and crayon resist.

Liquid Block-out Method

In this method, the screen is painted with a liquid block-out chemical which occludes the sections of the design you want left uncolored. You tape your design under the screen, and then trace onto the screen in pencil those sections you want colored. All the rest is painted with block-out. The screen has to be checked by holding it up to the light to make sure no pinholes have been left in the block-out. Characteristic of this method are soft edges, painting the block-out with a brush does not create crisp, hardline borders between the color and the fabric. This screen breaks down, and cannot be used indefinitely in production work.

Laquer Film Method

Laquer film is a plastic material in which two layers of plastic are adhered together. You cut your design through ONLY the top layer of the film, the backing film will later be removed. Use an X-acto knife with a swivel blade to cut the film, then peel off the cut out areas. This will be where the paint passes through. After cutting, the film is fixed to the silkscreen by wiping it with a special adhering chemical. Now the backing film is removed and the edges are touched up to block them out. A laquer film screen will produce sharp edged images, as contrasted to the painted on block-out method of silkscreen. Too, the laquer screen is very durable and lasts a long time.

Wax Resist Method   In this technique the area to be printed on the screen is first covered thoroughly with wax. The remaining sections are then blocked out with iron oxide. Finally, the wax is removed leaving clear the area for inking. This is the technique used for decorating the Cloud Cradle.

Tammy Kulamer
40 Zippers
Canvas, silkscreen dyes

43

Blueprinting on Canvas

Blueprinting on fabric is a fascinating technique, its potential in textile art is only recently being explored. The blueprinting process on fabric is exactly the same as it would be on paper, although using different fabrics will produce different results. Essentially, blueprinting is a photoprinting process whereby sections of fabric exposed to light turn a beautiful indigo blue. The sections blocked off from light remain white. On first glance, the technique may seem uncomfortably reminiscent of a high school chemistry class. However, a thorough reading of the particulars should assure the reader that it is well within grasp. Simply stated, blueprinting consists of saturating fabric with chemical emulsion in the dark, allowing it to damp-dry, and then exposing it to light. Whatever is placed on the surface of the fabric when it is exposed to light will leave a white image.

Blueprinting can be done on any white, 100% cotton or 100% viscose rayon fabric. When using canvas, you will have best results with 10 ounce or even lighter weights. Muslin will work, but be sure it has no polyester content. Very fine texture cotton lawn or viscose rayon render extremely precise and delicate images. Canvas, on the other hand, will give a fuzzier, less refined image, though nonetheless interesting.

The Blueprinted Images   The range of possible imagery that can be manipulated by use of the blueprint process is endlessly varied, and extremely exciting. And therein lies the art. A group of objects placed on the fabric will print in a straightforward way as solid white images on a blue background. However if you use objects with varying opacity, your images will reflect this in the degree to which they stay white. Glasses of water will print as transparent with the water level showing, since glass, and glass containing water transmit the light differently.

The printing of shadows is a fascinating area of discovery. Ordinarily, if you are blueprinting at midday, you will have the shortest exposure time for the fabric, but you will also have the fewest shadows. However, if you wait until later in the day when the sun drops in the sky, objects will cast fabulous, attenuated and softly shaded shadows.

How you lay out your objects for printing is an interesting part of the art of blueprinting. A group of kitchen utensils placed at random on the fabric will print in a fairly simple manner. However, a lineup of plastic cowboys with their shadows will print almost like a sculptured frieze. You can have great fun experimenting with the objects you choose, and the way you organize them on the surface of the canvas.

You can make images in other ways too. You can draw with a black, waxy Tusche crayon on a piece of clear acetate. Weight the acetate down on your canvas with clear glass and your drawing will be printed in white. Too, you can print strips of 35 mm film onto fabric. Just hold it down with a pane of glass. And the new color Xerox machines can enlarge your color slides and print them on acetate so your slides can be reproduced by the blueprinting process. Be sure to choose particularly direct and graphic images to print onto canvas. A certain loss of detail will occur due to the heavy texture of the fabric.

Tools for Blueprinting

- 100% cotton or viscose rayon, white or natural
- Potassium ferricyanide (see Supply Sources)
- Ferric ammonium citrate (see Supply Sources)
- Distilled water
- Electric fan (optional)
- Darkened room
- Tub, running water
- Board, thick foam rubber, or flat surface to rest fabric on
- Objects, drawings on acetate
- Clear glass to hold objects onto the fabric surface during exposure
- Gram scale
- 2 plastic light-proof bottles (available at photo supply stores)
- Plastic atomizer bottle
- Ultraviolet light source: sunlamp or sunlight

Sensitizing the Fabric

Use a gram scale and carefully measure 35 grams of potassium ferricyanide. Dissolve it in 250 cc. of distilled water. Pour this mixture into a light-proof bottle labeled A. Now measure 50 grams of ferric ammonium citrate, and dissolve it in 250 cc. of distilled water. Pour this into another light-proof bottle labeled B. *This must be done in a fairly dark room.*

When ready to use, mix equal parts of solution A and B in a tub, basin, or plastic baby bath. If you have a fairly small piece of fabric to work with, then dip it in the solution and saturate it completely. If you are working with a large surface of canvas, it is best to apply the solution with a plastic spray bottle. After the fabric is saturated it will be a bright lemon yellow.

Drying the Fabric

Keep the saturated fabric in a darkened room, or you will start the developing process. Hang it to dry, an electric fan set on "cool" will help speed this process. Fully saturated canvas should take an hour or more to reach the damp-dry state. Use your hand to press out the wrinkles as you hang the canvas to dry, or the wrinkles will print on the fabric too. When the cloth is damp-dry, it is ready to be exposed *immediately*.

Exposing the Fabric

If you are using a fairly small piece of fabric, spread it on a board, or a thick piece of cardboard. Do this in the dark room. Now arrange the objects to be blueprinted on this flat surface, and then carry it out into the sunshine. If you are blueprinting a large piece of cloth, spread it out in the sunshine first. Working quickly, then arrange the objects on it.

Watch the canvas. It will change color from yellow to a crusty, almost ashen grey-blue. Exposure time varies. Thick canvas will take up to 30 minutes or more at midday. Thin cotton will blueprint much more rapidly. Fabrics exposed earlier or later during the day will take up to 45 minutes to print. When the color is ashy blue, prepare a tub of cool, running water, out of the sun.

Rinsing the Fabric

When the fabric is ready, rush it into the shady tub of running water. Do not fuss with removing the objects from its surface, just dump them aside and run. Get the blueprinted fabric under running water *immediately*. Rinsing fixes and develops the blueprint. Thick fabrics, 10 ounce canvas for instance, take up to an hour to rinse. During this time, agitate and run cool water over the textile constantly. All the chemical must be removed from the cloth or the white areas will gradually fill in with blue. When the rinse water runs clear, hang your print to dry in the shade.

Blueprinted fabric cannot be ironed or the image will begin to fade. Smooth the wrinkles with your hand and hang it to dry. With thin fabrics, adhere them to a smooth wall or appliance surface so they dry without wrinkles.

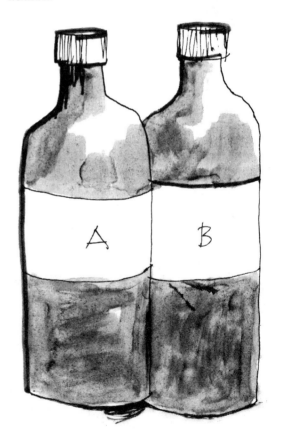

Margo Hoff
Red Block
Canvas, acrylic paint, wood

Painting on Canvas With Fabric Paints

Painting directly on canvas is easy and satisfying, particularly with the advent of several paints developed specifically for use on textiles. There are quite a few such paints on the market and they fall into two categories: oil- or water-base. Prang makes a good oil-base paint, however, you do have to use turpentine or solvent for clean-up. These paints come with an extender for diluting the colors, and are quite permanent when heat-set by ironing, according to the directions. Versatex, Dylon, and Hot Air are three water-base fabric paints that brush on easily and are also permanent to washing after being heat-set. In all instances, the manufacturers suggest washing the fabric first. As discussed earlier, this may be considered optional. A canvas item is not necessarily like a T-shirt which must be subjected to constant washing and drying in its lifetime. If necessary, a painted tote bag can be gently scrubbed with a brush in cold water. Some fabric paints are dry-cleanable though you must try a test sample at your cleaner's first.

Applying the Paint

All fabric paints are somewhat thick when brushed directly from the jar. This is not necessarily a disadvantage unless your design is an intricate one. Fabric paints work marvelously for flat areas of color such as printed letters and stencilled shapes. If they are to be used this way, paint with a stiff filbert brush rather than a pliable watercolor brush. The colors may be thinned, although if you thin them severely, you will want to add an extender to help hold the pigments on the fabric. If you dilute the colors to achieve a subtly blended or shaded wash effect, you may then switch to a sable watercolor brush for fine lines or details.

Most fabric paints are semi-opaque. This means that light-colored letters will only partially obscure a dark-colored background. For complete coverage you will have to paint the letters first in white, let them dry, and repaint with the light color. Fabric paints cover exceedingly well on light-colored or natural canvas, however.

Setting the Colors

When the paint is completely dry, set the color by ironing over the design with a hot iron on "cotton" setting. Insert a piece of white typing paper or tracing paper between the iron and the design, to protect the iron. When you are using water-base fabric paints, you can dry them as you work with a hand-held hairdryer. Besides speeding the drying process, this also begins to set the colors. Remember, however, that once the color begins to set, you cannot go back and correct errors, you can only paint over them.

Spray Painting

Spray painting is another method of applying paint to canvas. Airbrushing creates delicately shaded designs, and it can be executed with or without stencils. However, airbrush equipment tends to be expensive. I have found that a common plastic spray bottle, or a plant mister, filled with heavily diluted acrylic or fabric paint works very well for shading areas of cloudy color. You will want to practice on paper first, for it is hard to avoid sudden splats of color that drop on the canvas in the midst of a perfectly executed cloud. Wipe the nozzle of the sprayer often and hold it at an angle over the canvas. Try applying a rainbow in subtle gradations of color. With the spray bottle technique it is possible to achieve some spectacular effects. Then, after the sprayed colors dry, you can draw on top of them with inks, or stencil opaque designs on them.

Be sure to cover a large area surrounding your workspace with newspapers. The spray paint drifts, and will coat everything with a fine color mist if precautions are not taken.

Washing Colors onto Canvas   After you have painted a piece of canvas, you can take it outside and turn the hose on it. The water will wash across the surface of the painted designs, swirling the colors in abstract patterns. Use this method with acrylic paints or permanent watercolor dyes, and wash the canvas before the colors have had a chance to dry. To control the drift of colors on the canvas, merely lay the canvas flat again and allow it to dry, or carefully pat it with a clean towel. Try this technique also with pre-wetted canvas. The resultant color washes are beautiful by themselves, or they can become backgrounds to other designs that you draw or print on the fabric.

Canning   Canning is another fascinating method of applying color to canvas. A tin can full of paint is slid across the fabric leaving a bright band of color. Cut out the top and bottom of an ordinary can and place it on a piece of wax paper stationed at the edge of a length of canvas. Fill the can ⅓ with silkscreen ink or acrylic paint. Now slide the can across the canvas with an even stroke, end up on another sheet of wax paper at the opposite edge of the fabric.

By varying both the colors and the can sizes many outstanding designs can be created. Wherever the colors overlap, new colors will appear. Canning is particularly suited to curved, free-form designs that interweave continuous bands of colors. A series of throw pillows could be created by canning a long length of canvas and then cutting it into smaller sections for stuffing. It is also a versatile technique to use on awnings or hammocks, anywhere that a long expanse of yardage lends itself to a simple graphic statement.

Coloring with Marking Pens   Marking pens and canvas are made for each other. Markers are easy to handle, come in a wide variety of colors and shapes of nibs, and allow you more detail in design than paints. In fact, markers combine extremely well with paints. You can lay on a wash of colors with paints, then proceed to delineate an intricate pattern over the dry paint with fine line pens. Be sure to buy permanent markers, not watercolor ones.

There are a half dozen readily available brands of permanent color marking pens, among them Pantone, Design Marker, Magic Marker, and Dri Mark. They vary in permanency to washing and in price. A search of your local art or craft store, or a check on the stationers will give you an idea of the range of colors and prices available. In my experimenting, marking pens usually fade up to 30% in the first cold water washing. Be sure to test them on a canvas sample before starting a project that will be subjected to constant washing.

Marking pens, particularly the wide nibbed ones, have a tendency to bleed into the canvas in both directions, warp and weft. This is especially true of the natural canvas. To allow for this bleeding, work from the inside of your design out. Hold your pen almost upright as you work. Stop drawing at least ¼ inch before you reach the edge of your design to see how far the color will bleed out, then continue to the edge. Often it works well to outline areas of color with a black marker. Be wary of putting a dark color next to a light one, the darker one often runs into the lighter spoiling the precise design. Practice, and practice again before you start your actual project.

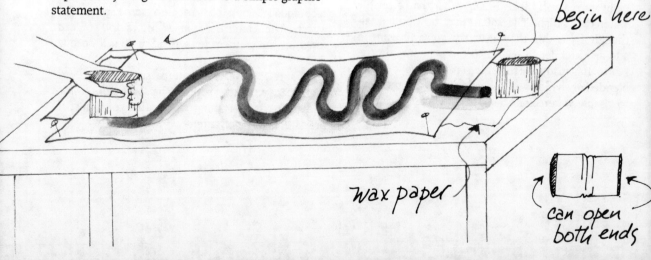

begin here

wax paper

can open both ends

Priscilla Young
Painted Chair
Canvas, fabric inks

Nancy Erickson
Sybil
Dyed canvas, marking pens,
muslin

Shirley Saito
Trees
Canvas, muslin

Quilting Canvas

The word quilting comes from the Latin *culcita*, meaning a stuffed cushion. Quilted garments were originally made of cotton or linen, and were layers of padding worn by Roman soldiers for warmth, protection and for comfort under metal armor. English quilting, in which three layers of fabric are stitched together in a design, is the most common type of quilting seen today. It is used for Appalachian quilts and coverlets as well as for wall hangings, and clothing. All of the quilted work in this book is English quilting because it is a technique that works well with canvas.

The principle of making a "sandwich" of canvas, batting, and backing is referred to constantly in the instructions in this book. The sandwich is stitched together through all three layers, thereby bonding the fabrics together and at the same time creating an interesting, dimensional design. Generally speaking, you will have more success if you use a lightweight cotton for the backing fabric, rather than another layer of canvas. With too much canvas, home sewing machines can strain, particularly if you have to turn under the edges or fold corners.

Canvas can be quilted by hand, but experience has shown that the results are often inferior to machine quilted pieces. The charm of handstitching is usually lost on heavy canvas. Before quilting, your design can be transferred to the fabric with dressmakers carbon and a tracing wheel. If you are quilting around pieces of applique, no patterns are needed. Freehand quilting is often charming and just as appealing as the more rigid traditional quilting.

50

sandwich ...   quilting inside...   defining quilting...

Some Quilting Hints

- Canvas quilts beautifully by machine if you use special machine embroidery floss, or heavy buttonhole twist for the top thread.

- Work with a quilting foot if you have a design laid out that requires careful following.

- When you make the sandwich of fabrics, cut the backing layer and the batting slightly larger than the top canvas piece. These have a way of shrinking when you sew on them, you can easily trim any excess after the quilting is completed.

- Be sure you study your piece carefully before you begin quilting. Canvas retains needle marks when the stitches are ripped out and these could mar your finished work.

- Pin basting is quite adequate when quilting canvas. Watch that the pins do not jab the heel of your hand as you guide the stiff canvas under the presser foot. Check underneath often to see that the backing is not rumpled.

- Stitch length should be from 6 to 12 per inch. I use the longest stitch length for working on canvas, but you may want to experiment.

- Always work from the center of the piece outwards. Pin the sandwich together from the center out, and as you sew, smooth the canvas constantly to assure an even finish.

- If you are appliqueing and quilting simultaneously, begin with the centermost piece to be appliqued and work towards the outer edges.

Two projects in this book that use quilting are the Rainbow Accordion Purse and Noah's Ark Wall Hanging. But study the other projects with an eye to embellishing them with quilting. Without a doubt you will find many places where quilting would be a fine addition to the finished product.

around shapes...   quilting lines alone....   storytelling...

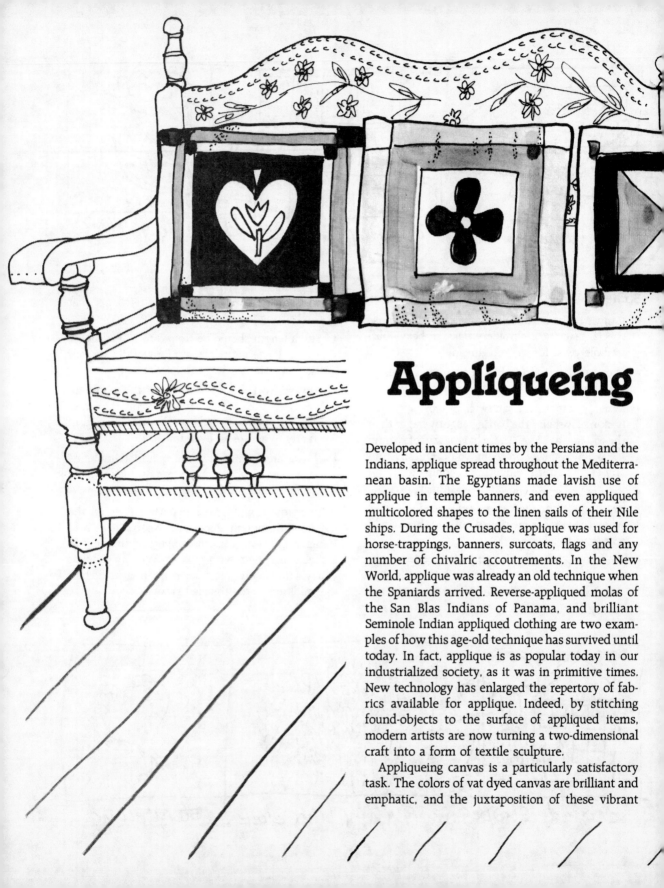

Appliqueing

Developed in ancient times by the Persians and the Indians, applique spread throughout the Mediterranean basin. The Egyptians made lavish use of applique in temple banners, and even appliqued multicolored shapes to the linen sails of their Nile ships. During the Crusades, applique was used for horse-trappings, banners, surcoats, flags and any number of chivalric accoutrements. In the New World, applique was already an old technique when the Spaniards arrived. Reverse-appliqued molas of the San Blas Indians of Panama, and brilliant Seminole Indian appliqued clothing are two examples of how this age-old technique has survived until today. In fact, applique is as popular today in our industrialized society, as it was in primitive times. New technology has enlarged the repertory of fabrics available for applique. Indeed, by stitching found-objects to the surface of appliqued items, modern artists are now turning a two-dimensional craft into a form of textile sculpture.

Appliqueing canvas is a particularly satisfactory task. The colors of vat dyed canvas are brilliant and emphatic, and the juxtaposition of these vibrant

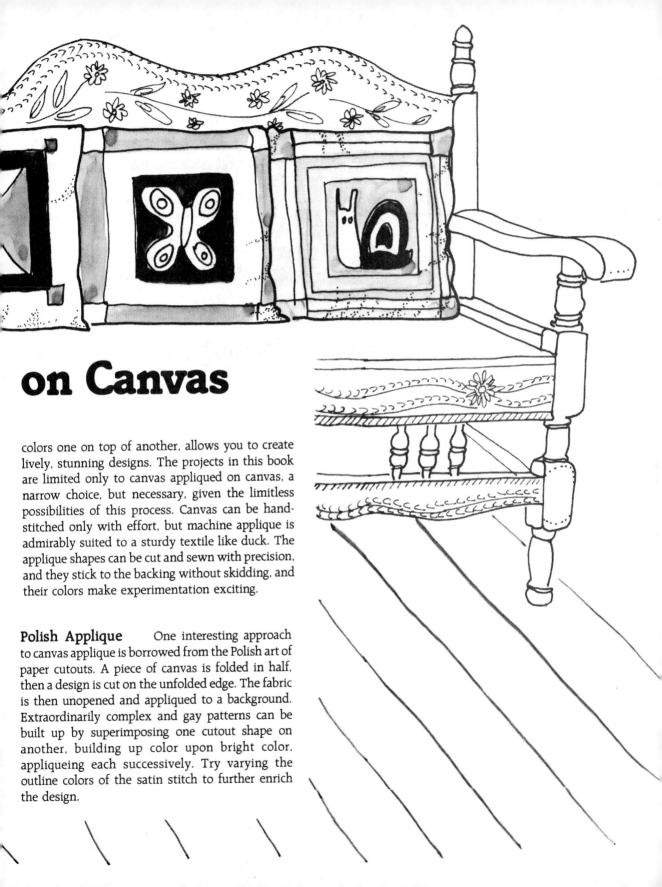

on Canvas

colors one on top of another, allows you to create lively, stunning designs. The projects in this book are limited only to canvas appliqued on canvas, a narrow choice, but necessary, given the limitless possibilities of this process. Canvas can be hand-stitched only with effort, but machine applique is admirably suited to a sturdy textile like duck. The applique shapes can be cut and sewn with precision, and they stick to the backing without skidding, and their colors make experimentation exciting.

Polish Applique   One interesting approach to canvas applique is borrowed from the Polish art of paper cutouts. A piece of canvas is folded in half, then a design is cut on the unfolded edge. The fabric is then unopened and appliqued to a background. Extraordinarily complex and gay patterns can be built up by superimposing one cutout shape on another, building up color upon bright color, appliqueing each successively. Try varying the outline colors of the satin stitch to further enrich the design.

A Few Applique Hints

- Applique shapes can overlap or not. Their edges need *not* be turned under, merely zigzagged down.

- Applique shapes can be held in place before sewing with a dab of rubber cement or fused to the backing with either fusible webbing or thin plastic.

- If the design is complicated, the applique shapes should be machine basted in place before zigzagging.

- When zigzagging the applique shape, be sure that at least ¾ of the stitching falls on the shape and not on the background. This is important, especially if the item will be washed frequently.

- Use lots of thread. Have lots of thread on hand when you begin so you won't run out just before the project is finished.

- Play with the effects of using different color threads. Hard edges will merge into the background if you use a thread the same color as the appliqued shape. Clean, standout shapes will result if darker threads are used. A luminous halo effect will be created if lighter threads are used in rows.

- Sew steadily and purposefully when you are zigzagging. There is a tendency to ease off on the presser foot while going around curves. Resist this. Sew, stop, lift your presser foot, turn the canvas. And so forth around the curve. Otherwise your stitching will become too open and weak on the curves.

- Inside curves are difficult. Study them carefully and approach with caution. Lift the presser foot and turn the fabric often.

- Applique with a straight stitch ⅛ inch from the outer edge, and let the raw ends ravel. Many imports from India are appliqued in this manner and the style has a casual charm.

Appliqued canvas looks especially handsome if you work with large shapes. Geometric patterns, enlarged shapes from nature such as stars, trees, rainbows, animals, leaves, clouds, or simple abstract areas of color are all good possibilities when you are designing. Be bold. Once you have cut your backing piece, you have the parameters of your project. It is very hard to make a mistake if you work *with* rather than against the spirit of the canvas. Let the excitement of the colors free your scissors and imagination. Don't be afraid to shout. Canvas is that kind of fabric.

Lane Neff
Emily's Sleeping Bag
Canvas, quilt batting, cotton

Altering the Surface

Karen Lucas
Quilt
Muslin, cotton cord, dye

Kathy Howe
Woven Painting D
Linen warp, canvas, paint

Unusual and often startling results may be achieved by manipulating the surface of the canvas before working it into bags, wall hangings, or banners. Tucking is especially attractive when used as a pocket treatment. You can pin-tuck the canvas by making lines of stitching on your sewing machine. Or you can pleat the canvas in horizontal, vertical or diagonal folds. These pleats can each be stitched down, or you can quilt across them in a grid pattern.

By ripping strips of canvas and weaving them in a pattern you can create canvas with great surface interest. The fringed edges are especially attractive if you rip strips, then wash and dry them. The soft, light-colored edges provide a contrast to the hard, dyed surface of the canvas.

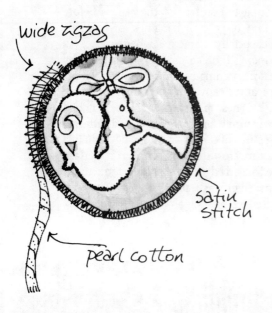

wide zigzag

satin
stitch

pearl cotton

A Simple Patch

It is easier to do extensive machine embroidery if your fabric is placed in an embroidery hoop, then machine stitched. You can control the direction of the stitches better if you have the hoop to hold on to. Draw your patch in the middle of the hooped fabric, then insert it under the needle. If your machine has an embroidery foot, use it. You can stitch over a piece of yarn for a raised look, or you can vary the width of the satin stitch as you work. When you have completed the design, remove the fabric from the hoop. Now lay a length of pearl crochet cotton cording along the edge of the patch. Change to a buttonhole foot. Go around outer edge of patch with a satin stitch, covering the cording as you work. Trim away excess fabric from edge. Now lay another length of cording next to the outside edge and go over it with a narrow zigzag. Press with a steam iron. When you applique the patch to a bag or jacket, sew over the outer edge with satin stitch again. This makes a luxurious edge for your patch.

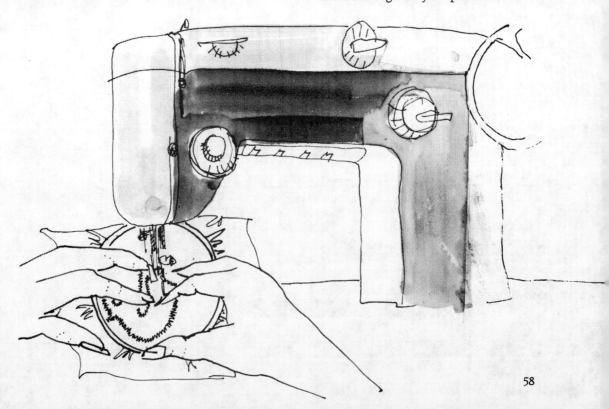

Outrageous Embellishments

Canvas lends itself to baroque forms of embellishment. These are limited only by your imagination, and though they are used sparingly in this book, your own lust for rhinestones may overwhelm you and you may choose to rivet several hundred to the flap of a tote bag. That's o.k. Canvas is sturdy enough and unassuming enough to take it . . . and look good in it.

- Shiny extras: Rhinestones come in bags of hundreds, and you can purchase pliers to apply them at fabric stores. They no longer simulate only diamonds, now you can buy fake rubies, emeralds and sapphires. Nailheads, rivets, stars and other metallic trims are worth considering for lettering or simple designs. They provoke a garish contrast to the spartan canvas.

- Iron-Ons: Iron-on letters come in a variety of sizes and colors, even calicos, and are simple to apply. They can be cut into applique shapes, ironed on, then zigzagged.

- Buttons: You may want to hunt for one perfect silver button, or mass dozens of them to form a design.

- Ribbons: Satin, grosgrain, plaid, or silken, these can be left to dangle free or woven into intricate designs to be stitched on your canvas.

- Feathers: Wrap in bundles with multicolored yarns, add beading for a colorful effect.

- Vinyl: Is great used as windows in tents, toys, bags. Use a wide open zigzag with the stitches fairly far apart to avoid cutting through the plastic.

- Leather: Looks superb with canvas. If you have leatherworking tools you can add it wherever you like for accent. Otherwise, consider using fake suede which can be sewn on your home machine.

- Beaded Rondelles: From Afghanistan, these softly padded circular decorations are available at import or specialized fabric stores.

- Found Objects: Anything you find, any object you wish to imbue with meaning, can become part of your art. Look around and find those magical surprises you want to add to your fabric.

Susan Dworski
Mandala
Muslin, silk, rayon stuffed and quilted

Soft Sculpture

Canvas is a splendid fabric for soft sculpture: it is durable and strong enough to assume any number of shapes. Its neutral surface invites the artist to paint, draw, color it in imitation of the images swimming in her subconscious. Soft sculpture is a grand enough subject for several books and as you become familiar with its properties you will inevitably want to experiment with three-dimensional shapes. Work with large and fairly abstract forms. Canvas's one drawback in this art form is its stiffness, you just can't manipulate it into fine or delicate shapes. But if your lines are simple enough, and your forms large enough you can create a whole mythology of people, animals, plants, whatever your imagination can conjure.

Stuffing large objects is a lot of work. Generally you should think of using polyester batting to stuff flat objects and polyester stuffing for dimensional shapes. However, if your scale is large, polyester may get expensive. You can use straw or crushed newspaper if you pack it tightly as inexpensive substitutes for polyester. For some objects, particularly squishy ones where the shape doesn't have to be clearly defined, you can stuff with plastic pellets. These give a nice feel to the object, but they are messy to work with and you will thank yourself later if you do the actual construction inside your garage.

Some objects may require wire armatures to add rigidity to the structure. Make your canvas pieces, place a wire shape inside, then stuff the object. You can also use wooden dowels, battens, or stiff cardboard as a kind of armature, for instance to stiffen the neck of a doll.

However you solve the technical aspect of soft sculpture, have fun! It can be a very evocative and charming art form.

Anne Sullivan
Look Mom, I've been to Africa
Canvas, batting

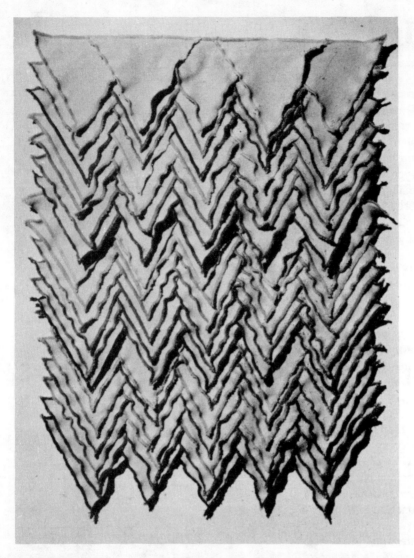

Linda Wellner
L'Arc en Ciel
Canvas and colored threads

Margo Hoff
Dove Descending
Cotton canvas, laminated canvas layers, acrylic paint

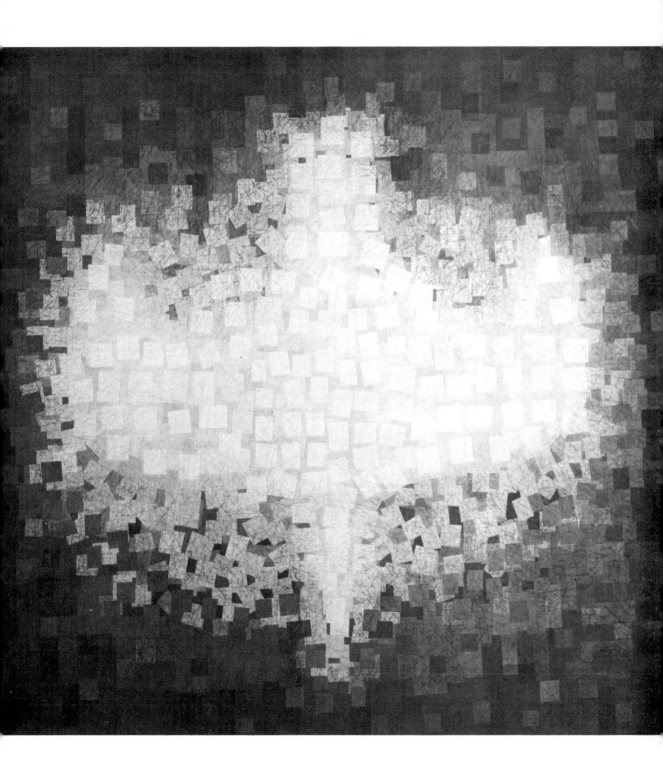

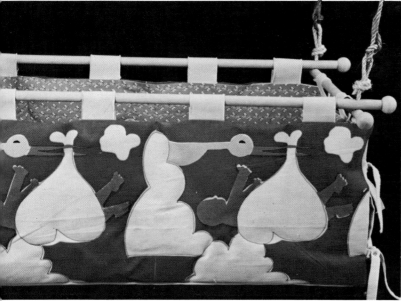

Top Left: Landscape
  Art Portfolio
Center Left: Cloud Cradle
Lower Left: Rainbow
  Accordion Purse
Right: The Stubby

Top: Seminole Ski Carrier
Above Left: Small Happy Purses for Small People
Above Right: Polish After-Ski Boots

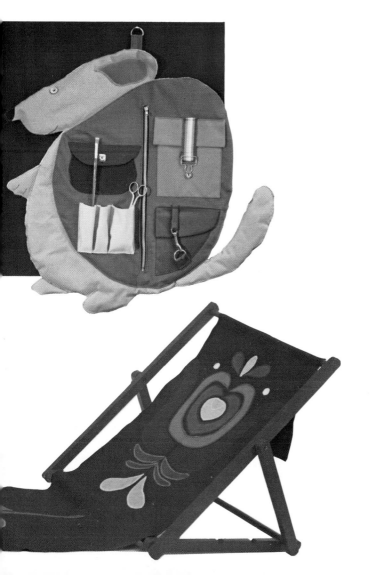

Top Left: Pack Rat
Lower Left: Ukrainian Backrest Carrier
Above Right: Viennese Puppet Stage

Right: Three Astonished People
Top Left: Ethnic mini-Purses
Lower Left: Ark Wallhanging

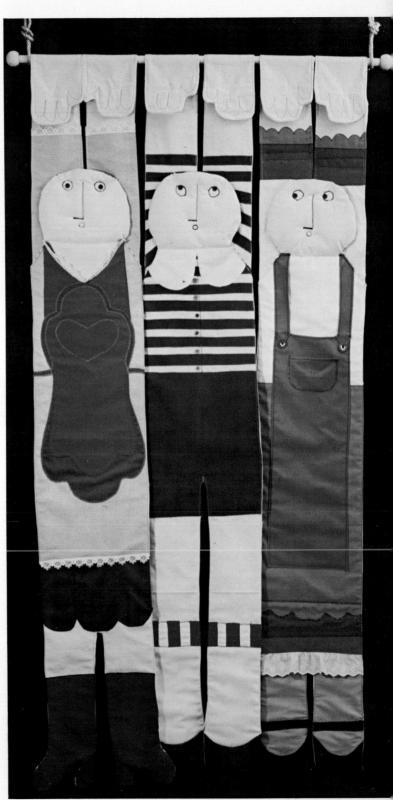

The Projects

Before beginning any project, make sure you read the instructions thoroughly. Many of the technical aspects of sewing canvas are explained in the second chapter, along with such instructions as how to enlarge a pattern. If any of the materials are unfamiliar to you, check the list at the end of the second chapter; it will tell you what kinds of stores to shop for everything needed to complete the projects. Complete instructions on the various embellishing techniques are included in the third chapter.

Organizers

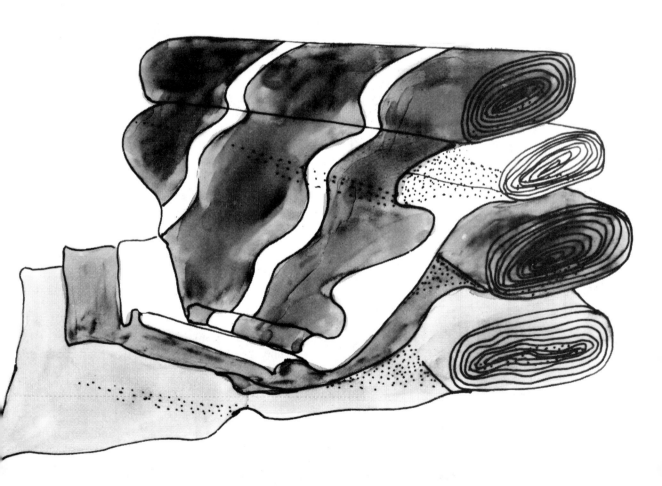

Baby-All

Preparing to travel anywhere with a baby is like outfitting an Arctic expedition. Babies are our newest mini-consumers whose necessities include disposable diapers, bottles, sterilizers, pacifiers, toys, jars of food, plastic pants, booties, teething rings, bibs, blankets, and a vast array of unguents and powders. In addition to needing a way to haul these things around, a mother is often faced with a lack of space in which to change the squirming child. The Baby-All is dedicated to every mother who has ever tried laying a cranky infant onto the wet tile of a public lavatory sink, pinioning him down with one hand while scrabbling with the other hand for a diaper pin.

The Baby-All is a tote bag, a changing table, and a wet clothes hamper too. Constructed on the flat, the Baby-All unfolds to reveal a softly padded changing table which can also double as a quilt to cover a sleeping child. On one side is a very large, waterproof pocket for wet or soiled clothes. On the other, a series of pockets conveniently hold a bottle, toy or diaper. The bag ties at the sides, and extra blankets and clothes may be carried in the folded Baby-All.

You might also make a scaled down version of the Baby-All for a child's doll, with pockets for pretend nursing bottles, doll clothes, and mini-diapers.

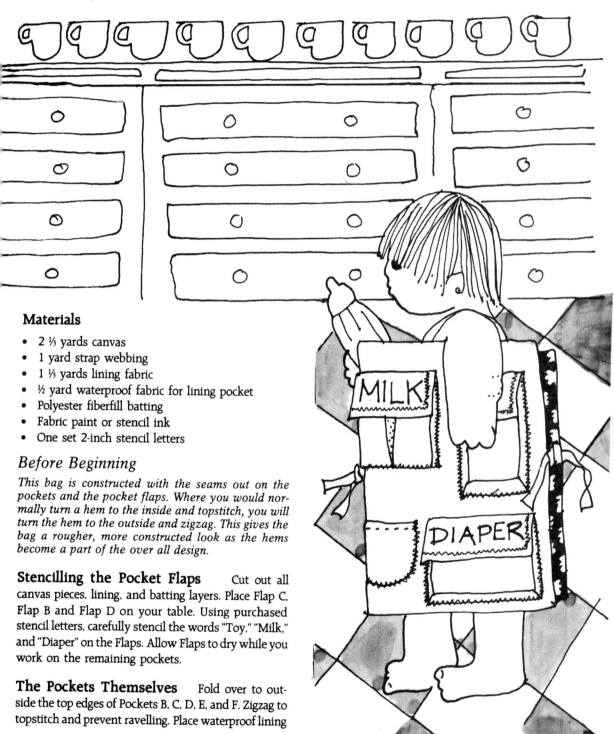

Baby-all

Materials

- 2 ⅓ yards canvas
- 1 yard strap webbing
- 1 ⅓ yards lining fabric
- ½ yard waterproof fabric for lining pocket
- Polyester fiberfill batting
- Fabric paint or stencil ink
- One set 2-inch stencil letters

Before Beginning

This bag is constructed with the seams out on the pockets and the pocket flaps. Where you would normally turn a hem to the inside and topstitch, you will turn the hem to the outside and zigzag. This gives the bag a rougher, more constructed look as the hems become a part of the over all design.

Stencilling the Pocket Flaps   Cut out all canvas pieces, lining, and batting layers. Place Flap C, Flap B and Flap D on your table. Using purchased stencil letters, carefully stencil the words "Toy," "Milk," and "Diaper" on the Flaps. Allow Flaps to dry while you work on the remaining pockets.

The Pockets Themselves   Fold over to outside the top edges of Pockets B, C, D, E, and F. Zigzag to topstitch and prevent ravelling. Place waterproof lining

Baby-All

and Pocket E together, *wrong* sides together. Baste around the outside, very close to the edge. Handling as one piece, zigzag large Pocket E onto one side of Backing A.

Turn Backing around so that the remaining pockets will be facing the other edge. Place Pocket B onto Backing. Zigzag right and left sides in place. You now have an excess of fabric which you fold into tucks, forming two separate pockets for bottles. Fold, pin and zigzag along bottom. Make a straight seam vertically between the center tucks to form two compartments.

Place small Pocket F onto Backing and zigzag in place.

Pockets C and D are both constructed the same way. Pin Sides to each side of Pocket D. Sew with a straight stitch. Now sew Bottom of Pocket D to bottom edge of Pocket. Seams will be to inside on Pocket C and D. Finish Pocket by stitching last seams joining Pocket Sides to Pocket Bottoms, forming a box shape. Turn right side out. Fold top edge of completed Pocket to outside ½ inch. Zigzag. You now have a squared-off Pocket 1½ inch deep. Pin this Pocket to the Backing as indicated in the pattern. Zigzag along outside edges. Repeat same procedure with Pocket C. Place C on Backing and zigzag.

If your Pocket Flaps are thoroughly dry, center each one above the appropriate Pocket and zigzag down. Flaps will overhang each Pocket by about ½ inch at the sides and should be positioned above each Pocket about 1 inch.

The Straps and Ties Cut four Tab Ties, 1 by 15 inches each, from scraps of canvas. Zigzag along all edges to prevent ravelling. Pin Ties onto sides of Backing 12 inches from top edges. Ties must be facing inwards to center of bag. Stitch in place. Cut two straps of webbing about 16 inches long. Pin as handles onto Backing A, loops towards center of bag. Sew in place.

The Changing Table and Quilt Make sure all straps and ties are pinned to center of bag so they will not get caught in the seams when you add the lining. Lay pocketed Backing on table face up. On top of this lay lining fabric face down. Then place the two layers of fiberfill batting on the lining, making sure the outside edges match. Pin through all layers, beginning in the middle and working out to the edges. Overpin, rather than skimp. With a straight stitch, sew around three edges of this sandwich, leaving one short end open for turning. If you find the batting is clogging up your presser foot, lay some tracing paper or newspaper over it and stitch right through the paper. This will keep your machine moving freely, and the paper will rip off easily when your stitching is done.

Turn entire Baby-All right side out, poking corners out with a sharp point. Handstitch final open edge with a blind stitch.

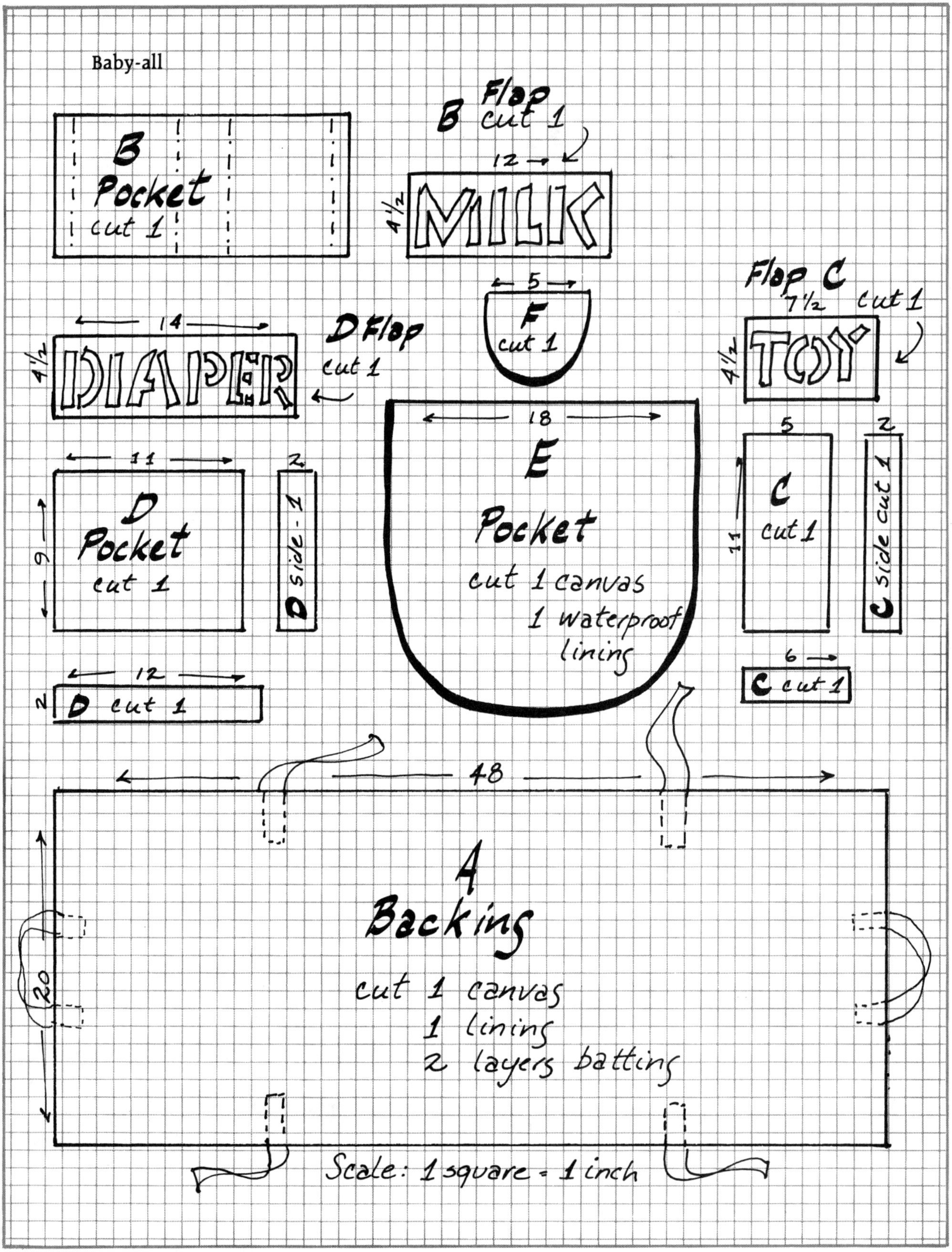

Baby-all

B Pocket cut 1

B Flap cut 1
12 →
4½
MILK

Flap C cut 1
7½
4½
TOY

14
4½
DIAPER

D Flap cut 1

5
F cut 1

D Pocket cut 1
11
9

2
D side - 1

E Pocket
cut 1 canvas
1 waterproof
lining
18

5
C cut 1
11

2
C side cut 1

12
2 **D** cut 1

6 →
C cut 1

48
20

A Backing
cut 1 canvas
1 lining
2 layers batting

Scale: 1 square = 1 inch

Hot Tub Organizer

Hot tubs are sybaritic, practical, friendly, luxurious, healthful and . . . sloppy. A recent dredging of ours proved astonishing: one gold hoop earring, a Venetian wine glass, 17 hairpins, a chess piece, three beer caps, a Navajo bracelet, and a mysterious wedding band which no one claims. The Hot Tub Organizer wraps around the perimeter of the tub, pocketing bathers' necessities while the revellers enjoy their plunge. Numbered pockets receive valuable jewelry, the larger pockets accomodate wine, loofas, hairbrushes, flashlights, eye glasses, massage oils, and deck shoes. A soft rope slung from the bottom keeps towels dry and out of snails' silvery pathways. The canvas is easily suspended from four cuphooks screwed into the redwood sides of the tub itself. A backing of waterproof fabric is added to help prevent possible mildewing.

Hot tub organizer

Materials

- 2 yards natural canvas
- 1 yard oilcloth or waterproof fabric
- 2 yards *each* red, yellow, and navy grosgrain ribbon, ¾ inch wide (fabric strips may be used for the stripes if you have scraps available).
- Twelve #3 grommets, and grommet setter
- 2¼ yards soft, natural rope
- Black fabric paint or permanent black marking pen
- 2-inch stencil letters (optional)

Preparing the Backing

Cut out all pattern pieces. Zigzag all edges of Backing to prevent ravelling. Cut waterproof lining in half lengthwise and piece together to form one long piece. Trim to match canvas Backing A. Place lining and Backing right

Hot Tub Organizer

sides together, and stitch around three edges. Trim, turn right side out. Fold remaining raw edges in towards each other. Stitch close to edge. Handle from now on as one piece.

With grommet setter, insert #3 grommets in each corner of Backing. Insert bottom grommets in Backing as shown on pattern.

Pocketing   Turn under long edge of Pocket B 1 inch and topstitch to hem. Pin lengths of grosgrain ribbon along Pocket, leaving a ¼-inch space between ribbons. Sew ribbons down, stitching close to edges.

Lay Pocket B onto Backing 8 inches from top. Turn under side edges ½ inch and topstitch in place. With the remaining Pocket fabric which is flopping loosely, fashion five tucked pockets, one for each numbered section. These may be the same size or they may vary, depending on where and how deeply you take the tucks. Experiment with the tucks until you have devised pockets that will meet your own hot tub needs. In some instances you may wish to take no tucks at all, but merely make a vertical seam thereby creating a flat pocket. When you have figured out your pocket sections, pin the tucking in place along bottom edge and zigzag with a wide stitch to hold. *See (a).*

Turn under the top edges of the small Pockets C ¼ inch and topstitch. Using purchased stencils or templates made from the numbers on the pattern layout, trace numbers "1" to "5" onto the small Pockets C. Fill in with fabric paint or marking pen. Allow to dry. Place Pockets onto Backing at even intervals. With a close zigzag or satin stitch, sew Pockets to Backing.

Roping the Bottom   Make a knot at one end of the rope. Beginning at one side, slip rope through grommets at bottom of canvas. Thread the rope through so that each section has a rope loop large enough to hang a towel. Tie off at the other side. *See (b).* There will be room enough in the corner grommets to catch a cup hook and hold the Organizer firmly at the bottom edge. When you attach the Organizer to your hot tub, don't put it on the same side people use to climb in and out of the tub. Put it on an unused side so its contents won't be knocked about by the bathers.

Fig. (a)

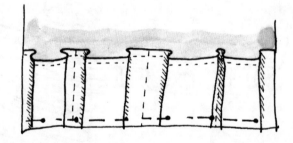

Fig. (b)

74

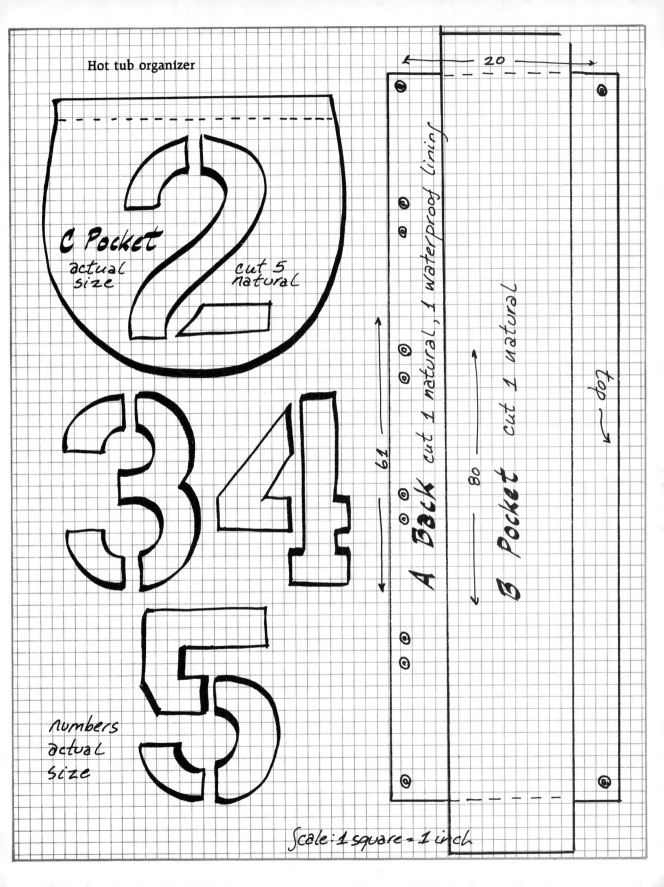

Hot tub organizer

C Pocket
actual
size

cut 5
natural

numbers
actual
size

A Back cut 1 natural, 1 waterproof lining

B Pocket cut 1 natural

20

61

80

top

Scale: 1 square = 1 inch

Jaws Pajama Bag

Benignly omnivorous, the Jaws Pajama Bag munches flannel nightgowns and Dr. Dentons with enthusiasm. His tastes are catholic, however, and he will accept jeans, T-shirts, dirty socks, or even a stuffed animal or two. Children delight in slipping their hands past his white felt teeth and diving to the bottom of his yawning maw to rescue a favorite toy. While the lurid pink figure disappearing into Jaw's throat may prove discomfiting to some adults, kids love it, invariably peering into the Pajama Bag to see if the legs are missing — chewed off, no doubt, by a hungry beast who missed his breakfast ration of P.J.'s.

Materials

- 1½ yards black canvas
- ¾ yard red canvas
- ½ yard pink canvas (or solid cotton)
- ⅓ yard white felt
- ¾ yard polyester fiberfill batting
- Two small brass rings

Making the Basics   Cut out all pieces. Tuck the white felt Teeth E under the top curve of the mouth and pin. Zigzag Teeth onto Head A around mouth. With black thread, zigzag or overcast straight edge across bottom of mouth on the Head to keep from ravelling. Place white felt Eyes F onto Head A. Place black eyeballs just underneath as shown in pattern. Zigzag eyes to Head.

Place Head A on top of Back G, matching top edges. Position disappearing pink Person onto inside of Back G so that the arms will show through the mouth of the Head. Remove Head A and stitch Person onto G with a satin stitch or zigzag.

Making the Tail   Cut one red canvas piece for the Tail, also cut one lining and one fiberfill batting. Make a sandwich of the lining (face down), batting, and canvas Tail. The Tail should curve to the *left* as you work so it will fit the Head when you are ready to join the top and bottom of the Bag. Pin this sandwich securely. With a straight stitch, quilt through all layers in a freely scalloped design, creating his scales. You may prefer to draw the scallop lines lightly in pencil first, but once you get the swing of it, you will find it isn't really necessary.

Completing the Behemoth   Lay Head A onto completed Tail C so it overlaps about ¼ inch. Zigzag carefully to join. Place the now completed front of Jaws onto Back G so that the Disappearing Person's hands show through the mouth. Pin around all edges. Trim so that the two pieces match exactly. Stitch around all the edges of the beast with a straight stitch ⅛ inch from the outer edge. Then go over this stitching again with an overcast or regular zigzag stitch. You may want to repeat for a neat edge.

Handstitch brass rings onto the back of Jaws so it can be suspended from hooks in the wall.

Feed with flannel, daily!

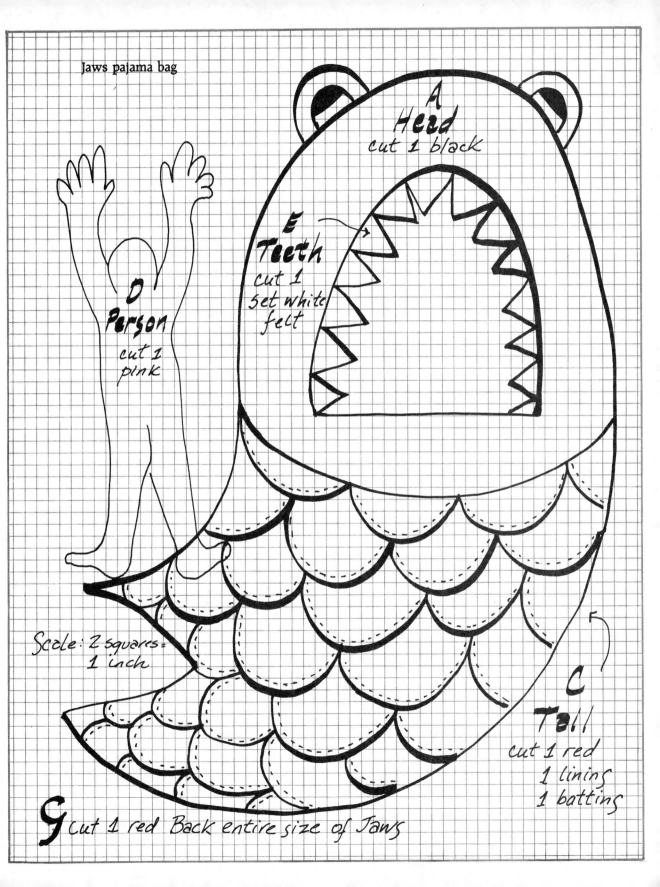

Jaws pajama bag

A
Head
cut 1 black

E
Teeth
cut 1
set white
felt

D
Person
cut 1
pink

Scale: 2 squares =
1 inch

C
Tail
cut 1 red
1 lining
1 batting

G cut 1 red Back entire size of Jaws

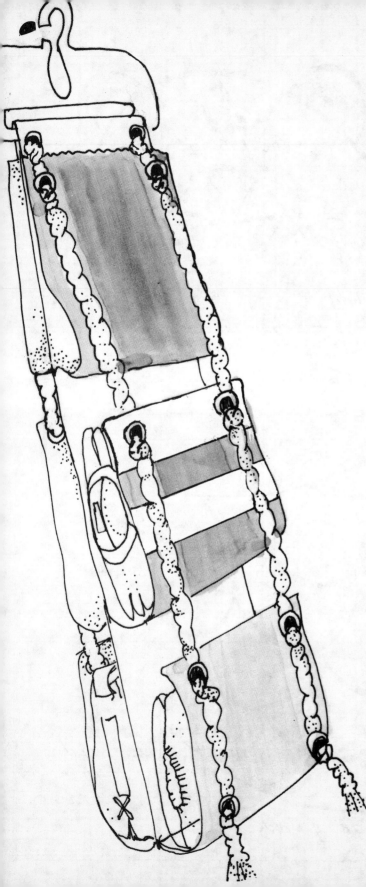

Soft Shelves

Simple, practical, colorful, easy to make . . . Soft Shelves can be hung in a closet, suspended inside the cabin of your boat, or hung prominently next to a child's bed as a not so subtle reminder to clean up. These Soft Shelves are made in modules and attached to both sides of a long strip of canvas, you may lengthen or widen them to suit your particular needs. They belong in the same category as all those other very simple things that help make our lives run a little smoother. They work well for storing soft things such as T-shirts, sweaters, jeans or underwear. Made narrower, they can hold pairs of shoes, toys, magazines, or help organize your skeins of yarn. Hung in a bathroom they neatly display towels and extra linen for houseguests. In your bedroom, scarves, belts, and accessories can be tucked into the pockets. They are a convenience in the garage or potting shed where trowels, seed packets, light tools and garden twine usually get tangled together. Scout around your house or apartment, and you'll find innumerable ways to put these canvas shelves to work.

Materials

- ⅔ yard natural canvas
- Twelve #3 grommets and grommet setter
- 1⅓ yards lining fabric
- Large plastic or decorative coat hanger
- 8 yards ½-inch rope or soft upholstery cording.

Preparing the Pockets   Cut out all Pockets and linings. Make first Pocket by placing Pocket and lining right sides together. Stitch around three edges, ½ inch from edge. Leave one long—16 inch—edge open. Turn, press. Fold in open end ½ inch and sew close to edge with a straight stitch. Make all six pockets in the same manner. With a grommet setter, insert a #3 grommet into the upper corners of each pocket. These pockets will be applied in pairs to either side of the canvas Body.

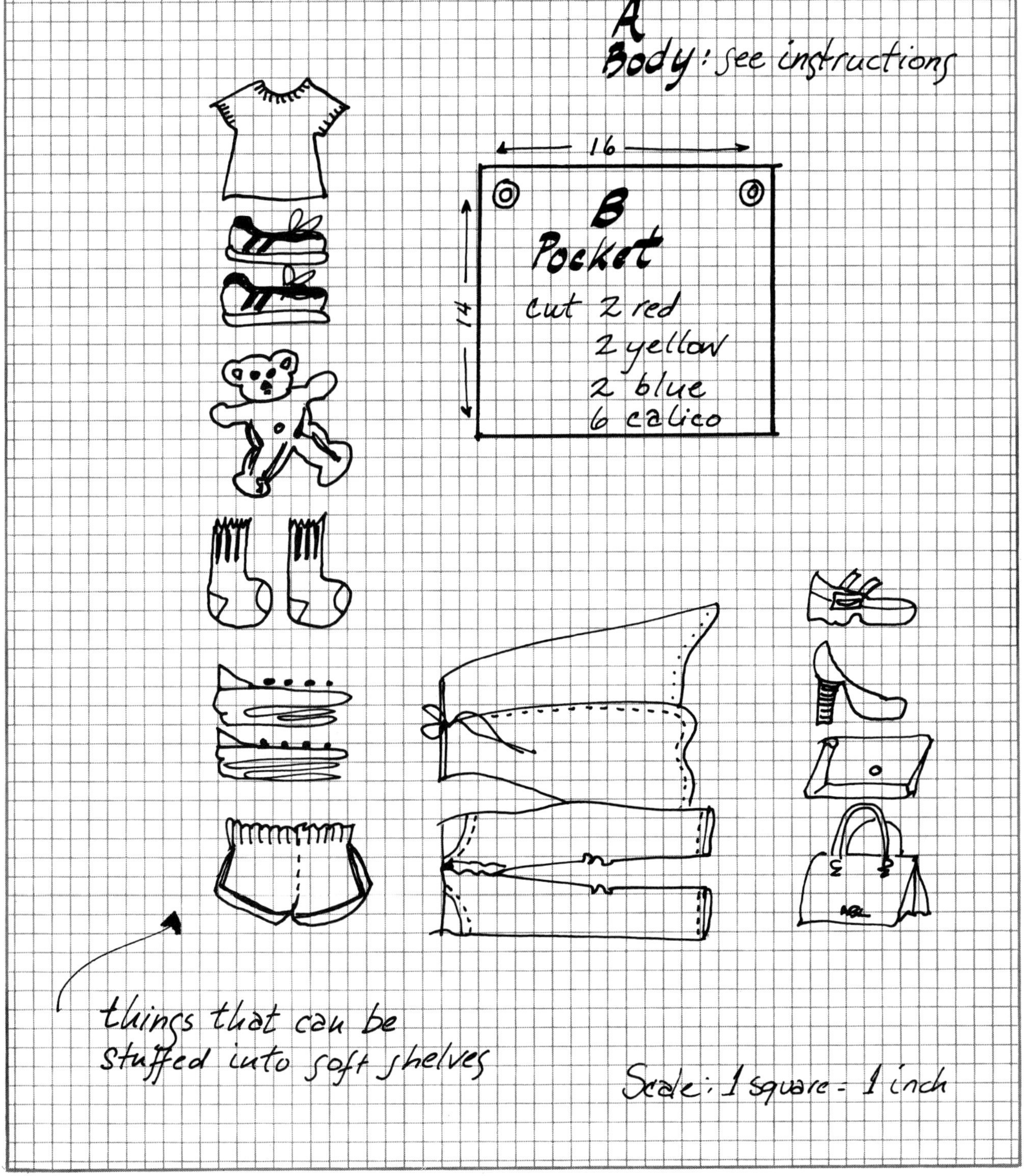

Soft shelves

A
Body: see instructions

<- 16 ->

⊙   ⊙

B
Pocket
cut 2 red
     2 yellow
     2 blue
     6 calico

14

things that can be
stuffed into soft shelves

Scale: 1 square = 1 inch

Soft Shelves

Making the Shelves   Cut out Body A. If you are using 54-inch wide canvas, simply cut one long strip 15 inches wide. If you are using 10 oz. duck which is 30 inches wide, cut one piece 27 inches long. Fold this piece in half lengthwise and cut in half, giving you two pieces each 15 inches wide. With a zigzag stitch, sew these two pieces together, overlapping the ends slightly. You now have a long strip 15 by 54 inches. Zigzag around all four edges of this Body to prevent ravelling.

Beginning at the bottom of Body A, sew one Pocket onto long Body. Now attach second bottom Pocket, with seam to inside. Fold Pockets up onto Body and pin. *See (a).* Leaving a space of 3 inches from the top of these Pockets, pin second tier of Pockets to Body and stitch. Sew with one seam.

Fold up second tier of Pockets and construct the top tier the same way.

Fig. (a)

Fold top of Body A through decorative hanger bar and topstitch in place. Insert two additional grommets two inches below hanger bottom, in Body A.

Hanging It Up   Lay Soft Shelves flat on floor or worktable. Fold all Pockets up towards the top. Cut two 3-yard lengths of rope or upholstery cording. Each length of rope will begin at the bottom Pocket, be pulled up through the grommets on the other Pockets, thence through the grommet in Body and continue down through the Pockets on the other side. It will be knotted off after going through the grommet on the bottom Pocket.

Insert rope through grommet in bottom Pocket in one side of Shelves. Knot. Now, make a simple loop knot in the rope approximately where you think the grommet hole for the middle Pocket will be. Draw rope up through this grommet, from the outside to the inside. Tighten your loop knot so that Pocket is held vertically. Make another loop knot about where the grommet will be on the top Pocket. Draw rope through top Pocket in the same fashion, tightening the knot when the Pocket is vertical. Pass the rope through the grommet near the hanger, and continue down other side. The second side will be easier because you do not have to make the knot *before* you slip the rope through each Pocket, but can do it afterwards. When you finish at the bottom Pocket, knot rope securely. Repeat this roping and tying on the other side of your Shelves.

Bedside Organizer

Bedside Organizer

The last few years have seen a revolution in domestic furnishings. Chairs have lost their legs, tables and desks are disappearing and reappearing connected to modular room dividers, traditional bureaus are becoming structurally integrated parts of beds and beds themselves are now respectable in the living room.

But with the simplification of our furniture has come a burgeoning of personal impedimenta which belies our move towards simplicity. It takes only one day spent in bed with a head cold to discover how complicated our lives have actually become: new Kleenex, used Kleenex, aspirin, bad novels, etc. all surround us with the paraphernalia of our lives. With the nightstand relegated to the endangered furniture list, we sit under our decorator sheets, miserable and overwhelmed.

The Bedside Organizer—one of the very simplest projects in this book—will provide soft, tuck-in shelving that eliminates a messy counterpane. The Organizer is simply a length of canvas with a series of pockets stitched onto it, you tuck it in between the boxspring and mattress. Or, in a waterbed, between the frame and mattress. The width of the Organizer, the depth and the variety of the pockets is up to you. This pattern is for a small caddy, but it could be enlarged to suit your particular needs.

Embellished with lace or satin appliques, the Bedside Organizer makes a sensible, and sensitive, honeymoon gift. Or piped with plaid bias tape, it makes an equally thoughtful houseguest present to leave at the home of a bachelor friend.

Materials

- 1 yard canvas
- 3 yards wide bias seam binding
- Assorted laces, ribbons, satins

Sewing   Cut out Background A and Pockets. Fold seam binding in half and stitch onto top edge of Pocket D. Sew binding onto diagonal edges of Pocket C. Place C on top of B and baste along top edge of C. Now apply bias binding across entire top edge of Pocket B enclosing all raw edges. Lay Pocket D onto completed Pocket C/B and sew around sides and bottom, ¼ inch from edge. Topstitch vertical seam in center to form another, center pocket section. Place entire completed Pocket section onto lower section of Background A so that bottom edges meet. Pin remaining seam binding all the way around A. *See (a)*. Mitre the corners as you go for a neat look. Sew binding in place.

For more elegant versions, you may wish to line the pockets in silk, substitute embroidered silk ribbons for the plain trim, or hand stitch a silk violet onto a pocket corner. Before presenting the Organizer to a friend, fill a corner pocket with a surprise sachet of pot-pourri to sweeten dreams.

Fig. (a)

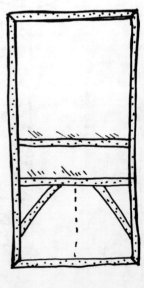

Bedside organizer

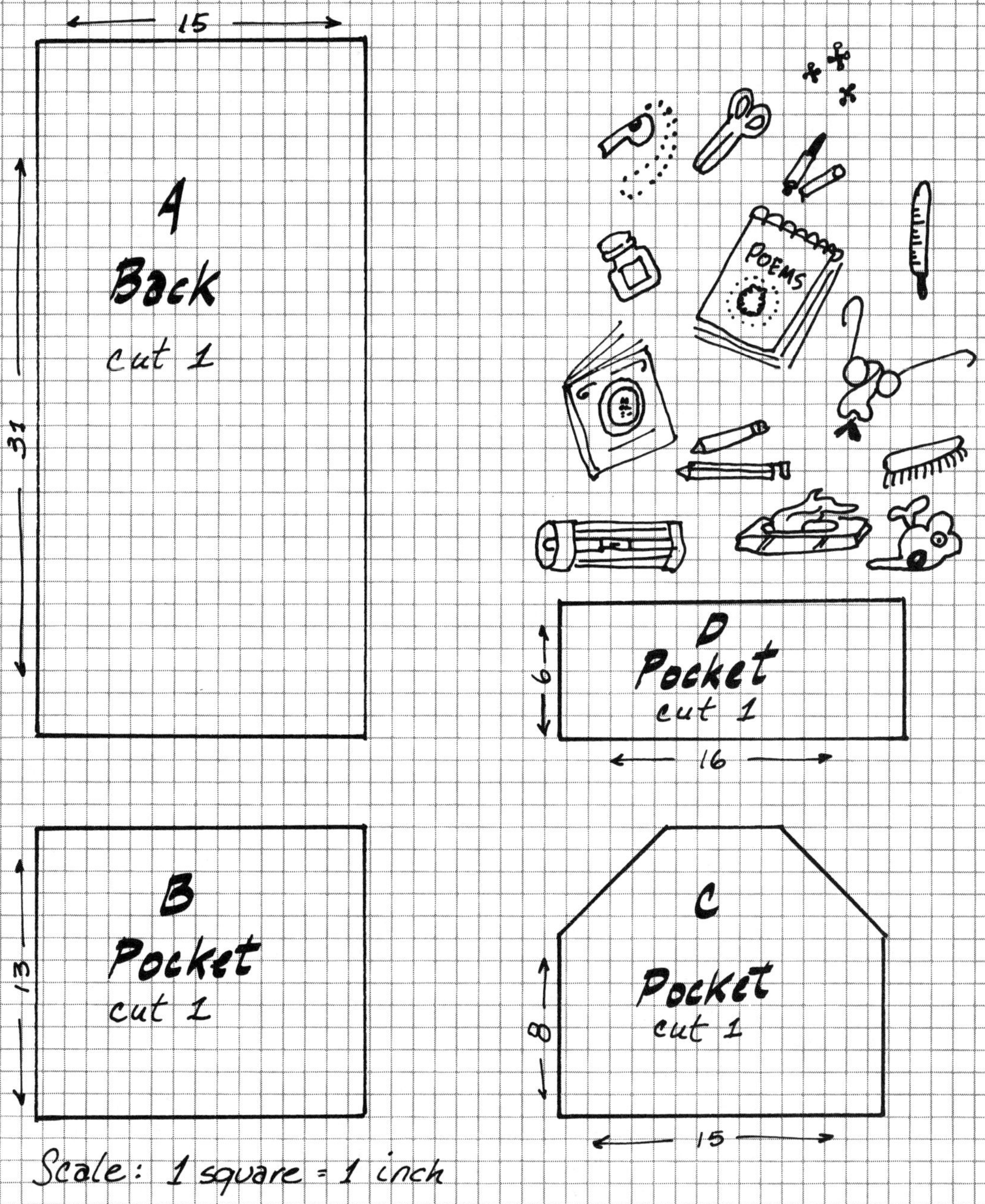
15
A
Back
cut 1
31
D
Pocket
cut 1
6
16
B
Pocket
cut 1
13
C
Pocket
cut 1
8
15
POEMS
Scale: 1 square = 1 inch

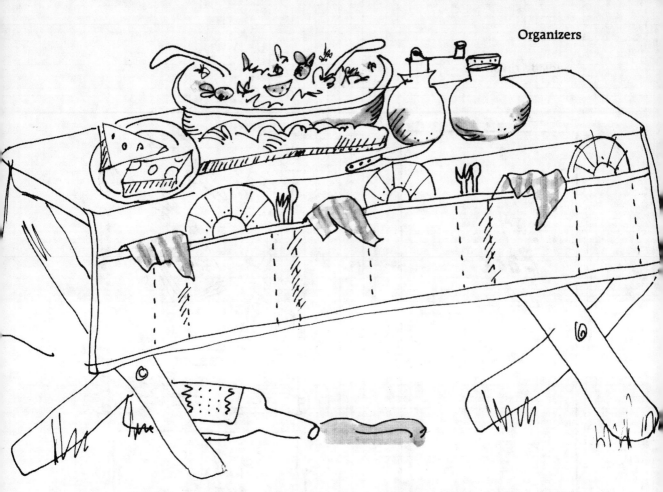

Park Gourmet Table-Setter

Nothing is as appealing to a weary traveler as a picnic table standing tranquil under a drifting pepper tree, its weathered wood benches inviting distraught parents to unpack their knapsacks and stretch out for a while. We gratefully accept the invitation, rolling out of the car, shirts stuck to our cramped backs, knees locked at right angles and our feet asleep. We spread the meal before us, ready to relax, when suddenly the wind comes up, gusting the paper plates like Frisbees across a nearby barbed wire fence. Baby Wendell screams, a splinter from the old table top lodged in his pudgy elbow. The peanut butter overturns, oozing over the ketchup

blobs left by the last gourmand.

The Park Gourmet ends all that turmoil. The Gourmet is a picnic table-setter designed to fit any standard 3 by 8 foot picnic table. It tops the table with bright canvas and has a series of pockets along the side flaps with room for eight place settings. Plates, utensils and napkins can be tucked away *before* you leave home. Then the entire cloth folds up and fits neatly into its own carrier envelope, ready to be flipped open when you sit down at your roadside retreat. Convenient, sanitary, and gay, the Park Gourmet makes a celebration of an everyday picnic.

Park gourmet table-setter

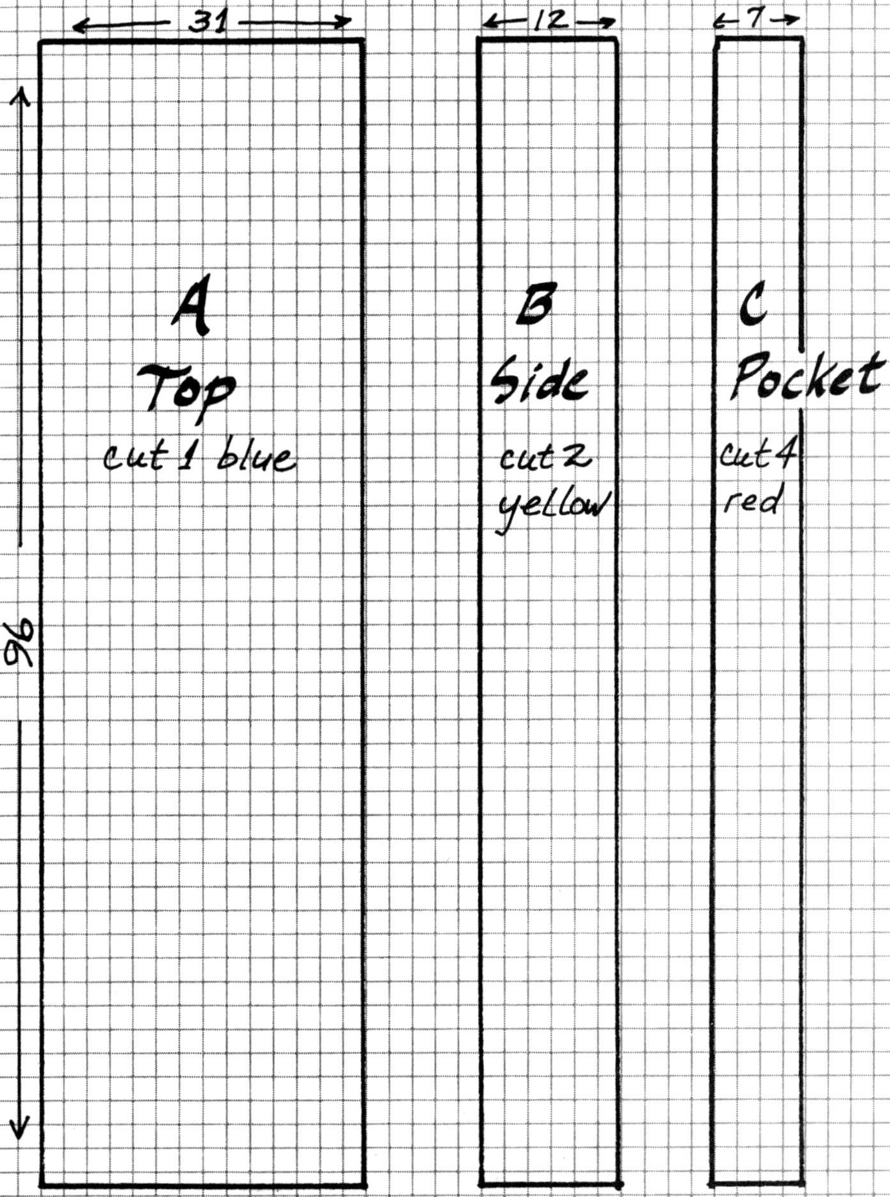

|← 31 →|

A

Top

cut 1 blue

96

|← 12 →|

B

Side

cut 2
yellow

|← 7 →|

C

Pocket

cut 4
red

Scale: 1 square = 2 inches

Park Gourmet Table-Setter

Materials

- 2 ⅔ yards blue canvas
- 2 ⅔ yards yellow canvas
- 1 ⅓ yards red canvas
- 14 yards wide blue cotton bias tape
- 1 ⅓ yards blue canvas for carrying case
- 12 inches Velcro

Assembling

Cut out all pieces of canvas, zig-zag all edges to prevent ravelling. Stitch Sides B to Top A along both long edges. Press seams towards Top and topstitch again for a trim look.

To form two long Pockets, join two pieces C together at narrow end and stitch with narrow seam. Repeat for second Pocket. Sew bias tape along one long edge of each Pocket, this will form the top of the Pockets. Pin Pockets on top of yellow Sides B, matching sides and bottom. Machine baste in place. Sew bias tape along the short sides of the entire Gourmet, enclosing the Pockets and the yellow Sides as you go. Now stitch Pocket C to Sides to form four individual pockets on each side. Bind lower edges with remaining bias tape.

The Carryall Envelope

Cut one piece of blue canvas 42 by 15 inches. Fold under the two short edges ½ inch and topstitch. Fold canvas in half lengthwise with topstitched seams to outside. Stitch around three edges to form simple envelope, leaving topstitched edges open. Turn right side out and press. Cut Velcro in three equal parts. Position these evenly along open edge at the ends and the middle. Stitch one half Velcro along one side. Match other half Velcro on other side and sew down. If you fold your table-setter in fifths lengthwise, and in fourths the other way, it fits easily into this carrying pouch, even when filled with picnic placesettings.

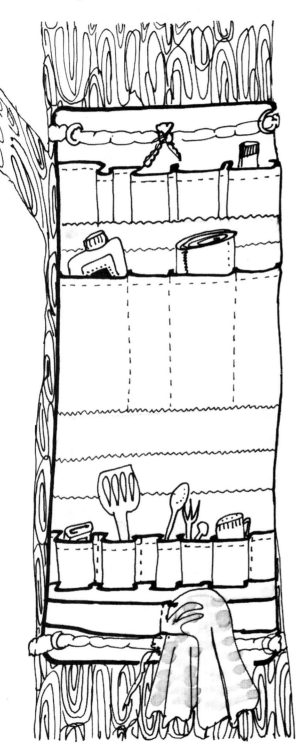

Roll-Up Tree Cabinet

As anyone who spends a good deal of time in the outdoors knows, the romance of camping dissipates quickly as the preparation of three meals a day becomes a chore. When our family camps out there always seems to be an incredible amount of miscellaneous cooking supplies and equipment that accumulates. I am usually the one who kicks the margarine into the coals or stabs the Granola bag on a pine branch while grabbing for a towel already alight in the fiery embers. Consequently, the Roll-Up Tree Cabinet was designed, selfishly, for me.

The Roll-Up Tree Cabinet is a sound answer to organizing kitchen supplies in the woods. It is constructed of a flat stretch of canvas with a welter of pockets stitched onto its front. To accomodate a variety of different items, some of the pockets are pleated and some are flat. Grommets at each corner allow rope to pass through and around the tree's girth, wrapping the Cabinet onto the tree. There are no nails to damage the living trunk, food is kept off the ground and away from animals, and the whole thing rolls and stuffs into your knapsack while you are hiking to Shangri-la.

Roll-Up Tree Cabinet

Materials

- 1¼ yards red canvas
- ½ yard orange canvas
- ¼ yard rust canvas
- ¼ yard yellow canvas
- ¼ yard olive green canvas
- Four #1, #2, or #3 grommets, with grommet setter
- Rope or clothesline appropriate to grommet size

Readying the Pockets   Cut out all pieces. On Pocket pieces C, D, and E turn under one long edge and zigzag to prevent ravelling. These will be the Pocket tops. The Cabinet is constructed so that the bottom edge of each Pocket section is enclosed by a strip of olive green canvas zigzagged on top and covering the bottom seam of the Pocket. For the bottom Pocket the green strip is left as a loose strap through which you hang towels or bandanas.

Sewing the Pockets   Lay Back A onto worktable. With hemmed edge at top, place yellow Pocket C onto Back 6 inches from the top. Match side edges of Pocket with side edges of Back. Machine baste sides to hold. Now there is extra fabric in the Pocket for you to tuck and fold into as many separate sections as you like. When you have devised your tucked pockets, sew along bottom edge of yellow strip to hold. Now place one green strip B along bottom edge of this tucked yellow Pocket so that it covers the raw edge. Zigzag entire strip to hold.

Place orange Pocket D onto Back about 2 inches below the green strip you have just sewn. Stitch down at intervals forming several pockets without pleats. Apply second green strip B across bottom edge of this Pocket as you did on the first.

Place rust Pocket E onto Back 4 inches below the green strip which bands the orange Pocket. Sew along both side edges. With the extra fabric, make a series of tucks to form small pockets suitable for spices, or kitchen utensils. Stitch tucks along bottom edge. Zigzag over these tucks to keep edge from ravelling. The bottom edge of this last pocket will not have the green strip banding it, but rather the strip will hang loosely in two loops for towels.

To make this towel strip take strip F and turn under the two long edges 1 inch. Zigzag around all four edges. Place this strip onto Cabinet so that its top edge covers the lower edge of the bottom pocket. Match side edges with Back side edges. Sew sides. Now sew the strip to Cabinet at center with one vertical seam, forming two towel loops.

Finishing Up   Turn under all four sides of Cabinet to the back ½ inch. Press and pin. Zigzag around perimeter of entire Cabinet to keep from ravelling. With grommet setter, insert one grommet into each corner of cabinet. Knot rope in each hole, leaving enough to wrap twice around the trees you might encounter. Obviously the Cabinet is not useful for camping in Giant Sequoia country, but elsewhere it is a joy to use.

Roll-up tree cabinet

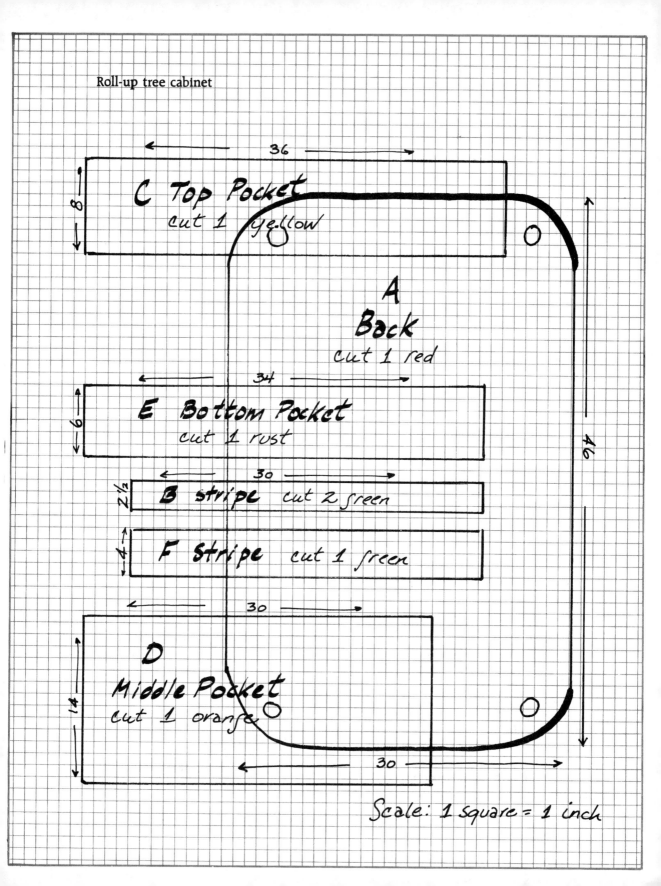

C Top Pocket
cut 1 yellow

36

8

A
Back
cut 1 red

E Bottom Pocket
cut 1 rust

34

6

B stripe   cut 2 green

30

2½

F stripe   cut 1 green

30

4

D
Middle Pocket
cut 1 orange

30

14

46

30

Scale: 1 square = 1 inch

Pack Rat

We are all of us pack rats, but surely the most obsessive and messiest collectors are children. Their collections of pebbles, stamps, broken springs, screws, shells, shark's teeth, rubber monsters, bone shards, false fingernails, jewels, postcards, empty make-up bottles and rubber bands rival the kitchen middens of the Neolithic Age. Yet, should a larger person dare suggest that a good cleaning under a bunk bed might appreciably lessen the burden on the floorboards, a cry goes up high enough to shake the throne of the gods.

The Pack Rat wall organizer joins this fray with his many treasure-ready pockets. A large zipper opens the center of the Rat's backpack into a pocket large enough to hide at least a dozen forbidden comic books. A smaller pocket is snapped into secrecy with an overall buckle. Another pocket is secured with a shiny gold button from an old Officer's coat. And on another, a snap-shackle is connected to a "D" ring for security. Observing it all, the Rat himself smiles, content that within his pouch reside the irreplaceable treasures of childhood.

Materials

- 1 yard tan canvas
- 1 yard rust canvas
- Scraps of blue, red, yellow, and green canvas
- 1 yard lining fabric
- Polyester fiberfill batting
- One 18-inch oversize decorative zipper
- One snap-shackle
- Three "D" rings
- One overall buckle, and one decorative button
- One wooden button for the Rat's eye
- 8 inches of decorative webbing
- Black fabric paint, or indelible black marking pen
- Scraps of cardboard for tail insert

Making the Rat Himself

Cut out entire tan Rat Body A. Place lining fabric on table *wrong* side towards you. Lay canvas Pack Rat on top of lining and cut out using Rat as a pattern. Now cut a layer of fiberfill batting the same way. Cut a piece of stiff cardboard for the Rat's tail as indicated on pattern. Make a sandwich of lining, fiberfill, and canvas. Pin together, starting from the center and working out to edges. Insert tail cardboard in place as you pin. With a straight stitch sew slowly around edges, sewing through all three layers. Trim excess fabric. Go over edge again with a close zigzag or satin stitch for a neat edge.

With a small brush and black fabric paint, or an indelible marker, draw in the Rat's nose, mouth and whisker dots. Sew on a wooden button for his eye. Cut a scrap of pink for his ear and applique to head.

Assembling Pack Rat's Backpack

Cut out all remaining canvas pieces. Prepare all Pockets and Flaps by stitching two pieces of each together. Stitch ¼ inch from outer edge, leaving the straight edge *open* in each case. Turn right side out. Press open edges in towards each other to hide raw edge and stitch. Position blue Pocket D, orange Pocket G and green Pocket I onto the rust Backpack B. Sew the bottoms of these Pockets in place, stitching ⅛ inch from edges. Pin two side edges of yellow Pocket J onto Backpack. Stitch down. With the extra material, make a series of small tucks in the yellow canvas to form three or four pouches. Pin tucks and press to hold. Stitch across bottom edge of Pocket J. Sew vertical seams between each tucked section forming separate pouches.

Place zipper in center of Pockets as shown. It may zip up or down, whichever you prefer. Slit canvas Backpack B the length of the zipper, making two diagonal cuts at each end to allow for a neat fold-back. *See (a).* Insert zipper into this slit, folding the

Pack rat

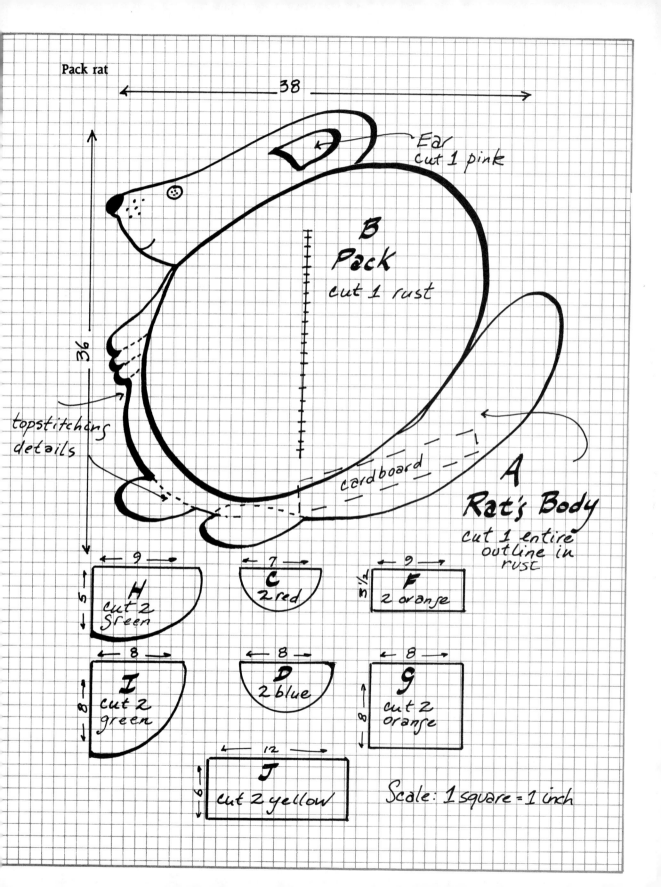

← ——————— 38 ——————— →

Ear
cut 1 pink

B
Pack
cut 1 rust

36

topstitching
details

cardboard

A
Rat's Body
cut 1 entire
outline in
rust

← 9 →
5 H
cut 2
green

← 7 →
C
2 red

← 9 →
1½ F
2 orange

← 8 →
8 I
cut 2
green

← 8 →
D
2 blue

← 8 →
G
8 cut 2
orange

← 12 →
6 J
cut 2 yellow

Scale: 1 square = 1 inch

Pack Rat

raw edges of the rust canvas under about ³/₈ inch.
Sew zipper in place, topstitching around all edges
with decorative thread if you like.

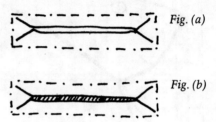

Fig. (a)

Fig. (b)

Pockets and Flaps
The Flaps are handled
differently for each Pocket. Make a buttonhole on
red Flap C to accomodate your gold button. Sew Flap
onto Backpack above blue Pocket D. Sew button
onto D. Insert one end of 8-inch length of webbing
into the overall buckle and sew in place. Position
orange Flap F over Pocket G. Tuck raw end of webbing over top of Flap F so that the buckle hangs
down onto Pocket below. Stitch Flap and webbing.
Sew button onto lower Pocket to fit overall buckle.

Cut a strip of green canvas 2 by 5 inches. Fold long
edges to inside. Press. Fold in half again. Topstitch to
form Tab. Insert a "D" ring into one end and stitch to
hold. Lay other end of Tab onto green Pocket I as
shown in pattern. Tuck end under to hide raw edge.
Stitch Pocket and Tab onto Backpack.

Make another Tab ½ inch wide and 7 inches long.
Into one end of this Tab, insert snap-shackle and
stitch Tab closed. Position Flap H over Pocket I and
pin. Tuck raw end of snap-shackle Tab over top edge
of Flap as you did with the webbing on the orange
Pocket. Stitch Flap across top, sewing through Tab
as well. Make another tab ½ inch wide and 2 inches
long and insert "D" ring through. Sew below Pocket
I, snap-shackle will attach to "D" ring.

Putting It Together
Place the completed
Backpack with all its Pockets onto the Rat's Body.
With a zigzag or satin stitch, sew onto the Rat. Make
another Tab, large enough for a "D" ring. Sew Tab by
hand onto the top back of the Rat's head for hanging
the organizer in your child's room.

Crafty Robber Shoe Bag

The shoe thief is here . . . and he is making off with your Mary-Janes, your sandals, and your hiking boots.

This Crafty Robber is able to hold four pairs of children's shoes while his wily eyes are on the look-out for more. The Robber's arms are striped canvas. If this is unavailable in your area, you can easily applique black strips onto natural canvas for the same effect. The pockets are designed for small footwear but they can be altered to fit larger shoes by widening the pocket strip.

And look out . . . the Crafty Robber loves jogging shoes.

Materials

- 1 yard yellow canvas
- 1 yard black and white striped canvas, or Sunbrella
- ⅓ yard black canvas
- ½ yard flesh colored canvas or cotton
- One pack narrow bias tape, yellow

Assembling the Robber   Cut out Robber's Head, Sleeves, Hands, Eyes, and Hat. Place his black Eyes onto the face as shown in pattern and zigzag in place. Using a slightly narrower zigzag, stitch lines indicating his eyelids and lashes.

Place two Heads G together. Zigzag around crowns to hold, On the *top* Head only, carefully cut out the Nose as shown by dotted lines on the pattern. Now place the two Hats H on the Head, one on front and one on back. Zigzag around all edges of Hat. This holds it onto the Head. Now slip the completed Head/Hat over the top (selvage) area of the Shoe Bag Back A. This Back will insert between the flapping Nose and the back Head. Pin in place.

Zigzag the front head onto the Back A, following under the eyes, around the droopy nose, and across the other side of his face.

Zigzag top Sleeve C onto Hand D at cuff. Place completed arm along top of Back A and curve hand over the top of the bag. Zigzag arm securely.

Pocketing   Stitch strips F and G together to form one long strip. Sew bias tape along one long edge to form the top of the Pockets. Pin this long strip onto Back A even with the bottom edge. At 4 inch intervals, fold under this strip ½ inch to form a tuck. Each tuck should be the opposite of its mate, and you should end up with eight equal shoe Pockets across the bag. Press these Pockets. Then zigzag down each side, and across the bottom edge to hold.

Making the Strong Arm   Applique striped Sleeve B on top of Hand E at sleeve cuff. Zigzag Sleeve and Hand onto bottom of bag, changing thread color when you reach the Hand. The Hand will block off the last Pocket slightly.

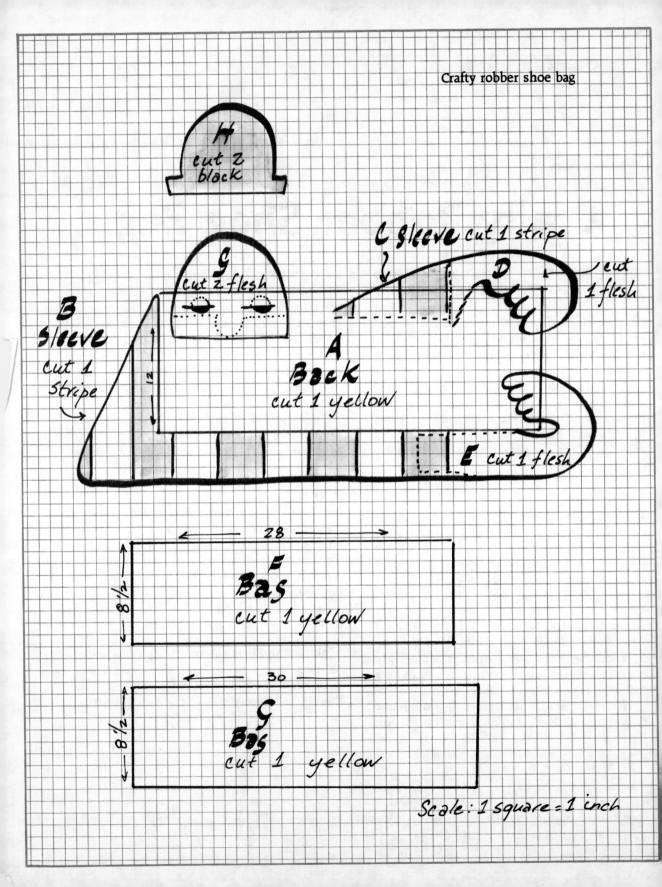

Crafty robber shoe bag

H
cut 2
black

C sleeve cut 1 stripe

G
cut 2 flesh

D
cut
1 flesh

B
sleeve
cut 1
stripe

12

A
Back
cut 1 yellow

E cut 1 flesh

28

F
Bag
cut 1 yellow

8½

30

G
Bag
cut 1 yellow

8½

Scale: 1 square = 1 inch

Totes

The Most Basic Bag

You will dream up endless variations on this basic design. Constructed on a flat surface, the bag has notched cutouts at the center bottom which make sewing it from heavy canvas an easier task for a home machine. The width and depth of the notches determine the amount of boxiness, or depth, that the bag has. You may want to experiment with creating a short, very wide bag for carrying gardening tools such as trowels or weeders. Or you may prefer a tall, thin bag for your needlepoint yarns. There are several kinds of plastic yarn holders on the market which accomodate up to twenty-four colors of yarn. You could attach two of these with Velcro straps to the inside of a tall, slender tote and stand it next to your fireside chair.

Use contrast webbing, striped or monogrammed tape, or canvas for the handles. Try appliqueing the outer pockets with a wildly personalized design. Applique the inner pockets with embroidered messages or hidden hearts and rainbows. Add double or triple pockets on the sides for a student carry-all. You might even stitch long skinny pockets vertically to the sides themselves for pencils and a slide rule or two. Once you begin elaborating on this basic tote, you will want to make one for everyone: friends, family, even foes. It is true, good tote bags make good neighbors. Have fun!

Materials

- 1⅓ yards canvas, add more depending on pockets
- 3 yards webbing
- Scraps of contrast fabric for applique (optional)
- Paints for stencilling (optional)

Pockets First   If you choose to pocket this tote bag, begin with the inner ones first. Turn under top edge of Pockets C and topstitch. Place these at desired height on the inside of Body A. Stitch in place. These seams will be hidden by the larger Pocket B on the

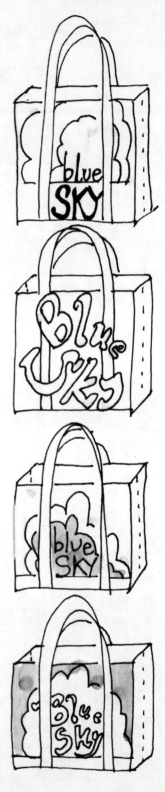

outside. Now turn under both short edges of Pocket B and topstitch. If you plan to add a monogram or other design to the outside of this long Pocket, do it now before sewing to the bag. Now place Pocket B onto the outside of Body A as indicated on pattern layout. Sew along both long edges with a straight stitch. This seam will be hidden by the webbing straps later.

Adding the Straps

Cut one long strip of webbing, allowing 12 to 15 inches on each side for the handle loop. If you want to make it a shoulder tote, you will have to measure the additional webbing accordingly.

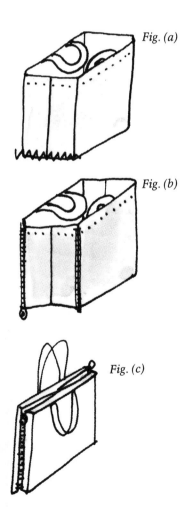

Fig. (a)

Fig. (b)

Fig. (c)

Begin with one end of the webbing at the exact center bottom of the bag, pin straps up one side and down the other. If you begin at the center bottom the loops for the handles will always be the same length. This is a nice tip to remember when making any bag. Nothing is more frustrating than to finish sewing on the entire strap, only to discover one loop is for a giant's hand, the other for a midget. Stitching close to webbing edges, sew straps to bag, boxing in the X's as shown on pattern. At the point where the strap ends meet, be sure to go over with a satin stitch to hold securely. You may want to applique some bit of whimsy, like a purchased patch in the shape of an ice cream cone, over the spot. Prepare the bag for sewing by zigzagging all edges to prevent ravelling. Then turn under ½ inch the two top edges of Body and topstitch.

Boxing It In

Since this is a very simple tote to make, and one that will probably get a lot of everyday use, it is worth making French seams along the two inside side seams. First zigzag all edges to prevent ravelling. Fold your bag so that the side seams match with *wrong* sides to inside. Stitch side seams very close to edges. Then turn bag inside out so that the *right* sides are to the inside, and stitch side seams again, enclosing the raw edges as you sew. Try not to make this French seam too thick and bulky, for it will be tough to sew up the final bottom seam if you do.

Now, with the bag still inside out, stand up and sew the two short bottom seams. Zigzag these twice for strength. *See (a)*. Turn bag right side out.

Polishing It Up

Press your tote neatly so all seams and folds are sharp. If you like a constructed look, a tote that will stand up on its own, then restitch the side foldlines ¹/₈ inch from the edge.

Another variation on this would be to insert an oversize plastic zipper between each set of side folds. I did this after completing a huge, bulky tote, and found it a successful solution to making the bag slimmer and more portable when it wasn't filled. *See (b) & (c)*.

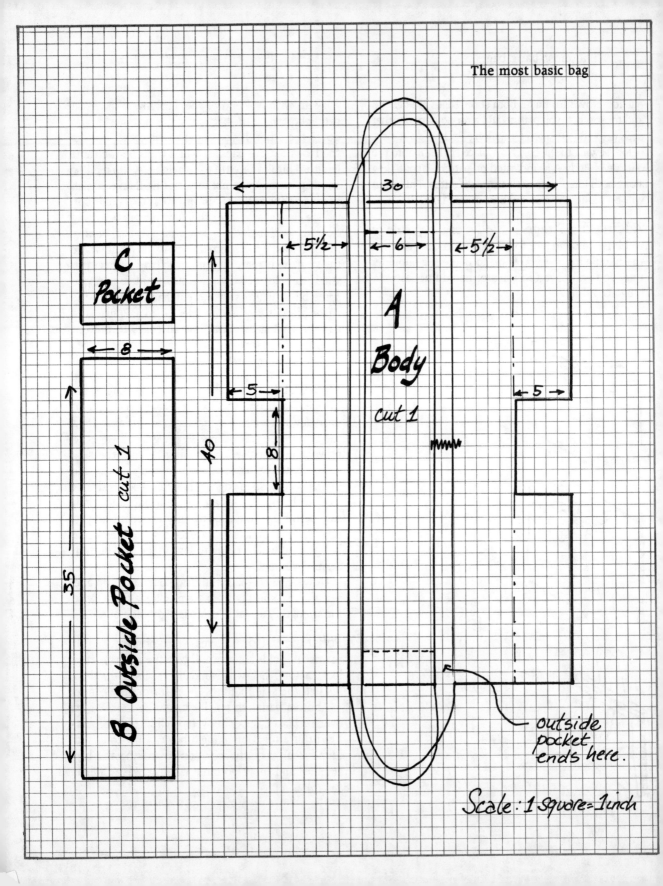

The most basic bag

C
Pocket

B Outside Pocket cut 1

35

8

30

5½   6   5½

A
Body

cut 1

40

8

5

5

outside
pocket
ends here.

Scale: 1 square = 1 inch

Flag Striped Duffle

There is nothing more quintessentially canvas than the duffle roll. Lightweight, stuffable, foldable, economical and virtually indestructable, duffle bags have been in existence in one material or another for over 500 years. Medieval knights used a form of duffle to carry their belongings during the Crusades against the Saracens. Gypsies strapped leather rolls onto the backs of their ponies on their wanderings through Europe. And, of course, the duffle has been the baggage of the seafarer and the military man. Its simple, soft shape makes it the most convenient and quiet luggage ever invented.

Bold red and green stripes on the Flag Duffle are a variation on an old, old theme. Contrast pockets on each end increase the "stuffability" of the bag. One pocket is zippered, the other is an expandable, patch pocket with a Velcro closing for last minute items. The large measurements, 12 by 24 inches, allow ample room for a whole family's vacation equipment.

Materials

- 1¼ yards natural canvas
- ⅓ yard green canvas
- ⅓ yard red canvas
- One 12-inch zipper
- One 24-inch oversize separating zipper
- 6 inches Velcro tape
- 3⅓ yards natural webbing

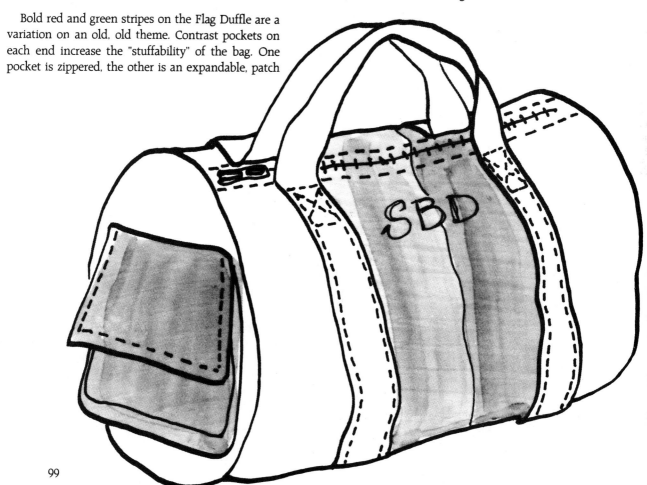

99

Flag Striped Duffle

The Round Body   Cut out all pieces. Zigzag edges of every piece to keep from ravelling. Sew red Stripe B and green Stripe C together lengthwise. Press. If you are appliqueing a monogram onto the stripe, do it now. Cut out letters in natural canvas and position them onto outside of middle Stripe AB, 3 inches from the top edge. With a satin stitch or close zigzag, applique letters onto Stripe. Now place Stripe onto Body A in exact center, according to pattern. Sew down along all edges. You do not have to turn under raw edges as the webbing will cover them.

Strapping the Duffle   Fold Duffle Body in half on foldline. Press with the palm of your hand to mark center bottom. Canvas marks easily this way, and it is a good trick to remember when working with patterns which require you to determine the midlines. At the foldline, begin pinning one continuous webbing strap onto bag. Cover raw edges of center stripe by ½ inch of webbing. Sew strap onto bag close to both edges of webbing, stopping at boxed-X so that handles are left loose. *See (a)* After stitching, pin handles towards center outside of bag so they don't interfere when you add the zipper.

Adding the Zipper   Fold short ends of Body A to the inside. Press firmly. Insert zipper between these edges and stitch in place. If you use a separating zipper it will be easy. If not, you will have trouble as you come to the end of the zipper but don't worry if you cannot get quite to the end. You can always zigzag over the zipper end later.

Pocketing the Ends   Place green E and natural E on worktable. Fold straight ends of each under ½ inch. Press. Insert 12-inch zipper between these edges and sew in place. Now close zipper. Place green and natural End face up on top of End D. Machine baste these two pieces together around

edges ½ inch from edge. This forms one zippered end Pocket.

Turn Duffle Body inside out. Place this Pocket into one end of tube, zipper side will be on inside. Pin. Stitching slowly sew Pocket onto Duffle, easing ripples as you go.

Now prepare other end Pocket. Pin long Strip I onto Pocket H. Sew around all three edges, turning with care as you come to corners. Clip at corner on inside to ease. Turn top edge of Pocket under ½ inch and topstitch. Center Pocket H onto remaining natural End D. Sew Pocket onto End close to edge, folding the raw edges of the Pocket under as you go.

Make the Flap for the Pocket. Place the two Flaps J together. Machine baste along three sides. Turn right side out. Press. Fold remaining raw edges in towards each other and press to hold. Now topstitch Flap around all sides ¼ inch from edges. The topstitching will close the open end of the Flap decoratively. Position Flap onto End D above Pocket. Sew Flap onto End stitching over topstitching. Pin a strip of Velcro to underneath of Flap. Handstitch. Align corresponding Velcro half on Pocket front and handstitch. Now pin this completed End into Body of Duffle and sew together according to instructions for other end. Turn right side out.

Fig. (a)

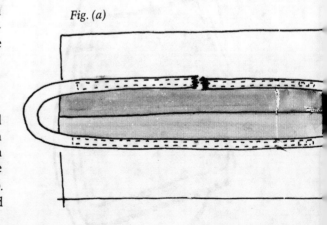

Flag striped duffle

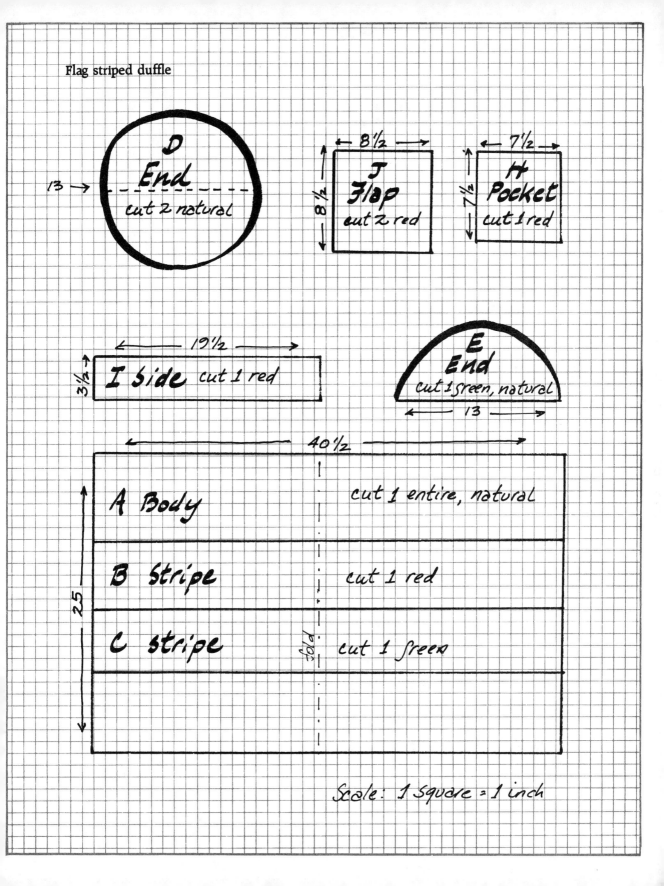

D
End
cut 2 natural

13 →

J
Flap
cut 2 red

8½

8½

H
Pocket
cut 1 red

7½

7½

19½

3½

I side *cut 1 red*

E
End
cut 1 green, natural

13

40½

A Body   *cut 1 entire, natural*

B Stripe   *cut 1 red*

C stripe   *cut 1 green*

25

fold

Scale: 1 square = 1 inch

Le Weekend

Stolen weekends are rare enough these days to deserve their own special carry-on luggage. This bag is large enough to carry everything you need for 48 golden hours. And by merely unsnapping the shoulder strap, you can use it as a tote and not feel as if you are wearing your luggage. Constructed from three pieces of canvas, it is one of the easiest projects to make. "Le Weekend" is stencilled on the side and gives it a Gallic personality that distinguishes it from its more mundane cousin, the anonymous seaman's duffle.

Materials

- 1 yard natural canvas
- One 20-inch oversize black zipper
- 6 yards webbing for straps
- 9 inches rainbow webbing, 1½ inches wide
- Stencil letters, 3 inches high
- Black ink, textile paint, dye or indelible marking pen
- Stencil brush, if using paint
- Two "D" rings
- Two snap-shackles

The Basic Body   Cut out all three pieces and the strap. Zigzag all edges to keep from ravelling. Lay straps onto Body A as shown in pattern, joining the ends in the middle of the bottom. Pin in place. Stitching close to the webbing edge, sew onto canvas as indicated. For reinforcement, stitch X's at the top of the edge stitching.

Stencilling   See the Embellishment chapter for complete stencilling instructions. Place letters on outside of duffle to spell out "Le Weekend" as indicated on the pattern. You will have to use the "E" more than once. If you are stencilling with paint, be sure to clean the "E" carefully and let it dry before using again.

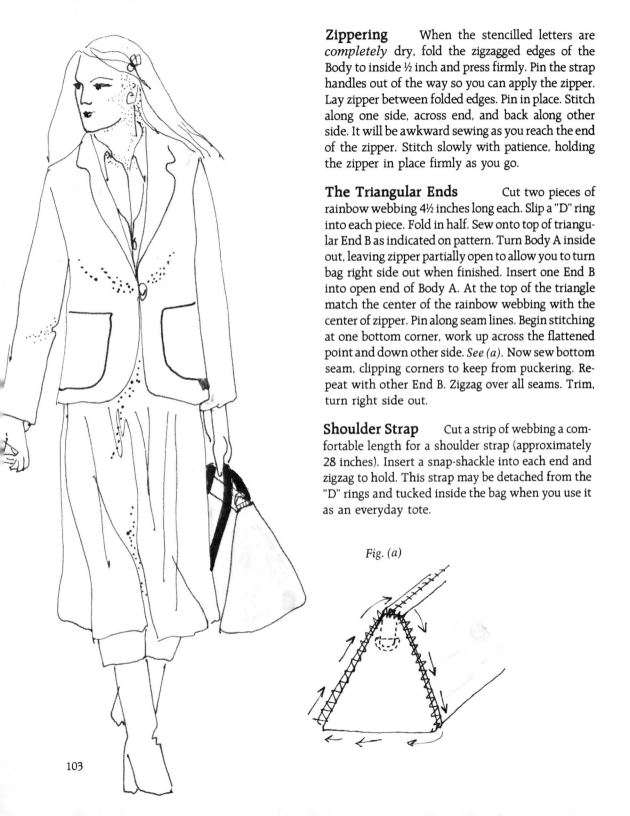

Zippering   When the stencilled letters are *completely* dry, fold the zigzagged edges of the Body to inside ½ inch and press firmly. Pin the strap handles out of the way so you can apply the zipper. Lay zipper between folded edges. Pin in place. Stitch along one side, across end, and back along other side. It will be awkward sewing as you reach the end of the zipper. Stitch slowly with patience, holding the zipper in place firmly as you go.

The Triangular Ends   Cut two pieces of rainbow webbing 4½ inches long each. Slip a "D" ring into each piece. Fold in half. Sew onto top of triangular End B as indicated on pattern. Turn Body A inside out, leaving zipper partially open to allow you to turn bag right side out when finished. Insert one End B into open end of Body A. At the top of the triangle match the center of the rainbow webbing with the center of zipper. Pin along seam lines. Begin stitching at one bottom corner, work up across the flattened point and down other side. *See (a)*. Now sew bottom seam, clipping corners to keep from puckering. Repeat with other End B. Zigzag over all seams. Trim, turn right side out.

Shoulder Strap   Cut a strip of webbing a comfortable length for a shoulder strap (approximately 28 inches). Insert a snap-shackle into each end and zigzag to hold. This strap may be detached from the "D" rings and tucked inside the bag when you use it as an everyday tote.

Fig. (a)

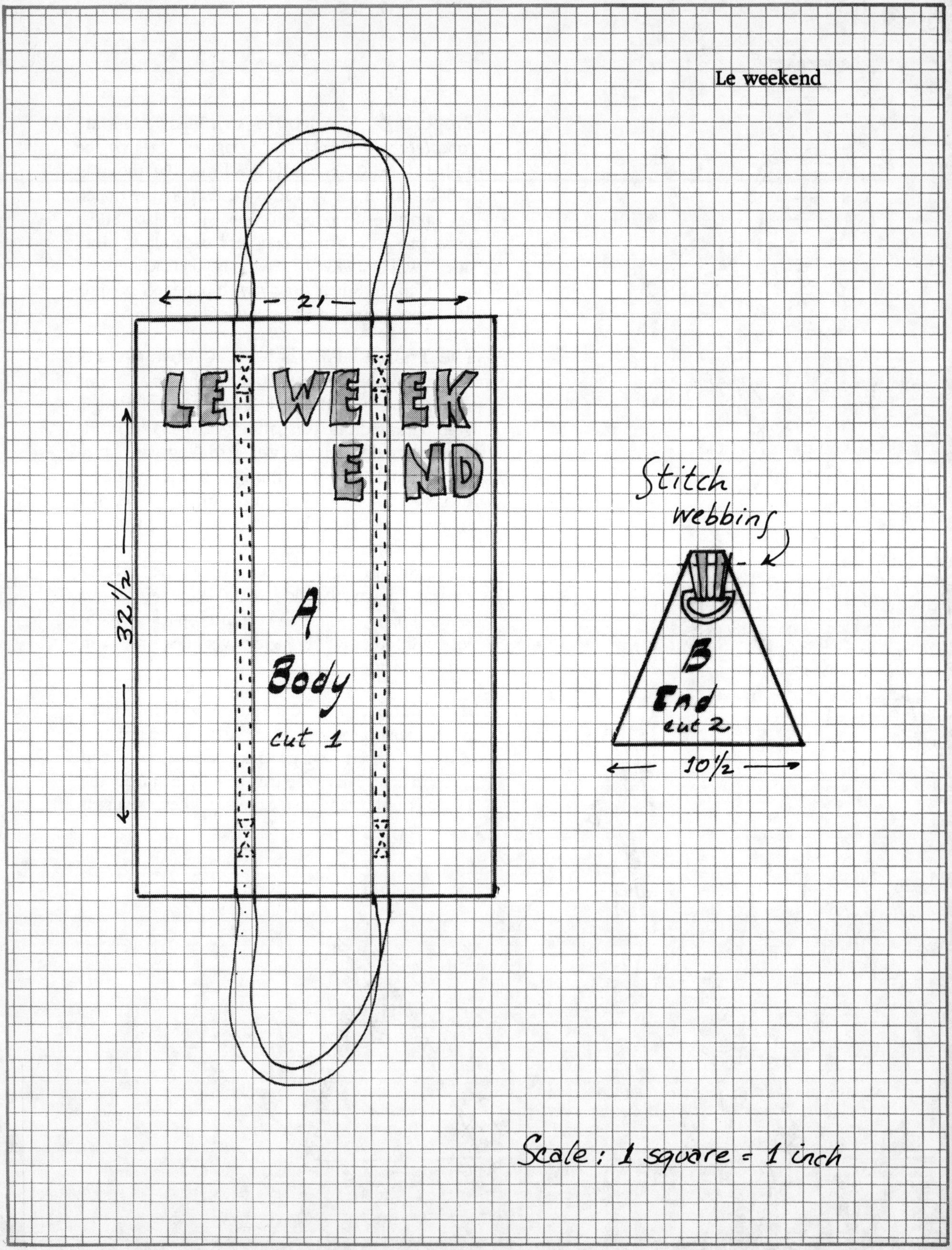

— 21 —

32½

LE WE EK
E ND

A
Body

cut 1

Stitch
webbing

B
End
cut 2

— 10½ —

Scale : 1 square = 1 inch

Four Star Shoulder Bag

The Four Star Shoulder Bag doubles as either a purse or an attaché case, suitable for carrying papers, scripts, schoolwork. The sides are fastened with zippers, allowing the bag to be opened from the side as well as the top. This makes it convenient to slip paperwork into the tote. It is constructed very simply: one long strip of heavy canvas folds twice and zips up the sides. The front flap is padded with batting, then the stars are appliqued. The padding gives them a gently rounded softness. A shoulder strap swings from webbing tabs, or you can make a shorter handle for a more businesslike look.

Materials

- 1¾ yards natural canvas
- Scraps of green, red, yellow, orange canvas
- ½ yard lining fabric
- 1 yard natural webbing or strapping
- ½ yard polyester fiberfill batting
- Two 14-inch oversize, plastic separating zippers
- Four brass or chrome rings

Pocketing, Lining, Starring   Cut out the long Body, the Pocket and the Strap. Zigzag edges to prevent ravelling. Fold under the top edge of Pocket B and topstitch. Lay Pocket on Body as shown in pattern and zigzag in place. Turn under top edge of Body 1 inch and topstitch down. Cut a piece of lining fabric the same size as the Flap. Cut *two* layers of batting slightly smaller than the piece of lining fabric. Make a cardboard template of the star shape. Use it as a pattern and cut out four stars of various colors. Lay Body face up on the worktable with Flap towards you. Lay lining fabric face down on top of Flap. Fold straight edge of lining back towards you, this will hide the raw edge when you turn Flap right side out. Pin lining to Flap all around. Sew lining to Flap with a straight stitch. Trim closely. Turn right side out.

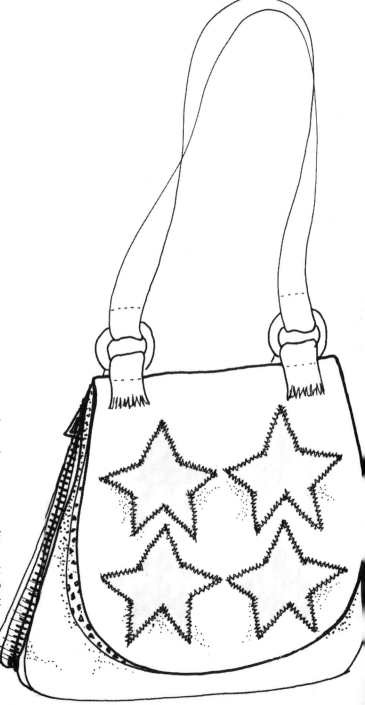

Four Star Shoulder Bag

Insert two layers of fiberfill batting between lining and Flap. Smooth out any bumps or lumps. Pin straight edge closed along foldline. Now, with the canvas side of the Flap facing you, position the four stars onto the Flap. Machine baste around the edges of the stars to hold them in place. With a close zigzag or satin stitch, applique the stars to the Flap. Be careful to feel under the Flap to make sure the lining fabric is smooth while you work. Now, with a straight stitch, sew the remaining edge of the lining to the Flap to enclose the batting.

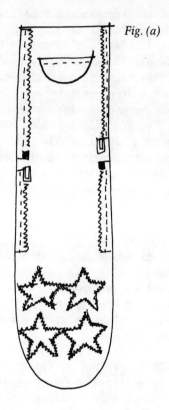

Fig. (a)

Zipping the Sides   Open the two 14-inch separating zippers all the way. With bag flat on table, pin zippers onto side seams with bottoms ¼ inch apart. Sew in place. *See (a).* Fold up sides of bag and zip up zippers. The zipper may be a little difficult to start, but if you use a large plastic YKK zipper, you should manage. Zigzag raw edges along edges of zipper tapes to prevent ravelling.

Tabs and Straps   Cut two 7-inch tabs from the webbing. Insert two brass rings onto each tab. Pin tabs on outside of bag as shown on pattern. Stitch down. Insert shoulder strap through rings and adjust for the correct length. You may zigzag the end of the webbing to prevent ravelling, although a ravelled edge has an appealing furry look to it.

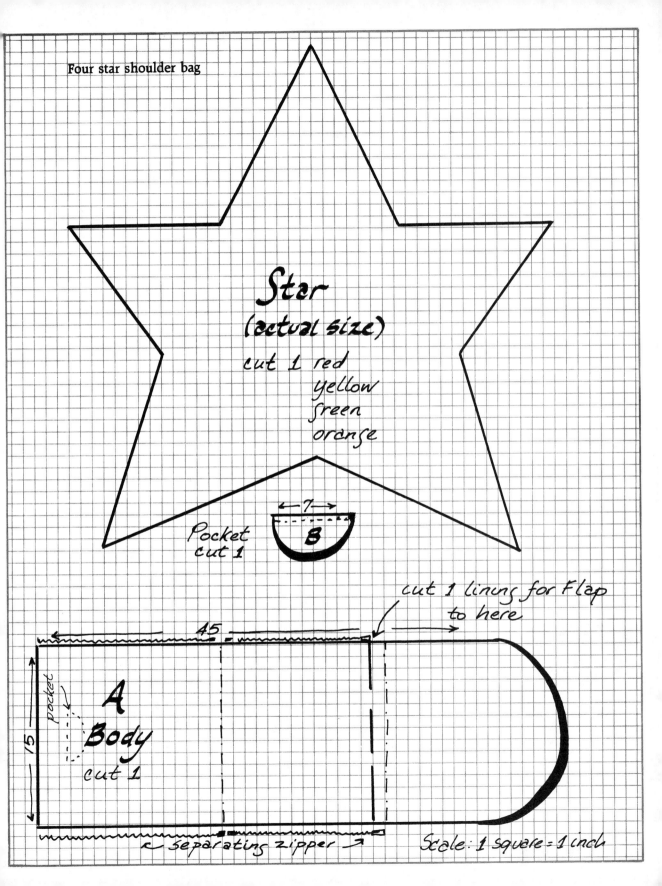

Four star shoulder bag

Star
(actual size)
cut 1 red
yellow
green
orange

Pocket
cut 1

← 7 →
B

cut 1 lining for flap
to here ✓ →

45

pocket

15

A
Body
cut 1

← separating zipper →

Scale: 1 square = 1 inch

Square Tiger Tote

The seriousness of this rectangular, dowel-handled tote is delightfully tweaked by a benign, be-whiskered tiger appliqued to the front and back. The tote holds stacks of books, papers or other heavy things, and the dowel handles make comfortable their carrying. The bag folds up completely flat and can be tucked into your luggage and unfolded later if you need an extra shopping tote. The flat, canvas sides of the bag make it an ideal place to sharpen your handpainting or machine embroidery skills. Once you have made the first version, you will see the possibilities for altering the pattern and may want to try making a long, skinny version or a short, chunky one to use as a city lunchbox.

Materials

- 1⅓ yards tan canvas
- ½ yard black canvas
- ½ yard orange canvas
- Scraps of deep orange and pink canvas or cotton
- Two ¾-inch wooden dowels, each 13 inches long
- Heavy cardboard for bottom stiffening
- Black permanent marking pens, both wide and fine-line
- White fabric paint or acrylic paint
- Small brush
- Black lacquer or stain for dowel handles

Dowel Handles   Depending upon your preference, paint the two dowels with black lacquer paint or stain them. Allow these to dry while you complete the canvas part of the bag.

Adding the Tiger   Cut out all pattern pieces, including the orange Tiger and his Tail. Zigzag all edges to prevent ravelling. Place the Tiger himself on one side of Body A with his head towards the top. Pin in place. Fold Body A along fold lines and position top edges evenly. Line up the Tiger's tail on the back of the bag, with the Tiger body on the front of the bag. Pin. Using black thread machine baste Tiger onto A, outlining his body near the edge. Now zigzag over the basting stitches, appliqueing Tiger to bag.

With a pencil, lightly indicate lines for his eyes, nose, muzzle, smile, legs, and paws. Cut two scraps of pink for his ears and one for his nose. Cut two deep orange eyeballs. Decrease your zigzag width slightly and sew ears, nose and eyes onto face. With white fabric paint, paint in his muzzle and nose. Use a fairly dry brush with very little paint on it. Zigzag

over the rest of your pencil lines to delineate body.

Step back from your Tiger and eyeball him. With a wide, black marking pen draw in his stripes. Do the same with his Tail. Paint them in firmly. Remember, the ink may not dry as quickly as you imagine, so be careful to not wipe your arm over the wet stripes as you work. Then with a very fine-line black pen, add whisker spots and eyelashes.

Adding the Yokes   When the Tiger is completely dry, place A face down on worktable. Pin Yokes C to Body A on the inside. Stitch along three sides of the squared opening. Clip corners. Fold Yokes to *outside*. Press. Zigzag Yokes onto front with a satin stitch.

Adding the Stripes   Sew two Sides B together along one long edge. Trim and zigzag seam. Repeat with other two Sides B. Position Sides between fold lines on A and sew to Bottom of A, seams to inside. Flip up Sides B forming box shape and Stitch to A along insides. Zigzag seams. Trim.

Dowel Handles   Trim top of Tote evenly on all sides. Overcast top edge with zigzag to keep from ravelling. Turn down tote top to inside 1½ inch and topstitch. This will form a tunnel for the dowels on the front and back. Turn bag right side out. Slide dowels into slots.

The Floor   Cover the piece of heavy cardboard with gay fabric by dabbing with rubber cement, stapling, or using white household glue. Insert into bottom of tote. This provides sturdiness and helps the bag keep its rectangular shape.

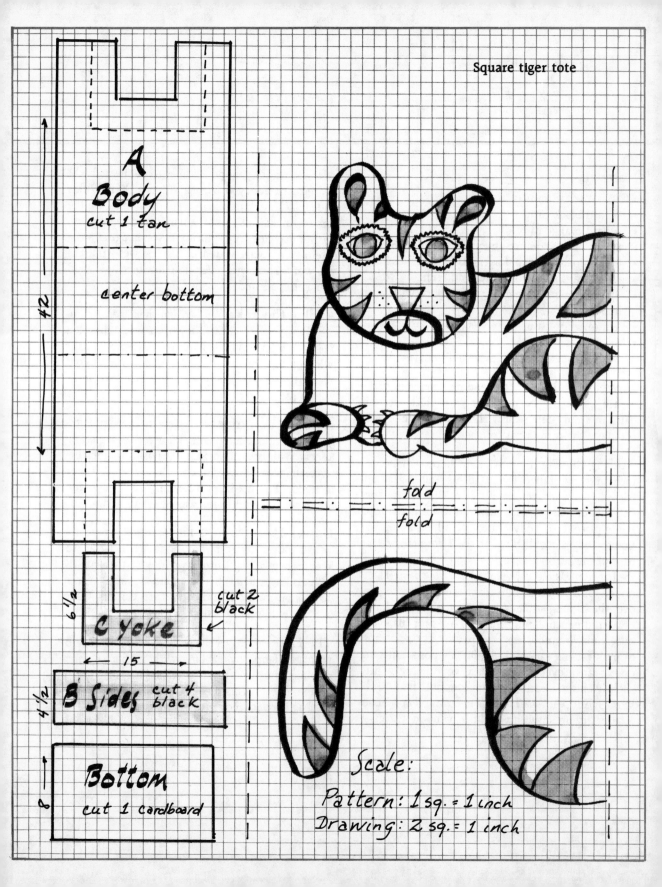

Square tiger tote

A
Body
cut 1 tan

center bottom

#2

6½

C yoke
cut 2 black

←15→

B Sides cut 4 black

4½

Bottom
cut 1 cardboard

8

fold
fold

Scale:
Pattern: 1 sq. = 1 inch
Drawing: 2 sq. = 1 inch

Tennis And Town Tote

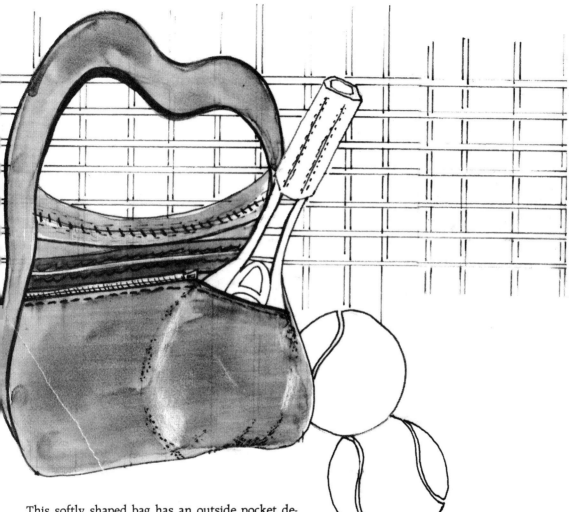

This softly shaped bag has an outside pocket designed to carry a tennis racquet, as well as plenty of room inside for a can of balls, an extra pair of tennis shoes, and a picnic lunch. It has a nice pouchy look, and is constructed with the seams to the outside. Contrast binding encloses these seams, giving the tote a crisp line. The body of this bag wraps around from front to back with no seam in the center bottom. The pockets also wrap around and are attached to the body in one piece.

Materials

- 2 yards canvas
- One 9-inch zipper for racquet pocket
- One 16-inch zipper for main body
- ½ yard decorative braid or webbing
- Two packages wide bias tape.

Tennis And Town Tote

The Pockets   Fold under one short end of Pocket B and topstitch to hide raw edge. On opposite end fold under one corner as indicated on pattern, and stitch down. These will be the tops of your Pockets. Now apply the lower half of the 9-inch zipper to the top edge of the Pocket that has its corner turned down. Lay Pocket B on top of Body A where indicated on pattern. Stitch the sides of Pocket and Body together. Position 16 inches of decorative braid or webbing over the upper half of the Pocket zipper and across the body of the bag. Stitch along both edges of the braid with a narrow seam, sewing the zipper and the braid to the bag.

Center Zipper   Cut Center C in half lengthwise and press center edges to inside $^3/_8$ inch. Press firmly. Apply 16-inch zipper according to package instructions between these two edges. Cut two 8-inch strips of bias tape and apply to each curved end of Center C. Turn your completed Body A inside out and stitch Center C in place. Turn and press.

Adding Straps   Sew Straps together, trim closely and zigzag for neatness. Pin Strap D to bag, seams to outside. Adjust to fit by trimming edges if necessary. Sew all around, trim seams to uniform ¼ inch width. This will make your seam binding application easier. Sew curved edge of Center C to Strap over stitching on bias tape.

Contrast Trim   Iron wide bias seam binding in half carefully and exactly. Pin to outside of bag. Beginning in an unobtrusive spot that will not get much wear (NOT the bottom of the bag), apply contrast trim over seams. Feed tape under presser foot gently and steadily, snugging the tape up onto seams as you go. Check underneath often, as it is easy for the binding tape to slip off the canvas, especially on the curves.

Tennis and town tote

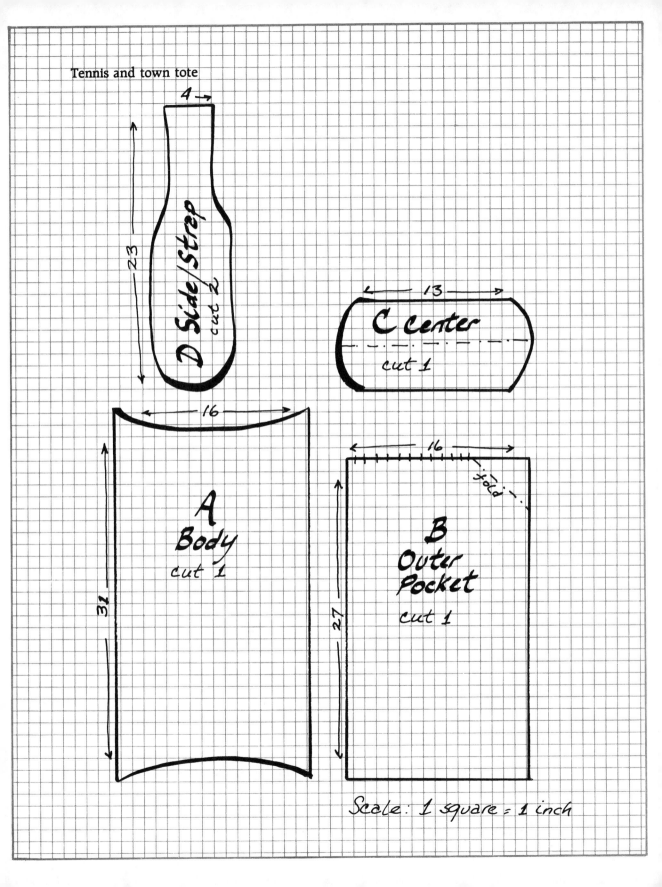

4 →

23

D Side/Strep
cut 2

13

C center
cut 1

16

A
Body
cut 1

31

16

fold

B
Outer
Pocket
cut 1

27

Scale: 1 square = 1 inch

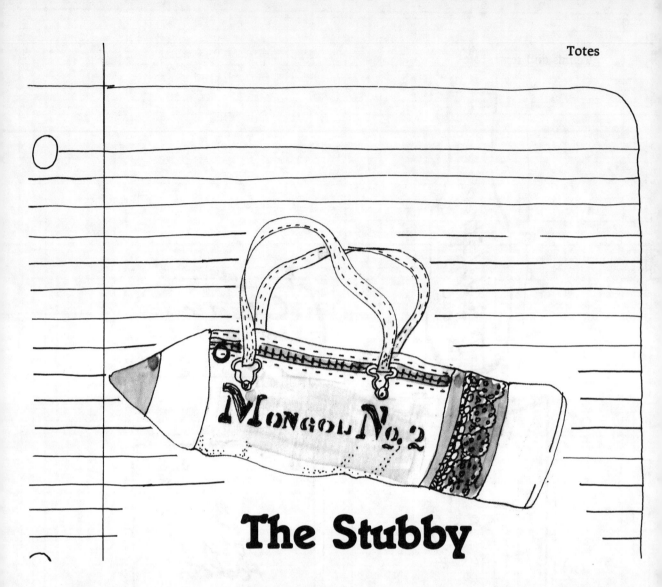

The Stubby

The Pop Art movement of the Sixties elevated the banal, the everyday object, to the realm of pure art. Andy Warhol's enthronement of the Campbell's Soup Can was a provocative attempt to force us to view the symbols of our culture with new eyes. Many artists of the last decade have played with American cultural symbols, blowing them up to gigantic proportions—Claes Oldenburg's thirty-foot high ice bag and his soaring lipstick sculpture—or miniaturizing and massing them—Warhol's seriagraph prints of famous people. In all, the spirit of play has been present, despite the more serious

intentions of the artist. We are meant to laugh first and reflect later. Laughter breaks down barriers in those who approach art with trepidation and hostility.

The Stubby tote has no ulterior motive beyond surprise and pleasure. It is meant to tickle the fancy, delight the spirit, and amuse the maker. It is constructed on the flat, embellished, rolled into a tube, and finally zipped. The point and eraser are stuffed with fiberfill. It can function as an ordinary handbag or overnight bag, providing a chuckle or two as it quietly serves.

The stubby

Materials

- 1 yard yellow canvas
- ¼ yard black canvas
- ¼ yard pink felt
- ¾ yard gold lace or ribbon
- Four overall fasteners
- One 12-inch oversize black separating zipper
- Polyester fiberfill stuffing
- Stencil, 2-inch capital letters and 1-inch small letters
- Permanent black marking pen, fabric paint, or silk-screen ink
- Stencil brush
- Protractor

Before Beginning

The yellow canvas forms the body of this bag. Both ends—the eraser and the pencil lead—are stuffed with fiberfill. Be sure to pack the stuffing in very tightly so that the ends retain their shapes! And, zigzag all edges before assembling to prevent ravelling.

Assembling the Eraser

Sew pink Eraser Side B to black Eraser Band C along the long edge. With right sides together, sew side seams to form a tube. With tube inside out, sew pink Eraser End E to the end of this tube. Ease the ripples evenly around the circle as you go. Trim seam and turn right side out. Stuff eraser end firmly with fiberfill. To enclose the stuffing, stitch one yellow Canvas E to end. The raw seam can be left outside since it will be enclosed when the Body of the pencil is attached.

Adding the Lead

Cutout black Pencil Lead G and beige Pencil Wood F. Sew together along seam line as indicated in pattern. This is difficult as you will have to twist the inside curve of the beige piece to fit the outside curve of the black piece. *See (a).* Pin it before you sew, and stitch slowly. With the right side inside, fold this piece in half and sew middle seam. This will form a funnel shape for your pencil point. *See (b).* Stuff tightly with fiberfill. Now stitch the other yellow canvas E onto this funnel to enclose the stuffing. Leave the seam outside. *See (c).*

Fig. (a)

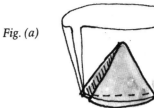

Fig. (b)

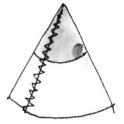

Fig. (c)

Fig. (d)

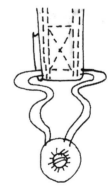

Fig. (e)

The Stubby

Stencilling the Body   Cut out yellow canvas Body A. Position stencil on the Body according to pattern. Letter "Mongol No. 2"* on the bag. You could do the lettering with a permanent black marking pen, fabric paint, or silkscreen ink. Allow the letters to dry.

Assembling the Body   On Body A, press the two long edges to inside ½ inch. Fold Body A into a tube, bringing these folded edges together. Insert zipper between these edges. Topstitch down according to zipper instructions.

Cut out Straps D. Fold the Straps along their length so the raw edges meet in the center. Press. Fold again in half and stitch twice along length. Slip each strap through a 2-inch overall buckle, folding ends under to hide raw edge. Topstitch in boxed-X. *See (d)*. Sew Buckle to each end of each strap. Position straps on Body as indicated in pattern. Sew the buckle buttons on Body A, sewing a smaller button on the inside at the same time. This will provide strength.

Adding Pen Point and Eraser   Open zipper and turn Body inside out. Push the stuffed Point into front end of Stubby Body. The Point will be inside the bag. Pin in place along seam line, the raw edges will be sticking out. *See (e)*. Stitching slowly, sew Point onto Stubby Body. Check seam, clip raw edges closely. Now push stuffed Eraser into other end of bag. Repeat stitching as with Point. Carefully pull bag right side out, gently easing out the stuffed Eraser and Point.

Handstitch gold lace or ribbon trim along the Eraser Band to give the effect of a metal eraser tip.

*Registered in the U.S. Patent and Trademark office by Eberhard Faber Inc.

The stubby

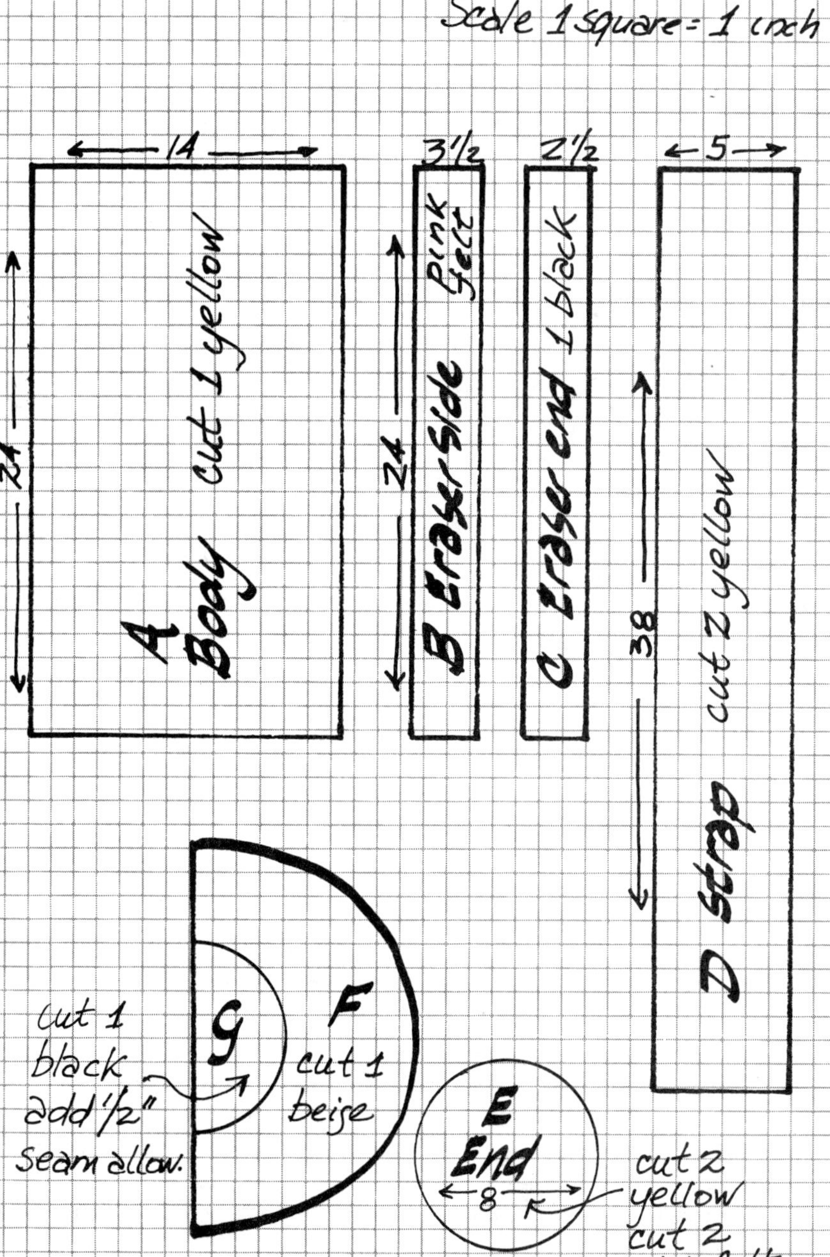

Scale 1 square = 1 inch

A Body cut 1 yellow
— 14 —
21

B Eraser Side Pink felt
3½
21

C Eraser end 1 black
2½

D strap cut 2 yellow
— 5 —
38

G cut 1 black add ½" seam allow.

F cut 1 beige

E End cut 2 yellow cut 2 pink felt
8

Giant Needleworker's Tote

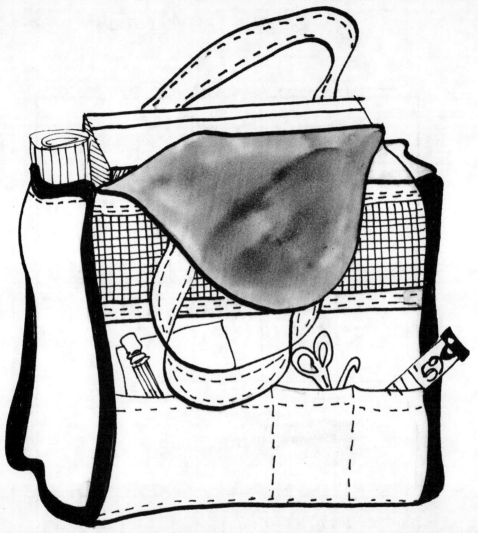

Every needleworker I know starts out in a small way with a simple pre-painted canvas. However, they rapidly advance to needing a huge selection of yarns, needlepoint mesh, markers, special rulers, scissors, crochet hooks, instruction books, frames . . . the list is endless. This large tote bag (21 by 16 by 8 inches) is designed to carry all the accoutrements of the serious needleworker. A series of outer and inner pockets and a large, zippered compartment hold every conceivable kind of equipment. Two vertical pockets at the ends are convenient for rolled mesh, and a flap over the top tucks in to protect your work from rain or small, curious fingers.

As an added surprise, the top flap flips up to reveal photos of your children or grandchildren. The images are heat transferred by ironing onto the canvas. You have the heat transfers made from your favorite slides on a color Xerox machine.

Giant needleworker's tote

Materials

- 2¾ yards canvas
- 2¾ yards lining fabric (optional)
- One 20-inch wide, plastic zipper
- Two packs wide bias tape
- ¼ yard needlepoint mesh, any gauge
- Color slides of your family
- Color Xerox machine, usually at least one copy shop or offset printer in town has one of these new machines

Before Beginning

This bag is a box shape with a top flap added on. If you decide to line the bag, cut out three additional A's—one for the Front, one for the Back, and one for the Flap—and two additional D's—one for each side. With the wrong sides together, machine baste lining to canvas on all pieces except one section A. This remaining A will become the Top Flap which tucks in loosely over the open bag, protecting your needlework-in-progress. Prepare Flap by placing canvas A and lining A with right sides together. Sew along three sides, leaving one long side open. Trim, turn. Press. Press raw edges inside, topstitch along outside edges.

Back Section   The back of the bag is made of two pieces of canvas joined together. The Inside Back has pockets applied to it [See (a)] and the Outside Back has a zipper in it [See (b)]. When the two completed pieces are sewn together, they will form a large, zippered pocket.

Cut Outside Back apart on dotted line as indicated in pattern. Fold under raw edges ³/₈ inch and press. Insert zipper between these two pieces and stitch in place.

Cut out Inside Pocket F and fold long edges under. Topstitch for a neat hem. Place this strip along lined side of Inside Back at desired height. Stitch Pocket down along sides and bottom edge. Now sew as many vertical seams as you need to form separate sections for crochet hooks, scissors, ruler, knitting needles, etc. Above this long Pocket you may want to stitch a strip of felt or embroidered ribbon which has been lightly padded with fiberfill. This would act as a pincushion for embroidery or needlepoint needles and pins. Now lay the two Back sections

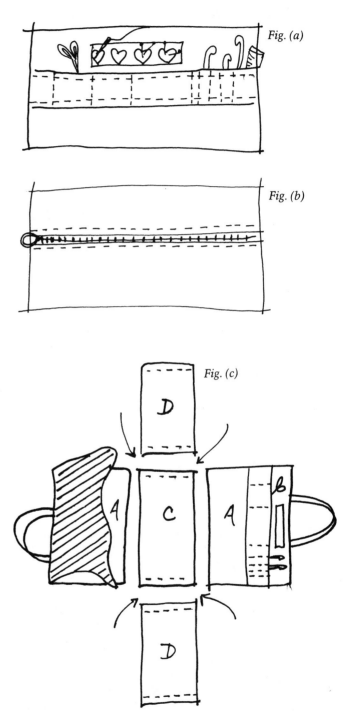

Fig. (a)

Fig. (b)

Fig. (c)

119

Giant Needleworker's Tote

together, *wrong* sides facing each other. Baste around all edges ¼ inch in.

The Front
The front pocket is constructed the same way as the Inside Pocket. Cut out Outside Pocket C and fold down along one long edge. Topstitch the hem. Press. Lay this Pocket along the outside of Front A with the raw bottom edges matching. Stitch along sides and bottom. Stitch vertically through all layers to form three (or more) sections in the Pocket.

Pin needlepoint mesh (or completed needlepoint) onto top of Front A, top edges matching. Cut out Band H and fold raw edges inside along seam line. Press firmly. Place Band over bottom of needlepoint mesh and topstitch in place covering edge of mesh. Leave top edge of bag unfinished. You will cover this after you have added the Handles and Flap.

The Handles and Flap
Cut out two Handles G and fold long sides to center along seam line. Press. Fold in half and press. Topstitch. Sew Handles to Back and Front as indicated on pattern. Stitch Handles at least 1½ inches below top edges of bag to allow for seam binding later.

If you have not lined the Flap A, turn in raw edges on three sides leaving one long side raw. Topstitch a hem neatly. With right sides together, lay Flap onto Back. Have the raw edge of the Flap meet the raw top edge of Back. Stitch along top edge, sewing over the seam line attaching the Handles to the bag.

Assembling the Tote
Sew remaining Bottom C to Front and Back of bag, seams to *inside*. Zigzag and trim closely. This forms the bottom of the bag.

Apply seam binding across top short end of each of the four Sides D. These will become the top edges of the two vertical side pockets which hold rolled

needlepoint canvas. Place two Side D's together. Baste around the three raw sides. Repeat for other two pieces. Now sew Sides to Bottom C, seams to *outside*.

Apply seam binding to top of Front A. Fold up Sides and join to Back and Front sections. Pin. Sew with seams to *outside*. You have now completed the basic box shape, with its flap. *See (c)*.

A Few More Details
Apply seam binding along Back top edge. The binding will enclose the raw edge of the Flap where it joins the Back. Trim binding closely at corners.

Now sew seam binding to cover the side seams. Begin at one top corner and continue down and around the other corner. Remember to tuck raw ends of binding under at corners as you begin and end. You may like to add a nailhead or rivet at each top corner to finish. These are available at any fabric store.

Printing the Images on the Flap
Take a selection of your favorite slides to a copy shop that has a color Xerox machine. There have your pictures enlarged and made into heat transfers. The slide is projected by mirrors onto a flat photo-plate where it can be enlarged up to 8 x 10 inches. You might want to vary the size of your photos to achieve an interesting arrangement. After enlargement, the image is imprinted on a sheet of white paper with a waxy surface, just like the heat transfers available in T-shirt shops. You can cut the paper any size.

Now arrange the heat transfers on the flap. Iron for at least 3 minutes with a HOT iron. For even better results you can take your transfers to a T-shirt shop and, for a small fee, they will adhere them to the canvas with their mounting machine. They are usually quite cooperative about this.

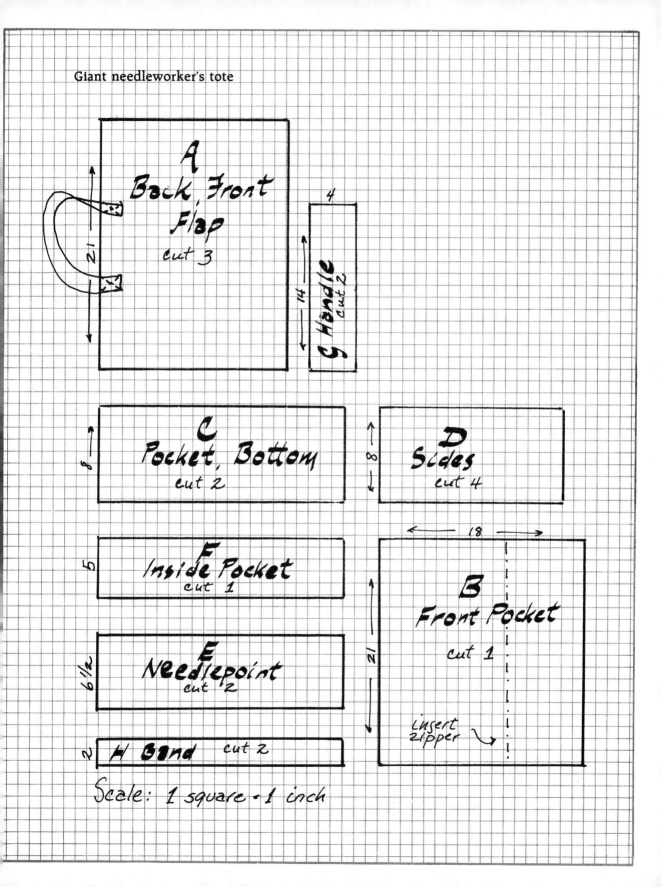

Giant needleworker's tote

A
Back, Front
Flap
cut 3

4
G Handle
cut 2
14

C
Pocket, Bottom
cut 2
8

D
Sides
cut 4
8

F
Inside Pocket
cut 1
5

18
B
Front Pocket
cut 1
21
Insert
zipper

E
Needlepoint
cut 2
6½

H Band   cut 2
2

Scale: 1 square = 1 inch

Plain Brown Wrappers

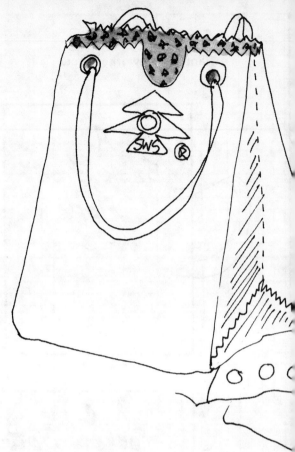

There is something enormously satisfying about brown wrapping paper, whether it is used for mailing or carting things home from the market. It has much of the unobtrusive, everyday quality of canvas itself. Recently, though, I notice that its anonymity has been threatened by a new trend — the personalization of the grocery bag. You may wish to personalize your Plain Brown Wrappers as well. Or, you may want to print the standard logo on your bag by stamping it with a carved potato or lino block. Either way, the Brown Bag and the Window Envelope offer an opportunity to show off your sewing talent in a subtle, tongue-in-cheek fashion.

Brown Bag

Materials

- 1 yard tan canvas
- ¾ yard lining fabric
- Four 1-inch grommets, and grommet setter
- Leather or rope to length for straps
- Lino block, or large potato
- X-acto knife or lino cutting tools
- Lino inks, fabric paint, acrylic paint, or drawing inks
- Rubber cement or plastic bags

Making the Bag   After cutting out, zigzag all edges to prevent ravelling. Since a well-joined top edge is essential to this bag, affix lining to one side of all pieces. This may be done with rubber cement. Another way to laminate two fabrics together uses plastic bags. Either from grocery store produce bags or from the bags your cleaning comes home in, cut plastic to fit all pattern pieces. With right sides of the fabric outside, sandwich canvas and plastic and lining. Now iron together with a warm iron. If you mis-position any pieces, they can be peeled apart and ironed together again.

Now zigzag a Triangle D to the outside of the bottom of each Side B. This applique lends a brown bag authenticity without adding bulk. With the lining to inside, stitch Bottom C to Front A and Back A forming one continuous piece of A-C-A. Pin one Side B to large piece A-C-A, folding up to form bag. Sew with seams inside. Zigzag over seam, trim closely. Insert the other Side B the same way. *See (a).* Now stitch Bottom into bag and finish the seam. *See (b).* Turn bag right side out, press.

Carefully pink the top edge of the bag, making a small scoop on the front like a market bag. Now topstitch ⅛ inch from the edge of the outside on all four side seams. Topstitch ⅛ inch in from the edge. This will give your bag a crisp definition and make it stand up without sagging, something no respectable grocery bag would dare do.

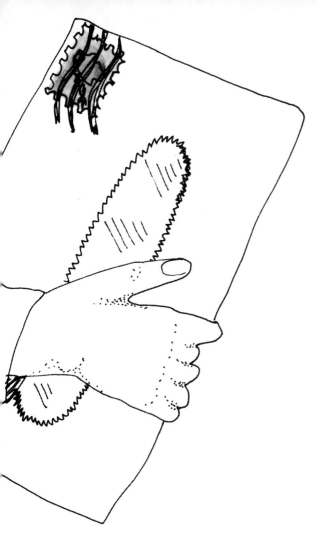

Handles Position 1-inch grommets on each side of bag. Set them according to package instructions. Cut Straps to length from leather or rope. Insert through grommets and knot to hold.

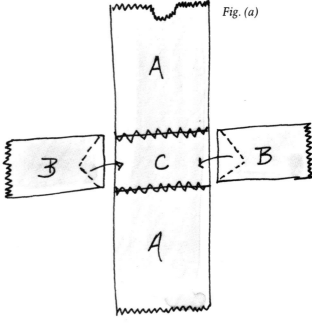

Fig. (a)

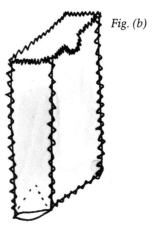

Fig. (b)

Imprinting the Logo Carve a logo on a lino block using linoleum cutters. Blocks and cutters are available inexpensively at most craft or hobby shops. Or, using a sharp knife, carve the raw edge of a potato half. Potatoes tend to get mushy if you do not print immediately, so carve your logo when you have your inks ready. Use lino inks, fabric paint, acrylic paint, or drawing ink and test your stamp first on a piece of scrap canvas. You will find that your bag prints well if you insert the end onto the point of the ironing board. The padding on the board allows you to exert good pressure as you roll the block or potato with the heel of your hand. Make sure the entire design is well inked. Now add details with a marking pen or black India ink.

Plain Brown Wrappers

Window Envelope

Materials

- 1½ yards tan canvas
- ¾ yard lining
- 12 inches cording
- Clear vinyl, 12 by 40 inches
- One potato, or 3 by 3 inch lino block
- X-acto knife, or lino cutting tools
- Printing ink

The Basic Envelope   Cut two Envelopes of canvas and one of lining fabric. Make a sandwich of canvas, canvas, and lining in that order. The right side of the lining should face the canvas. You are using two pieces of canvas for sturdiness. Tuck 12 inches of cording between the lining and the canvas at the point of the envelope flap. The long ends should be hidden inside. Stitch all around, leaving the bottom edge open. Trim, turn right side out so that the lining is on one side, the canvas the other. Press.

Inserting the Window   Fold your purse into thirds and press gently. Re-open, the fold marks should now show. Place canvas side up on the table, and with a sharp pencil outline the window on the middle section. You may want to cut a template of the window shape out of cardboard and use it to trace around. Now, with *very sharp* scissors, cut through all three layers to form a window. Cut a piece of clear vinyl in a rectangle about 2 inches larger than the window itself. Insert this vinyl between the canvas layer and the lining. Pin. With a satin stitch sew around the window edge, sewing through all layers. Now fold the open bottom edges into themselves so that the raw edges are hidden and press. Sew close to the edge.

Printing the Stamp   Using a lino block or a potato carve a stamp design. It can be a rough profile of a head, nothing too detailed. Carve a second block or potato with the wavy cancellation lines. Ink and press your stamp in red on the corner. After the first ink dries, print the cancellation lines over it in black.

Sew a button on the point of the Flap. Sew another button on the back of the envelope just below the point of the Flap. Wrap cord in a figure 8 around the buttons to close the purse.

Plain brown wrappers

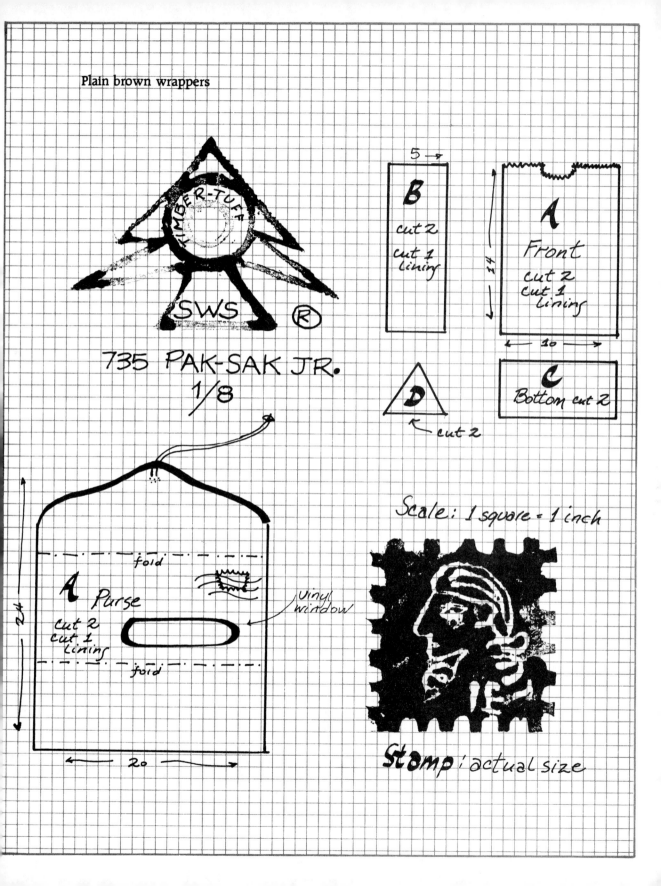

TIMBER-TUFF

SWS ®

735 PAK-SAK JR.
1/8

B
cut 2
cut 1
lining
5 →

A
Front
cut 2
cut 1
lining
14
10

D
← cut 2

C
Bottom cut 2

A Purse
cut 2
cut 1
lining
fold
fold
vinyl
window
24
20

Scale: 1 square = 1 inch

Stamp actual size

Small Happy Purses For Small People

Nothing speaks of springtime more than a Japanese kite whipping gaily in the breezy sunshine. Its brilliant, primary colors emblazon the breeze with a silent, dancing song. Why not make a small version to remind you of April's promise even during the darkest winter months? Or perhaps you remember another kind of promise — the twelve, shiny, perfectly pointed promises inside a new box of Crayolas? For me, as a child, new crayons were always secret harbingers of new beginnings, a clean slate. I took deeply-felt, internal vows not to let anyone dull them or break them. Times have not changed, and hardly a birthday passes in our house without that ubiquitous box of Crayolas being exchanged. The design on the flap of this Crayola purse is actually colored in with crayons and a marking pen, though you may prefer to use crayons exclusively, sacrificing a certain sharpness of line for purity.

Japanese Kite Purse

Materials

- ½ yard beige canvas
- ½ yard lining fabric
- ½ yard polyester fiberfill batting
- One 12-inch zipper
- Silk cord for handle
- Fabric paints and small brushes, or marking pens

Painting the Fish   Cut out two Fish of canvas and two of lining material. Zigzag all edges to prevent ravelling. On one canvas piece draw the design onto the Body. Try it first with a pencil, lightly, letting your wrist relax in a swooping motion. If you do not like what is happening, you can always use that side on the inside of the bag. Many people panic when confronted with free-hand work. But remember, it doesn't have to be perfect, so have fun! Sit down with some good music on a quiet evening and lay out your paints or marking pens and create the gayest carp imaginable. If you use fabric paints, use them full strength. You will probably want to go over the reds twice, as this color tends to be more transparent than others.

Quilting   Make two sandwiches of canvas, fiberfill, and lining: one for the Front and one for the Back of the purse. Be sure to wait until your fish is completely dry before you work with the Front. You will sandwich the layers together with right sides of the lining and the canvas to the outside. Baste to hold, along the edges ¼ inch from outside. On the painted Front section, quilt freely following the lines of the fish scales and the gills. Don't worry about being too exact, a sense of freedom and play is right for a kite.

Zippering   Following the instructions on the package, apply zipper as indicated on the pattern, seams to inside. Pin a braided, silken cording to either end of the zipper for a strap. Make sure the strap is facing the *outside* of the purse. Now place right sides of fish, Front and Back, together and stitch all around. Remember to open the zipper halfway before sewing so you can turn the bag right side out.

126

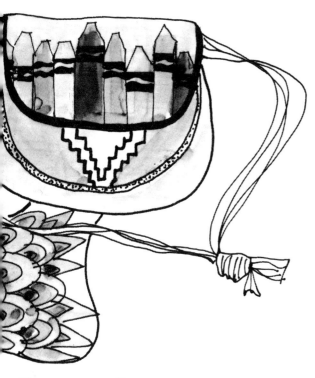

Crayon Purse

Materials

- ½ yard canvas
- ½ yard lining fabric
- ¾ yard piping cord
- ¾ yard wide calico bias tape
- Ribbons for strap
- Permanent marking pens with wide tips

Coloring the Design   Cut out Back A and Front B in both canvas and lining. Zigzag canvas edges to prevent ravelling. With a pencil, sketch crayon design onto canvas Flap section of Back A. With sharp crayons fill in the design, using a black marking pen for details. The rough texture of the canvas makes it impossible to fill in the color solidly. But, this adds a pleasant, childlike look, not unlike the effect of crayons on the newsprint in a coloring book.

Piping the Edge   Open the bias tape and lay the piping cord in the center. Fold tape tightly around the cord, and using a zipper foot, stitch close to the cord for a neat piping. Now lay this piping around the edge of the completed Flap with the corded part facing in towards the center of Flap. *See (a)*. Stitch between X's.

Place Back A on your table, right side up. Place lining on top of it, face down. Pin. Stitch around edges, leaving an opening at side to turn right side out. Feel with your fingers as you nurse the machine around the curved piping. Be careful not to catch the piping in the seam, and don't leave too big a space between the piping and the seam. Turn and press, slip stitch opening.

Finishing   Place Front B and lining right sides together. Stitch around edges leaving the straight, top edge open. Turn, press. Fold top edge and lining together to hide raw edges. Press and stitch. Now lay Back A and Front B together, right sides facing. Sew, leaving Flap free. Make sure to tuck the raw edge of the piping into the seam where the Flap folds. Hand-stitch several narrow, multicolored satin ribbons as a strap. Leave their ends flying freely at the side.

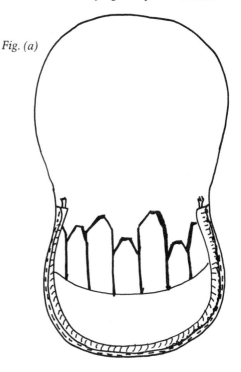

Fig. (a)

127

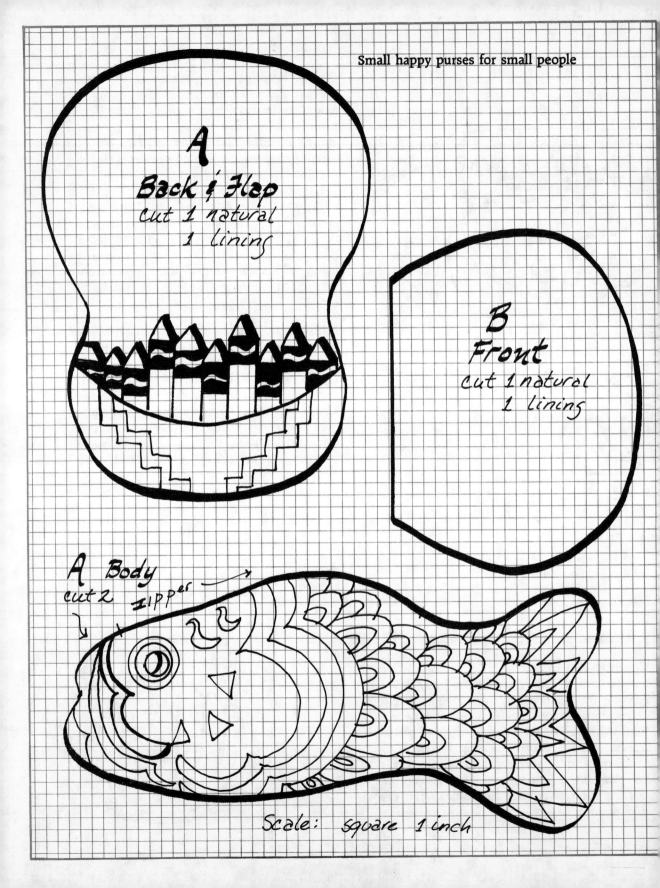

Small happy purses for small people

A
Back & Flap
cut 1 natural
1 lining

B
Front
cut 1 natural
1 lining

A Body
cut 2   zipper

Scale: square 1 inch

Landscape Art Portfolio

Art portfolios tend to be uninspired muslin carryalls or grim, black cardboard folios. How much more exciting and cheerful to arrive at a gallery with your work in a colorfully appliqued canvas portfolio. The construction of this bag is very simple. Although the appliqued landscape may look complex, it too is simple. By laying one colored shape on top of another, you create a bold mountain vista. The pattern sketch is intended merely as a guideline. As you cut out the design elements follow the dictates of your own, inner landscape and create a work of art that is completely yours.

The portfolio is made like a box. Double zippers meet at the center top and extend halfway down the sides for easy access to artwork. It measures 23 by 30 inches and will accomodate an illustrator's clipboard, large drawing folder, and even a stretched canvas or two. You may want to add pockets for pencils, pens, and brushes on the inside of the back. If so, remember to stitch them on *before* you begin assembling.

Materials

- 4 yards black canvas
- ¼ yard lemon yellow canvas
- ½ yard natural canvas
- ¼ yard orange canvas
- ½ yard brown canvas
- Scraps of dark green, turquoise, marine blue, tan canvas
- 1 by 31 inches of hot pink canvas or cotton
- 30 inches black webbing for handles
- Two 24-inch oversize zippers
- Heavy cardboard, one or two pieces 23 by 29 inches

Before Beginning

As canvas colors are limited, you may wish to substitute heavyweight solid color cottons for the pink. Be sure as you applique the substitute fabric that it doesn't buckle or pull on the bias while you work.

Appliqueing the Landscape   Enlarge the drawing of the landscape. Since the finished portfolio measures 23 by 30 inches, you will need to use a sheet of butcher's paper, wrapping paper from your laundry, or even an old sheet. Actually, sheets work very well for designing patterns for applique. They are easy to draw on with pencils or markers, are large enough for almost every project, and don't flutter off the table in the breeze.

After enlarging the landscape draw it on paper or fabric. Number the pattern pieces as indicated. Cut out the tree shape and its leaves first, then trace this tree onto another piece of paper or sheet. This second tree will be the pattern you use when cutting the canvas. Place the original tree back onto your landscape and tape it in place with clear tape. Now proceed to cut the rest of the landscape pieces. Cut right through the tree as necessary, and use these pieces to cut out the canvas.

The *top* edges of each shape in the canvas landscape are the definitive ones, with the exception of the tree, rock and clouds. The background pieces will be layered over each other, and each of these shapes, from the sunset strip of pink down, tucks under the other. When you cut out the shapes you may leave an extra ½ inch or so at the bottom of each of these pattern pieces. Zigzag all edges to prevent ravelling. They will tuck neatly under the piece above and there will be no danger of the edges slipping out later and unravelling.

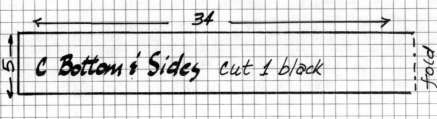

← 34 →

C Bottom & Sides cut 1 black

5 (left side) fold (right side)

← 27 →

3 **B Sides & Top** cut 4 black

Color code for Applique

1. orange
2. pink
3. white
4. marine blue
5. turquoise
6. yellow
7. brown
8. green
9. tan

A: cut 2 black panels 24 x 31 inches

Scale: 1 square = 1 inch

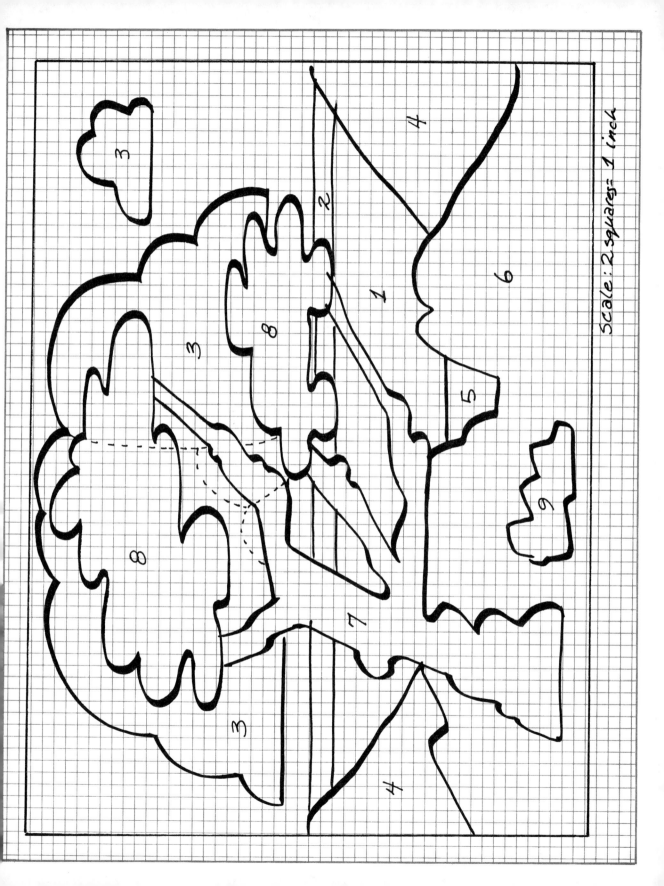

Scale: 2 squares = 1 inch

Landscape Art Portfolio

When all your canvas shapes are cut out, lay them onto one black Side A. Arrange them so that all ravelling edges will be well hidden by the machine applique.

If you wish to personalize the portfolio, cut out the necessary initials now, and have them ready to sew on when the landscape is finished.

Now machine applique the shapes onto A with a tight zigzag stitch. Work according to the numbered order of colors. You will tuck one shape under the other as you proceed, but if you move slowly, the order and logic will become apparent. The final touch will be the monogram in the lower right hand corner. Zigzag the initials onto the yellow desert when you finish the applique. Trim outside edges neatly.

Attaching the Handles   Cut two pieces of webbing 15 inches long. Beginning 3 inches from each end, fold in half and sew edges together. This forms a small, rounded handle which will be comfortable when carrying heavy loads. *See (a)*. Stitch handles onto Sides A as indicated on pattern. Handles should be facing in towards center of portfolio.

Sides and Bottom   Turn under ½ inch each short end of Bottom C, and hem with zigzag. Fold C in half on foldline indicated on pattern and press. With appliqued Front A on table facing you, place crease in middle of C at exact center bottom of A. Pin C to A, right sides together. Begin pinning at center bottom and work up sides. Clip corners as needed. Sew C in place. You now have the Front A with a low, boxy wall standing along the bottom and partially up the sides.

Zippers   Sew two sections B together along short ends. Do this twice forming two long strips. The zippers will be inserted between these. Trim the seams closely. With seams to inside, fold one long edge of each strip under ½ inch. Press firmly. Lay these strips along your worktable, folded edges under. Pin the two zippers between these strips so that the zipper tops meet at the center seam. There will be extra fabric at the bottom of each zipper but that will not matter since it will be hidden by the overlap of C. Sew zippers in place. Now pin completed Zipper section B onto appliqued Front A. Match the center top of the bag and the zipper tops. Make sure the seams face the inside of the bag. Sew around all edges and across handle seams, clipping corners as you go. Tuck the zipper ends of section B to the inside, under the ends of section C.

Closing the Box   Lay completed A on table with the face up. Open the zippers. Place remaining section A like a "roof" onto the "walls" formed by B and C. Pin in place carefully. Clip corners. Now begin sewing the Back on the portfolio. This will be awkward, as the appliqued landscape has made the front piece quite heavy and unwieldy. Holding the portfolio upright and leaning it against your left shoulder will facilitate sewing. If kept flat, the bag has a tendency to skid off the sewing table. Check seams for missed spots, then restitch seam with zigzag to cover seamline. Turn right side out. Insert cardboard pieces into bag to keep the portfolio upright and flat when not filled.

Fig. (a)

Ethnic Mini-Purses

Almost everyone has a treasure drawer in which they collect odd lengths of ribbon, swatches of old embroidery salvaged from a long-ago tablecloth, or perhaps a silk scarf whose edges are tattered beyond recall, but whose magnificent heliotrope roses are simply too lovely to throw away. I have a passion for bits of fabric memorabilia and derive enormous pleasure recycling them in new ways. Some treasures, particularly the glittery, sequined ones take a long time to find their home. There aren't enough of them for a quilt, they are too delicate for a jacket, they are too good to use for a doll's dress. But they can become the heart, the design center of a tiny evening bag.

For one of these mini-purses I used Thai silk patches, gently puffed and quilted. The bag was clasped with a shiny, gold frog fastener and lined with striped, Guatemalan cotton. On another I blindstitched a small Mola patch made by a Cuña Indian woman, then added a large silver bead from India and a tassle of yarn in brilliant colors.

You will find it a delightful challenge to work very tight and small, particularly if you have been wallowing in yards of canvas. Approach each bag as the delicate, unique jewel that it is, and you will find your mind flying as it plays with color, textures, and novel combinations. You may even find yourself raiding other people's treasure drawers in search of the right actors for your miniature fabric dramas.

Mola Tri-Color Purse

Materials

- ⅓ yard green canvas
- ¼ yard orange canvas
- 2 yards yellow bias tape
- ⅓ yard lining fabric
- Small, decorative embroidered patch or Mola
- Assorted yarns
- Bead for closure
- Ribbon
- Polyester fiberfill batting

Quilting the Front   Cut out all pattern pieces, including the linings. With right sides together, sew lining to Front B at top edge. Fold right side out, press. Machine baste other three edges to hold. Handle this as one piece. Cut a piece of fiberfill batting the same size as Front Stripe D. Make a sandwich of Front B, fiberfill and Stripe D all facing up. Center the Stripe D on Front B. Machine baste around edges of D to hold. Using bias tape, cover raw edges of D by topstitching tape over the edges. Make sure you begin at a top corner so that the tape joint will be covered by the Flap. Lay aside.

Preparing the Flap   Lay green Flap A on table canvas side up. Place orange Flap Strip C onto

133

Ethnic Mini-Purses

center of A. Stitch in place. Place yellow bias tape over raw long edges and topstitch as in preparing front of bag. Now lay Flap A face up on table. Place lining on top. Stitch around three sides, leaving one short side open. This will be on the bottom back of the bag. Trim seam, turn and press. Handstitch embroidered patch in place above the closed seam.

Finishing   Place A and B right sides together. Pin. Sew around all three edges. Trim closely. Turn right side out. Press. Sew on a ribbon strap of desired length.

To make the yarn closure, lay a bundle of yarns about 9 inches long on the table. Cut a length of cording or clothesline about 5 inches long and lay alongside yarns. With yet another piece of yarn 15 inches long, begin wrapping your bundle. Work evenly and tightly, not allowing the central cording/filler to show. Wrap until you have a length long enough to make a loop for your button. Now curve the wrapped cord forming a loop. Wrap the yarn around both thicknesses at the bottom of the loop, leaving the yarn ends dangling. Now slip the end of your wrapping yarn back through the bundle by threading it on a large needlepoint needle and pulling it tightly back into the core. Trim protruding end of filler cord. Sew button onto the edge of the Flap and fasten the bag shut with yarn wrapped loop.

Oriental Purse

Materials

- ½ yard black canvas
- 6 inches yellow canvas
- ½ yard lining fabric
- Polyester fiberfill batting
- Silk patches, old scarves, velvet scraps, etc. Enough to cover an area 6 by 7 inches.
- Satin or embroidered ribbon for trim and strap
- Gold frog fastener

The Patchwork Flap   Cut out all pieces, including one lining for A and two linings for B.

Using your silken patches or other treasures, fashion a central design for the Flap. After sewing your patches together, cut a piece of fiberfill batting to fit its measurements. Center the patchwork over the fiberfill on the Flap. Pin in place. Using long stitches, quilt over your patchwork as the design dictates, working from the center out. Repin along edges, adjusting for puckers. Baste around all four sides. Trim off any excess fiberfill or wandering threads. Using a satin or embroidered ribbon, topstitch this trim around all four sides of the quilted patch.

Place Flap A and lining right sides together. Stitch around three sides, leaving one short side open. Trim corners carefully. Turn right side out. With a

134

bamboo collar pointer or a pencil, poke into corners, working the canvas until the edges are square. Press gently. Now fold raw edges of the open end in towards each other and stitch close to edge.

Completing the Pouch

Center yellow C onto front of one Bottom B. Zigzag in place with satin stitch. Place one lining B and one Bottom B right sides together. Sew around three edges, leaving one short end open. Trim, turn, press. Repeat process with second Bottom B except don't applique with yellow C. Place lined Bottoms B with canvas sides together, raw edges at bottom. Sew down side, across raw bottom edges, and up other side. Trim bottom edge only. Turn right side out. Press.

Fold Flap on foldline and handstitch to back of pouch with blindstitch. Tack Flap again at top of pouch on inside. Hand sew ribbon strap at side using an antique gold button or other decorative trim.

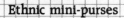

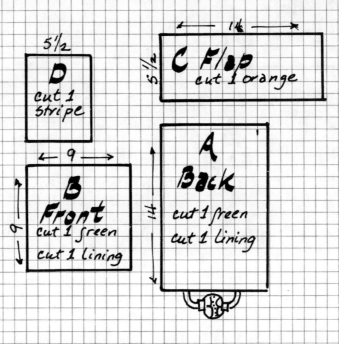

5½

D
cut 1
stripe

1¼

C Flap
cut 1 orange

5½

9

B
Front
cut 1 green
cut 1 lining

9

A
Back
cut 1 green
cut 1 lining

11

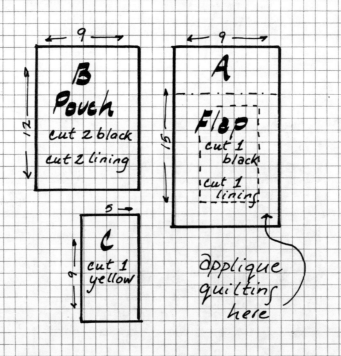

9

B
Pouch
cut 2 black
cut 2 lining

12

9

A

Flap
cut 1
black
cut 1
lining

15

5

C
cut 1
yellow

9

applique
quilting
here

Scale: 1 square = 1 inch

Rainbow Accordion Purse

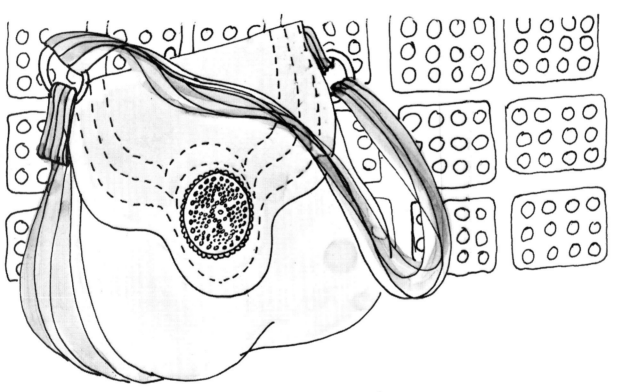

The glowing, multi-colored pouches of this shoulder bag are not only a pleasure to look at, they hold a staggering amount of personal equipment as well. The bag expands to almost ten inches when full. The top flap is decorated with a shiny, beaded Afghani Rondelle purchased at an import store. Lines of topstitching with machine embroidery thread heighten the effect of the Rondelle as they gently quilt the surface of the bag's front. A strap of rainbow webbing echoes the arrangement of the bright pouches and is fastened to the bag's side with shiny brass rings.

Materials

- ¾ yard red canvas
- ½ yard each blue, green, yellow, orange canvas
- ½ yard calico lining
- 1 yard rainbow webbing, 1½ inches wide
- Two 2-inch brass rings
- One Rondelle, or any other bit of beading, needlework or memorabilia
- Polyester fiberfill batting
- Machine embroidery thread for quilting the front, the color will depend on your choice of decoration

Rainbow Accordion Purse

Before Beginning

Cut the Red A and Red B and lining B ½ inch larger than the pattern to accomodate an extra seam.

Quilting the Flap   Cut out the pattern pieces. Cut two layers of polyester batting slightly smaller than B. Place canvas B and lining B right sides together. Stitch around edges leaving an opening for turning as shown on the pattern. Turn, trim seam and press. Insert batting layers between canvas and lining. Slipstitch the opening closed. Pin Rondelle to canvas front of Flap and sew by hand. Using machine embroidery thread, quilt around Rondelle in pattern indicated, or create your own design.

Pouching the Accordion   The centers of the Pouches A will be cut away as shown on the pattern by dotted lines. But *Do Not* cut away the center of one blue Pouch. This will form the front of the purse. Lay all the Pouch Sections on your worktable in a rainbow: begin at the bottom with orange, yellow, green, then blue. Sew the same-color sections together along the curved outside edge to form four Pouches. Trim seams neatly and then turn right side out.

Line up your completed Pouches on top of red Flap pieces. These Pouches will be sewn together along the center curves. Begin with the center Pouch, the yellow one, and work out to each side. Zigzag the Pouches together along center curves. This is tricky work. If one Pouch becomes off-center, the others

Fig. (a)

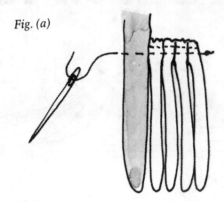

will follow and it will be impossible to realign them later.

When you have joined all the Pouches, expand the bag and trim the tops of the sides neatly. Turn side section to inside and topstitch ¼ inch hem to prevent ravelling. Refold accordion Pouch at top and, using a thimble and a quilting needle, pass a doubled thread through this thick, top section to hold it together. *See (a)*. Be careful not to sew through the padded red back.

Adding a Strap   Cut two strips of rainbow webbing 5 inches long. Insert a brass ring in each, fold in half. Zigzag ends closed. Place onto the top sides of the accordion, aligning the colors of the strap stripes with the pouch colors. Stitch ring tabs onto purse by hand using a doubled thread. Cut a shoulder strap to desired length and slip through rings. Zigzag closed.

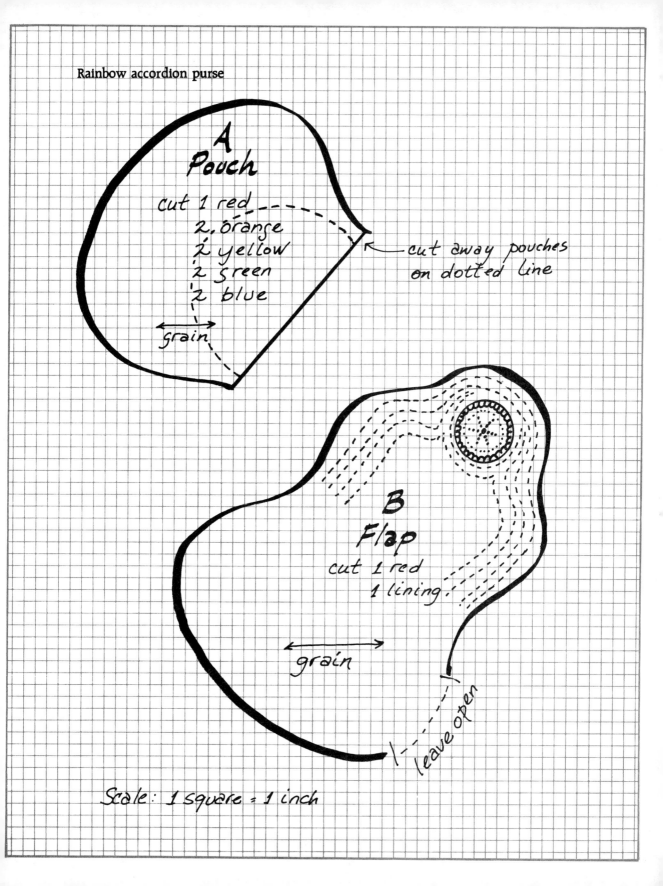

Rainbow accordion purse

A
Pouch

cut 1 red
2 orange
2 yellow
2 green
2 blue

grain

← cut away pouches
on dotted line

B
Flap

cut 1 red
1 lining

grain

leave open

Scale: 1 square = 1 inch

Beaching It

Dolphin Beach Travois

The travois was like a pick-up truck to the Plains Indians. Indian women would load the travois, usually made of birch branches with a leather covering, and they would set off on their yearly migrations following game animals. If she were lucky, the squaw would have dogs or ponies to pull the travois. Often though, she would pick up the long poles herself and drag the heavy load behind as the tribe moved.

The travois is still an extremely practical way to transport a collection of bulky, awkward items that could not be handled in one trip. A large family outing to the beach, for instance, often means lugging an ice chest, beach chairs, an umbrella, extra clothes, food, surf mats, and beach balls. The Dolphin travois can handle 100 pounds of equipment in its canvas bed. One adult can drag it up sand dunes and down trails to that secret cove tucked away from the main beach. When the poles are propped up off the sand it can conveniently double as a comfortable cot for napping children.

Materials

- 2 yards natural canvas, heavyweight, 48 inches wide
- Two 1¼-inch poles, 8 feet long
- Two 1¼-inch poles, 5 feet long
- Four #1 grommets, and grommet setter
- Electric or hand drill, with ³/₁₆-inch bit
- 2 yards ¼-inch cord
- Rasp and sandpaper
- One pint each turquoise, dark gray, and light gray acrylic paint
- Medium paintbrush

The Travois Bed   Cut out Travois Bed and four canvas strips as pole Casings. Zigzag all edges. Turn under ½ inch all four edges of Travois Bed, and zigzag. To form Casings for 8-foot poles, sew two long canvas strips on back of Travois Bed. Sew these strips close to the long edges on the *back* of the Travois Bed. Cut one remaining strip to a length of 18 inches and zigzag along top *front* of Travois Bed. Cut final strip 30 inches long and sew along *back* of end of Travois Bed. Insert a #1 grommet in each of the four corners of the Travois.

Dolphin beach travois

Painting the Dolphin Lay the Travois Bed onto a flat surface. With a soft pencil, draw the dolphin and the waves. If you begin with the waves and use a free-swinging arm, you will find that you are warmed up when the time comes to sketch in the dolphin. Drawing on a large scale is easier if you stand up from time to time so that your eye encompasses the entire surface. Once the waves are drawn in, you can use them to guide you in placing the dolphin. Perfect accuracy is not important! Mistakes can be covered by the paint. Achieve a rhythmic swinging line so the dolphin appears to leap out of the waves.

Paint the design on the canvas. Use a fairly wide brush for acrylic paints. Thin your paint down enough so that it has a transparent quality and will move rapidly over the canvas without clogging. Painting on canvas will not create the same results as silkscreening. Painting has a looser, freer quality, so let yourself go when you are working. Don't expect a perfect opaque finish. The rough effect will have a charm of its own.

Putting it Together With a rasp or very rough sandpaper, round the ends of the poles gently. On the 8-foot poles, drill holes 24 inches from one end. Now drill holes 12 inches from the other end. On one of the 5-foot poles, drill holes 6 inches from either end.

The other 5-foot pole won't be fastened to the dragging poles so it needs no holes drilled. If it is left loose in the top casing, then the long poles can be pulled closer together for easier transport. Slip all poles through the appropriate casings. With short lengths of cording, tie the bottom corners of the Travois Bed through the grommets and the holes drilled in the poles. Tie cording through the grommets on the top of the Travois Bed and the holes in the dragging poles.

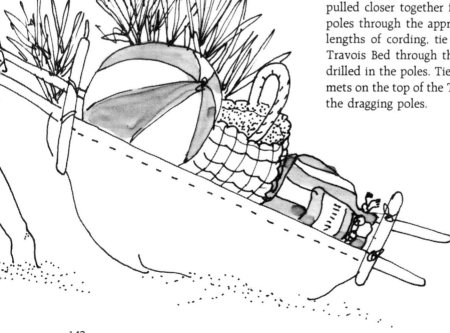

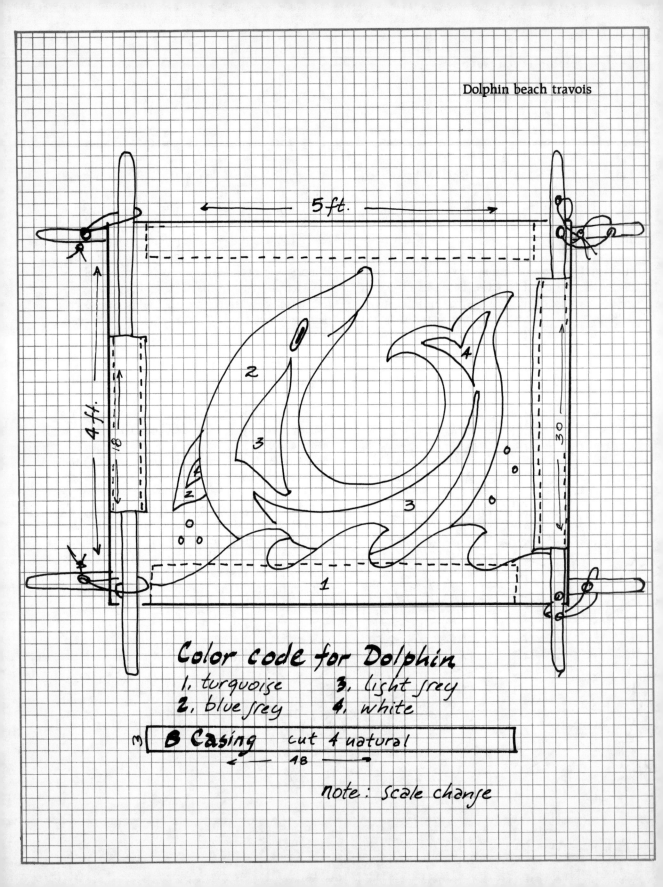

5 ft.

4 ft.

18

30

2

3

2

4

3

1

Color code for Dolphin
1. turquoise   3. light grey
2. blue grey   4. white

B Casing   cut 4 natural
18

note: scale change

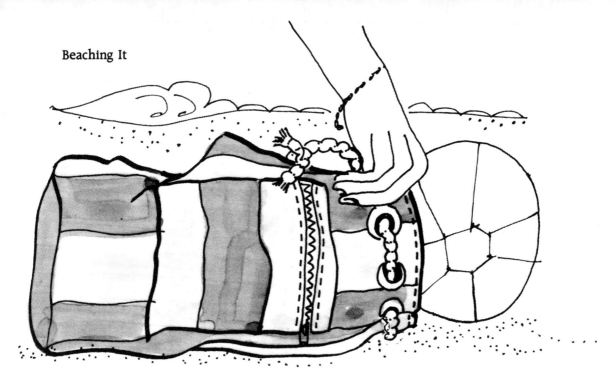

Volleyball Swim Roll

All across America volleyball aficionados are spiking, digging, and dunking with gusto. In Southern California alone, an estimated two hundred thousand volleyballs were sold in 1977. Even if you are not yet a volleyball nut, the Swim Roll will prove a practical adjunct to your summertime activities. Made of boldly striped canvas, it hosts a zippered pocket on the outside to carry your valuables and is roomy enough inside to hold a towel, change of clothes and a volleyball. For the serious sportsperson, one who never travels without two or three balls—leather for indoors, rubber for beach—the sides of the Roll may be lengthened another 12 inches to accomodate an additional volleyball. And if you are a coach and need a whole team's worth of balls, just tack on the necessary inches while you are cutting out the main body of the bag.

Materials

- 1 yard boldly striped canvas
- 4 feet of ³/₈-inch rope
- One 12-inch plastic zipper
- Six #2 or #3 grommets, and grommet setter

Making the Roll   Cut out canvas, and zigzag edges to prevent ravelling. Zigzag top edge of Body A. Fold this edge over 3 inches to inside, forming a deep hem. Stitch. Insert six grommets along top in middle of hem as indicated on pattern.

Cut Pocket B into two sections as indicated on pattern. Fold raw edges under and press firmly. Insert zipper, face up, between these two folded edges. Stitch in place, trimming end if necessary. Fold under ¼ inch all edges of Pocket. Press. Place Pocket onto Body A and topstitch onto bag.

Stitch side seam of Body, right sides together, to form tube. Go over again with zigzag. Trim closely.

Place End C into tube formed by Body, seams to outside. Pin. Stitch around End, adjusting gathers as you go. Zigzag. Trim seam closely. Turn right side out.

String length of rope through grommets and knot at end.

145

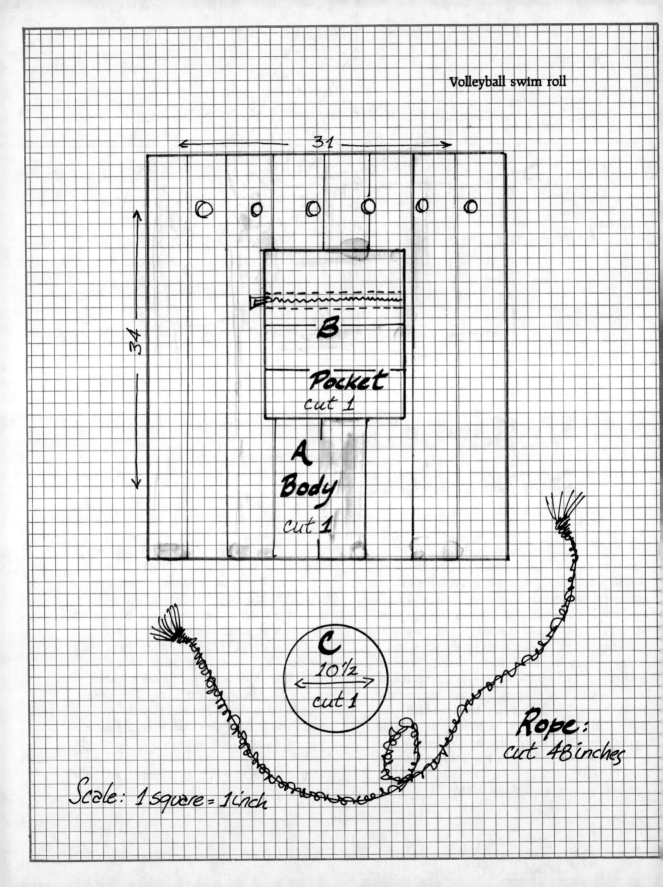

Volleyball swim roll

31

34

B

Pocket
cut 1

A
Body
cut 1

C
10½
cut 1

Rope:
cut 48 inches

Scale: 1 square = 1 inch

Ukrainian Backrests

A backrest is a simple thing: a few dowels, some paint, and a length of canvas slung between. Hundreds of thousands of them are sold each year and propped up on hot July beaches. It seems altogether right that such a utilitarian item should be emblazoned with brilliant, primitive designs. The ones I have used are enlargements of the motifs so often found in Ukrainian textiles. Ukrainian peasant needlework is one of the loveliest expressions of beauty and skill, indeed, the Ukrainians are masters in all the textile arts. The multitude and abundance of their designs is staggering.

The appliqued shapes ornamenting these backrests have been made in much the same fashion as those on the Polish After-Ski Boots. Shapes are folded in halves, or quarters, and then cut out. The appliqued canvas sling is then hung on a purchased backrest frame. This is a good chance to let your imagination and sense of color have free rein. The patterns provided here are just suggestions, you might want to search out a book on folk costume and create your own brilliant display of color and design. The backrest is merely an excuse for you to play — with scissors, thread, and scraps of colored canvas.

Materials

- Pink Backrest:
    1½ yards hot pink canvas or cotton
    Scraps of lilac, heliotrope, green, orange, yellow for applique. You will need to use some cotton other than canvas for some of these.
    6 inches Velcro
    Small can green enamel paint, and brush
    Sandpaper
    White glue
    Purchased backrest

- Burgundy Backrest:
    1½ yards burgundy canvas
    Scraps of red, orange, hot pink, light pink, green, and yellow canvas or cotton
    6 inches Velcro
    Small can red enamel paint, and brush
    Sandpaper
    White glue
    Purchased backrest

- Blue Backrest:
    1½ yards blue canvas
    Scraps of yellow, red, green, hot pink, and lilac canvas or cotton
    Small can yellow enamel paint, and brush
    Sandpaper
    White glue
    Purchased backrest

Preparing the Frame Gently twist the dowels on your purchased backrest and loosen them enough to slip the existing canvas off the dowels. With sandpaper, sand down the backrest frame to remove rough edges. Dust off with a damp rag. Paint the frame with a thin coat of enamel. Watch out. The frame is tricky to paint. It has lots of hidden niches and angles that can catch running paint or get forgotten. Work rather methodically and you'll have the best luck. You'll need to turn the frame upside down to paint the opposite side. Have a large box ready to set it on. Allow the frame to completely dry. Sand lightly, and repaint with a final coat.

A word of warning: study your backrest frame intently, and with respect, as you work. It looks simple. It is and yet it isn't. I had a hard time putting one back together when it fell apart. I just couldn't figure it out once it was pulled apart.

Ukrainian Backrests

Assembling and Appliqueing   Cut out Backrest A and Pocket B. Zigzag all edges of Backrest A. Fold under top edge 1½ inches and topstitch to form a tunnel for the top dowel. Make a pinch-tuck of 1½ inches at the center, towards the back, to form a tunnel for bottom dowel. Fold under bottom edge ½ inch and topstitch.

Cut out applique shapes and arrange them onto the canvas backing. Use the numbered guide on the pattern. Remember, however, there is no perfect way to design these patterns. The shapes are easily cut out by folding a piece of canvas in half, drawing a half-shape with a pencil and then cutting. If you feel unsure, experiment with paper first, and then use the paper as a pattern for your actual canvas.

With a dab of rubber cement, affix the shapes to the backrest canvas. Using a straight stitch sew each shape very close to the edge to hold it onto the backrest. Applique each shape onto the backing with a close zigzag stitch. Try different colors of thread for this. A color slightly lighter than the appliqued shape will add a radiant glow to your design. A darker color will add definition.

Adding the Back Pocket   Fold under the short edges of Pocket ½ inch and topstitch. When the sides are sewn together these short edges will form the top of the Pocket. Now apply Velcro strips to the inside of these hemmed edges so your Pocket can be fastened closed. With right sides together fold Pocket in half horizontally, matching top edges. Stitch side seams. Turn Pocket right side out and pin onto Backrest just under the top dowel tunnel. Sew down along one top edge. Now the Pocket will hang loosely from the back, providing you with a place to keep your snacks and suntan oil away from the sand.

Finishing   Slip completed canvas over the appropriate dowels. Before inserting dowels into backrest frame, fill the recesses with a squirt of white glue. This will hold the wooden pegs securely when the chair is assembled.

Ukrainian backrest

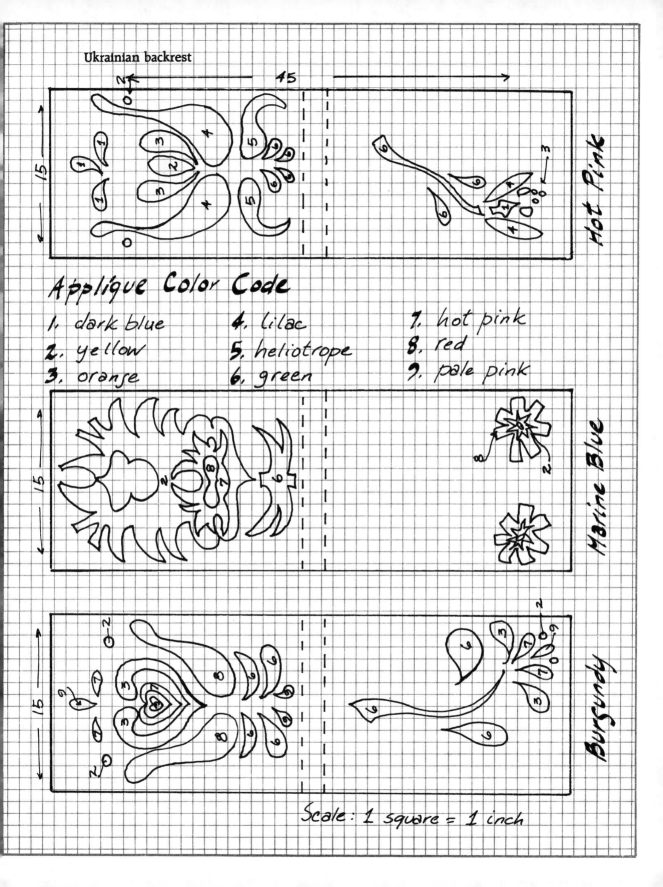

Hot Pink

Applique Color Code

1. dark blue
2. yellow
3. orange
4. lilac
5. heliotrope
6. green
7. hot pink
8. red
9. pale pink

Marine Blue

Burgundy

Scale: 1 square = 1 inch

Backrest Carrier, Windscreen, Gameboard

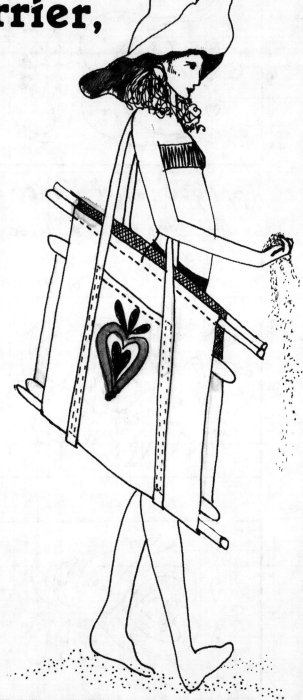

It is always a pleasure when a simply designed, utilitarian item can serve more than one function. This Carrier began as an attempt to answer a real beachgoing need. As anyone knows who has tried to ride the bus to the beach while laden with a swinging backrest, it always seems to flop open just as you step down from the last step, setting your teeth on edge and sharply rapping your ankle. This Carrier is an over-the-shoulder tote for your backrest, and the simple addition of three dowels will allow you to set it up as a sunscreen. It also sports two deep pockets large enough to carry your magazines. On the inside, the Carrier is a gameboard with room for playing three different games. Appliqued black and white strips form a Chess or Checkers board, and canvas triangles are sewn down to become a Backgammon surface. Not only will this Carrier help you get to the beach, but it will entertain you once you are there. The Backrest Carrier-Windscreen-Gameboard is decorated with Ukrainian peasant designs so it will coordinate with the Ukrainian Backrest in this same chapter.

Materials

- 2½ yards canvas (burgundy, blue, or hot pink if you are matching the Ukrainian backrest)
- Scraps of assorted canvas colors for applique
- Chess-Checkers Board:
    ⅓ yard black canvas
    ⅓ yard natural or white canvas
- Backgammon Board:
    ⅔ yard black canvas
    ⅔ yard natural or white canvas
- Three ½-inch dowels, 36 inches long
- Small can enamel paint for dowels (optional)

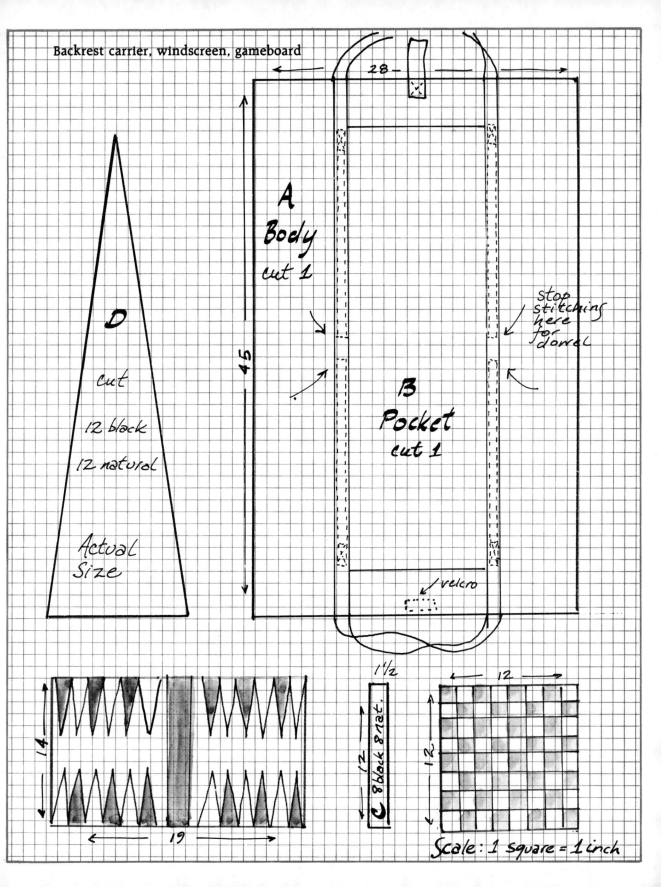

Backrest carrier, windscreen, gameboard

28

A
Body
cut 1

D
cut
12 black
12 natural

Actual
Size

45

stop
stitching
here
for
dowel

B
Pocket
cut 1

velcro

14

19

1½

12

C 8 black 8 nat.

12

12

Scale: 1 square = 1 inch

Backrest Carrier, Windscreen, Gameboard

The Basic Body Cut out all pieces. Zigzag all edges to prevent ravelling. Fold under the long sides of Body A ½ inch and zigzag to form hem. Fold under each short end of A 1 inch to form a tunnel in which to insert dowel. Zigzag tunnel in place. The third dowel will be inserted on the *outside* of the Carrier, slipping under the straps as they pass the bottom center.

The Gameboards If you choose to embellish your Backrest Carrier with gameboards, they must be appliqued before any other sewing is done.

For Chess-Checkers: Cut out strips C. Each should be precisely 1½ by 12 inches. The finished gameboard will be 12 by 12 inches, and the stitching will be hidden by one side of the Pocket when it is applied later. Weave the strips to form board. Pin the weaving in place. With black or white thread, neatly zigzag the strips down to complete gameboard.

For Backgammon: Cut out triangles and median strip. Position to form gameboard on other half of inside of Body A. The board fits between the strap seams of the Pocket and measures 14 by 19 inches. Applique median strip and triangles in place.

Pocketing Turn under ½ inch each short end of Pocket B and topstitch. Cut out applique design from scraps of canvas. Place on Pocket at desired height. Applique in place with a close zigzag or a satin stitch. Position this Pocket on the front of Body A as indicated in pattern. Sew to Body with straight stitch along outside edges.

Strapping From remaining canvas, cut two Straps 3½ inches wide and approximately 16 feet long. You will have to piece the Straps in order to get the length you need, and this length will depend on your height. When you have pieced the strapping to form one strip, join the ends so you will have a continuous circle. Fold the edges of the Strap to the middle, pressing with a hot iron as you go. Fold again in half to hide raw edges. Press. Topstitch along edges. Lay Body A on your worktable or floor. Pin strapping to it as indicated on pattern, making sure that the edges of the Pocket are hidden under the Strap. Check that handles are the same length. Sew Strap to Body, stopping stitching when you reach center bottom. Leave a 1-inch gap in the handle stitching at the center bottom, this will form a tunnel for the third dowel.

Dowelling the Windscreen Paint, stain or varnish the three dowels as you like. Insert into Tunnels as shown. You may want to make a Tab to hold the carrier shut. Cut a scrap of canvas 3½ by 6 inches, and make it as you did the Strap. Stitch Velcro on the end of the Tab, and on the top of the Carrier. Sew Tab to one side of Carrier as indicated on pattern.

Cabo San Lucas Sunshade

The Cabo San Lucas Sunshade provides a blissful oasis of shade to hide over-cooked sunbathers from the noon heat. Tropical beaches always look gorgeous and inviting on the glossy pages of travel magazines. However, after about ten minutes under the broiling equatorial sun, most people long for the cool shadow of a clacking palm and the clink of ice in a fruited drink. The Cabo San Lucas Sunshade is much simpler and lighter than an ordinary beach umbrella, and it works well when a wind is blowing. By adjusting the side cords, you can change the slant of the Sunshade to follow the path of the sun. Too, it has no center stake to reduce the shady area. A family of four can picnic comfortably under the rectangular Sunshade with no crowding. And when you are ready to pack up, the Sunshade rolls up like a furled flag and stows under the car seat.

Materials

- 1¾ yards red canvas
- 1¾ yards orange canvas
- ¾ yard yellow canvas
- ¾ yard green canvas
- Two 1-inch dowels, 72 inches long each
- Two 1-inch dowels, 52 inches long each
- 24 feet ⅛-inch nylon cord
- Electric or hand drill with ³/₁₆-inch bit
- Rasp
- Fine sandpaper
- Varnish or shellac (optional)

The Canvas Top   Cut out all canvas pieces. Zigzag all edges to prevent ravelling. Stitch Sides B to long edges of Body A to form a rectangle with red striped sides. Cut out small diamond-shaped holes

Cabo San Lucas Sunshade

on Body. Zigzag around edges of this diamond to prevent ravelling.

Fold under the outside edges of red stripes ½ inch and topstitch for a neat hem. Fold under the short ends of Body AB 2 inches to form a tunnel for the dowels. Zigzag to hold. Lay AB on the floor and pin triangular sections C to it. The green and the yellow triangles will meet at the center, overlapping slightly. The pointed ends will meet the corner formed by the small, cut-out diamond. When you have pinned these large triangular C sections to the main Sunshade, zigzag along their outer edges to join them to the main Body AB. Work slowly, taking care to avoid puckering. It helps to roll the excess canvas as you work.

Assembling the Sunshade

With a rasp, shave off one end of each 72-inch dowel to form a point. This end will stick into the sand. Smoothly round off the other ends with sandpaper. Using a hand or machine drill, drill one hole in each dowel 2 inches from the top of the *rounded* ends. Drill two more holes in *each* dowel 36 inches from the rounded ends. These holes should be about 1 inch apart. These will be your "tie-down" holes, through which the cord will pass that enables you to adjust the angle of the sunshade.

Insert a 12-inch length of cord through the hole at the rounded end. Make a knot at one end to keep the cord from slipping through the dowel. With the free end of the cord, make a loop about 6 inches long and knot it to hold. This loop will pass through the diamond hole in the canvas shade, around the dowel

in the Sunshade itself, and then back around the top of the rounded dowel. *See (a).*

With a rasp and sandpaper, gently round the ends of the two remaining dowels. Drill a hole 2 inches from both ends of each dowel. Slide these dowels through the tunnels on the Sunshade. Cut the remaining cord into four 6-foot lengths. Tie one length of cord through each hole in the dowels.

Putting the Sunshade to Work

Poke the two 72-inch pointed dowels into the sand at about the width of the Sunshade. Affix the canvas Sunshade onto these dowels by slipping the knotted loop through the cut-out diamond and over dowel. Then pass the long 6-foot lengths of cording through the holes on the upright dowels and tie down at the correct angle.

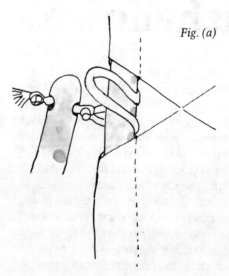

Fig. (a)

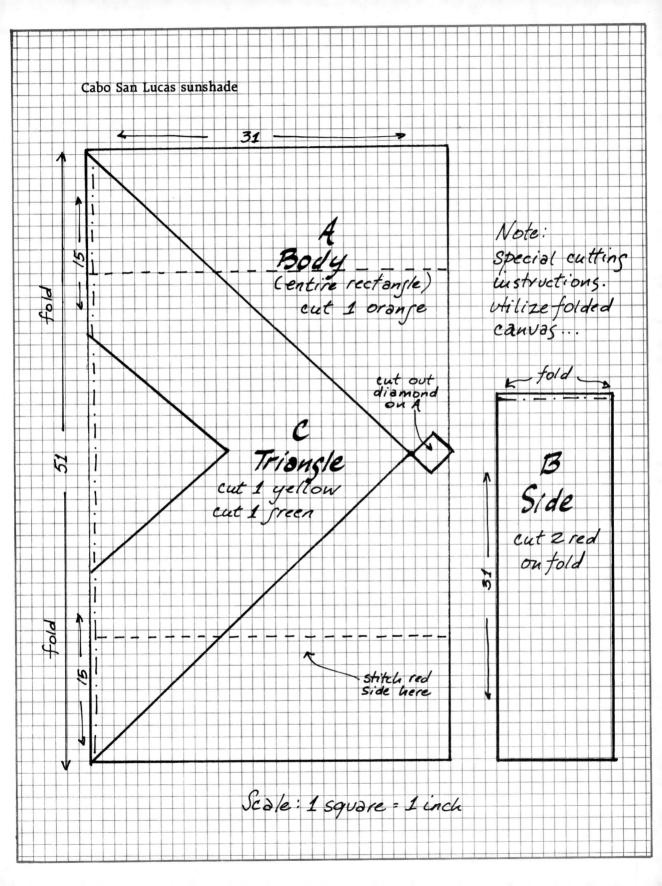

Cabo San Lucas sunshade

31

A
Body
(entire rectangle)
cut 1 orange

fold

15

51

cut out
diamond
on A

C
Triangle
cut 1 yellow
cut 1 green

Note:
special cutting
instructions.
utilize folded
canvas...

fold

B
Side
cut 2 red
on fold

51

fold

15

stitch red
side here

Scale: 1 square = 1 inch

Supergraphic Windscreen

Afternoon Westerlies are the enemy of the beach-goer, forcing the sunworshipper to pack up and steal away, a coat of gritty sand cloaking his oiled skin and his reading material in disarray. The Supergraphic Windscreen, its dowels driven deeply into the sand dunes and supported by four sand-filled "deadmen," makes a large cozy shelter to protect you from the wind. A series of pockets holds thermos, towels, clothes, radio, books, magazines and any other supplies needed for an all day beach expedition. If the bottom edge of the Windscreen is tucked into the sand, no cold air can creep underneath. Too, if the Windscreen is propped into the sand in a triangular shape, you can use it as a portable dressing room. The Windscreen can be rolled up tightly and carried under one arm.

Materials

- 1½ yards wide stripe blue canvas
- 4 yards natural canvas, 48 inches wide
- ½ yard solid blue canvas, to match stripe
- Thirteen #1 grommets, and grommet setter
- Four ¾-inch dowels, 6 feet long
- 9 yards ¼-inch nylon rope
- Rasp, sandpaper

Pockets First

Cut three panels of canvas 3 by 4 feet each. Cut out all Pocket pieces and lay out on table ready for assembling. Zigzag all edges to prevent ravelling.

Pocketing Panel A: Applique diagonal Stripes E onto Pockets D. When you are laying the Stripes on the Pockets, leave ½ inch of Pocket free at the inner

Supergraphic windscreen

corners. *See (a)*. That way, when you fold the edge of the Pocket under to sew on the Backing, the point of the diagonal Stripe will come exactly to the point of the Pocket. Now fold over top edges of Pockets D to inside ½ inch and topstitch. Turn under all remaining edges of Pockets D ½ inch and press firmly to hold. Pin Pockets onto Panel A and topstitch close to edges.

Pocketing Panel B: Turn under the top edge of Giant Pocket F ½ inch and topstitch. Insert one #1 grommet in center of Pocket 8 inches from bottom edge. Turn under all remaining edges ½ inch and press to hold. Pin Pocket to Panel B at desired height and topstitch close to edges. Turn under all edges of Flap G ½ inch and zigzag. Insert one grommet in Flap G close to point. Pin Flap above Pocket F and stitch down along top edge. Thread a 15-inch length of rope through each grommet and knot to hold. This will tie down the pocket Flap.

Pocketing Panel C: Turn under both long edges of Pocket J ½ inch. Topstitch. Pin the sides of Pocket J to Panel C at the correct height. Stitch sides in place.

You now have extra canvas flopping out on Pocket J. To create the two, small side pockets in the larger J, take a tuck 1 inch from side seams. Pin tuck down. Take another tuck in the opposite direction, this one 6 inches in from the first tuck. You should do this on each end to form two pockets. Sew the bottom of the two pockets formed, but stop sewing at the end of each pocket. This will leave the center of Pocket J unsewn, now sew one vertical seam through the middle of the unsewn section. This will form two loops next to the pockets through which you can hang towels or clothes.

Fold under top edges of Pockets H and I ½ inch. Topstitch. Fold under ½ inch all remaining edges and press firmly. Pin these Pockets to Backing C and stitch in place close to edges.

Making the Windscreen
Sew Panels A, B and C together, seams to the back. Turn under ½ inch the bottom edge and zigzag. Turn side edges to back ½ inch and zigzag also.

Cut four strips, 3 inches by 4 feet. In one end of each strip, insert two grommets. Fold long edges of strip under ½ inch and press. These long strips will form the casings to hold the poles and will be sewn on the back of the Windscreen. Center a strip over each back seam on the Windscreen, wrong sides together and with grommet ends at the top. Stitch strips to Backing, sewing close to edges of strips. Now sew the remaining two strips along the outside back edges of the Backing to make two remaining casings. Sew across tops of all casings to close.

With a rasp, shave one end of each 6-foot dowel to a rough point. Sandpaper smooth. Insert a dowel into each casing, pointed ends protruding from the bottom.

The "Deadmen"
On exceptionally windy days, the Windscreen can be kept upright by "deadmen," little sandbags. Cut out eight section K's. Place together, two at a time, and stitch around three sides to form pockets. Zigzag top edge to prevent ravelling. Insert a grommet in one top corner of each bag. Tie a 6-foot length of cord through the two grommets on the back of each pole casing on the Windscreen. *See (b)*. Run this same cord through the grommet in a "deadman" and tie. Fill the "deadmen" with sand when you get to the beach, and bury them in the sand on the windy side of the Windscreen. When buried in the sand, these four pockets make the Supergraphic Windscreen capable of withstanding a strong breeze without toppling over.

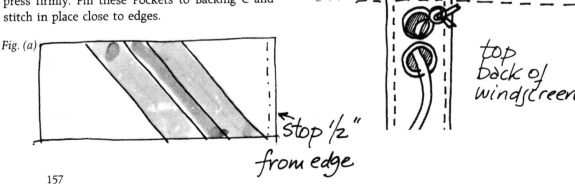

Fig. (a)

Fig. (b)

stop ½" from edge

top back of windscreen

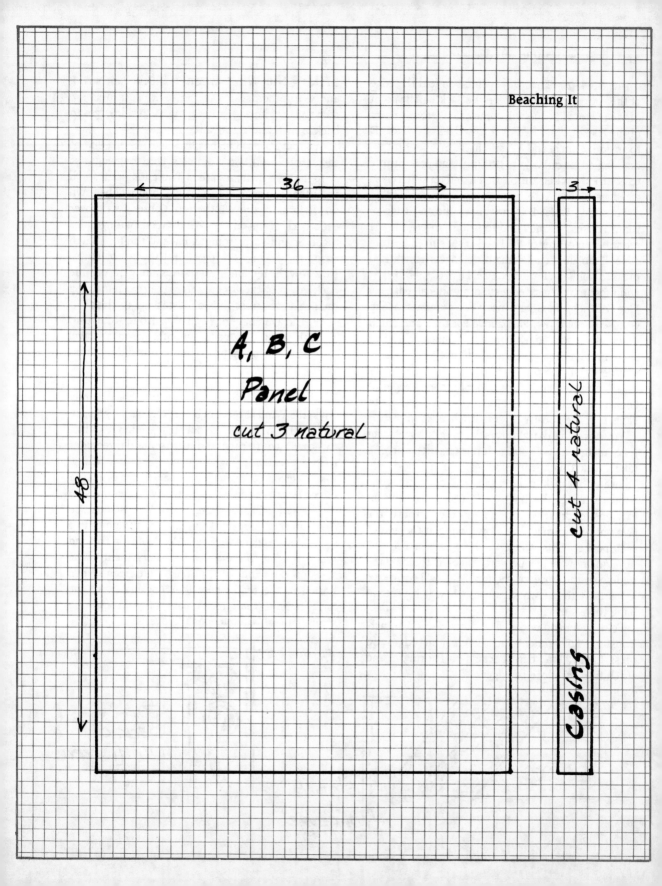

Beaching It

36

3

48

A, B, C
Panel
cut 3 natural

Casing   cut 4 natural

Supergraphic windscreen

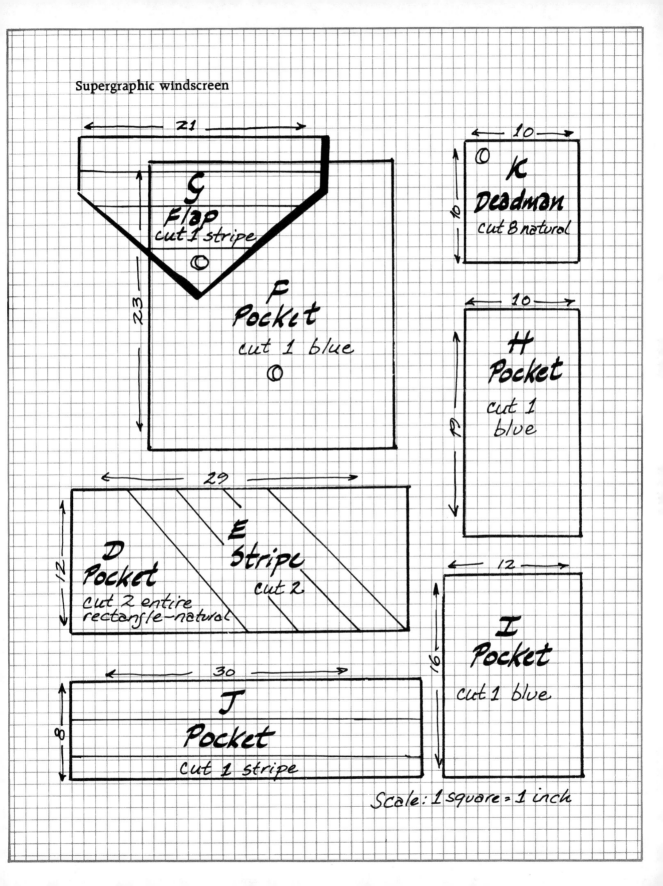

21

G
Flap
cut 1 stripe
○

23

F
Pocket
cut 1 blue
○

10

○ K
Deadman
cut 8 natural

10

10

H
Pocket
cut 1
blue

12

29

D
Pocket
cut 2 entire
rectangle-natural

E
Stripe
cut 2

12

16

12

I
Pocket
cut 1 blue

30

J
Pocket
cut 1 stripe

8

Scale: 1 square = 1 inch

Habitations

Haunted Playhouse

This A-frame playhouse is constructed of 1 x 2's hinged at the top to form a triangle. A canvas house is sewn in a giant A and slips over the hinged frame, to remain sturdy during the ghostliest games. Vinyl windows allow those inside to peer out, the eerie ghost and bat eyes are actually peepholes too. A miniature striped door on one side closes with Velcro when danger threatens. Hang a rubber spider from the top to warn off would-be invaders.

Materials

- 5½ yards black canvas, 48 inches wide
- 2 yards white canvas
- ½ yard striped canvas
- 1 yard red canvas
- ¼ yard rust canvas
- ½ yard vinyl, 24-36 inches wide
- Two 1 x 2's, 47 inches long each
- Four 1 x 2's, 54 inches long each
- Two sets folding hinges, 1 by 2 inches
- Electric or hand drill, 1/8-inch bit
- Hammer, saw, nails
- Screwdriver
- Sandpaper

Beginning   Cut out pattern pieces A, B and two C's. Zigzag all edges to prevent ravelling. Turn under one 48-inch edge of Sides A and B ½ inch and topstitch to hem. This will become the bottom edge of the playhouse. Turn under the short edge of triangular C's ½ inch and hem along bottom edge. Cut out doorway from one C and zigzag around opening.

Making the Ghostly Front

Cut out Eerie Fringe D for front door. Cut fringe strips about ½ inch wide leaving a 2-inch strip across the top. Zigzag this fringe to the inside of the Front at the top of the door opening. Zigzag along outside of Front again where Fringe joins for neat edge.

Cut out Ghost. Cut out Ghost's eyes and mouth. Cut scraps of vinyl larger than these three openings and zigzag into openings using widest zigzag stitch and medium length. Trim excess vinyl on inside. Now pin Ghost to Front A and zigzag to Front. Ghost overlaps the front door slightly so you will have to pull fringe to inside while you stitch. When the Ghost has been appliqued to the Front, restitch zigzag around eyes, then carefully cut out the black canvas covering his eyes and mouth so the vinyl shows.

Making the Bat and the Trapdoor

Cut out pieces for Bat. Cut eyes out and sew vinyl to inside as with Ghost. Pin white Bat Body to Side of Playhouse. Place rust Wings in position with red Head covering edges of Wings. Pin entire applique in place. Zigzag onto Side. On inside, cut out eyes and let vinyl show, taking care not to cut into vinyl.

Cut trapdoor opening on Side B and zigzag around the edges to prevent ravelling. Cut out piece of striped canvas to cover the trapdoor. Zigzag edges. On bottom of Striped Trapdoor sew 10-inch strip of Velcro. Sew corresponding half of Velcro to bottom inside edge of door opening. Seal Velcro, sew top edge of Trapdoor to inside of B above door opening. Now this door can best be opened from the inside. Cut out Cupola and Tower. Zigzag Cupola above Trapdoor, tucking red Tower under at center top as you sew. Zigzag Tower onto Side.

The Haunted Window and Trailing Ghost

Cut out all applique pieces for Side A. Cut out Window opening and zigzag edges. Cut a piece of vinyl slightly larger than Window. Sew with a wide zigzag stitch of medium length the window frames on the vinyl Window. Now zigzag Window in place on inside of Side. Zigzag again on outside. On each Shutter topstitch as indicated on pattern. Place Shutters on outside of Window and zigzag to

Haunted Playhouse

hold. Zigzag red Cupola onto top of Window.

Pin trailing white Ghost body onto Side A. The Ghost should wrap around from front to back of the Playhouse when the side seams are sewn, so make sure the two Ghostly halves match before you sew. Zigzag to hold.

Finishing the Canvas Triangle   Sew Side A and Side B together at top, keeping seam to inside. Right sides together, pin Back C to Sides A and B beginning at top and continuing down sides. Sew firmly with small stitches. Now install Front C in the same manner. You now have a giant, canvas A.

Making the Frame   Place two 54-inch 1 x 2's side by side, wide side up. Place hinges between these boards 6 inches from one end and 13 inches from the other. Drill holes and screw hinges into boards so that they open towards you. *See (a).*

Nail one 58-inch 1 x 2 to the end of each hinged board, matching corners as you nail. With frame opened flat on ground, lay a 47-inch board underneath the 58-inch stringers, matching the corners. Nail firmly. This forms an adjustable A-frame for the Playhouse. Slip completed canvas house over this frame and you are ready for haunting.

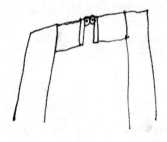

Fig. (a)

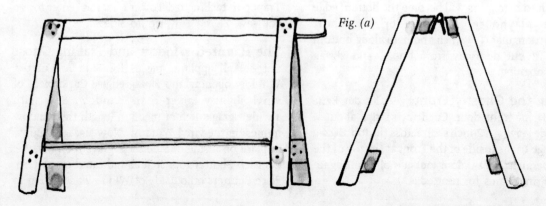

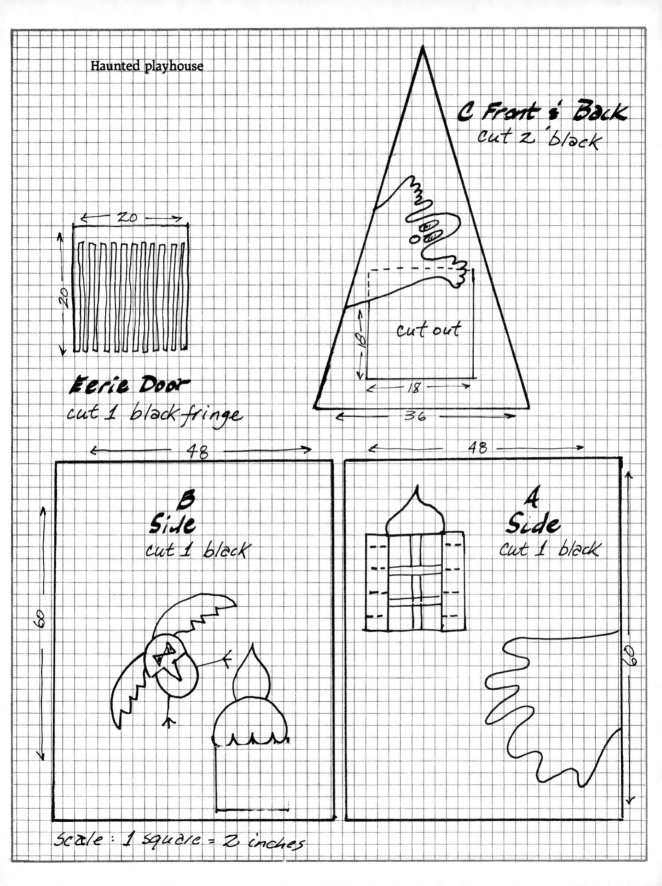

Haunted playhouse

C Front & Back
cut 2 black

cut out

18

18

36

20

20

Eerie Door
cut 1 black fringe

← 48 →

B Side
cut 1 black

60

← 48 →

A Side
cut 1 black

60

scale : 1 square = 2 inches

Cat Castle

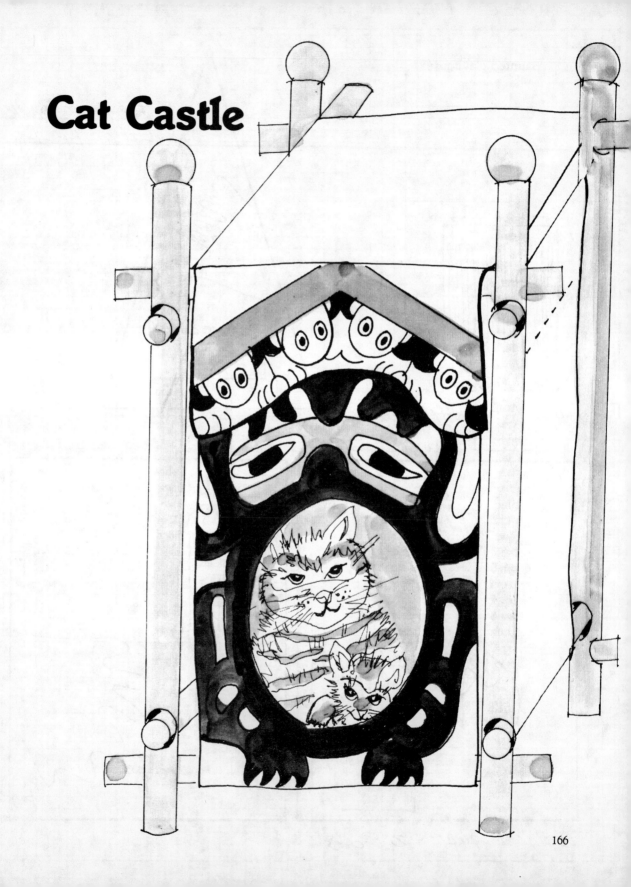

Every independent feline needs her own castle, and this easily constructed canvas one will provide shelter and privacy for your pet. No nails are needed and it can be disassembled and rolled up in a minute. The painted designs are adaptations of totemic paintings of the Haida Indians. These tribes dwelt along the fogbound Northwest coast, and are renowned for the elaborate animal imagery of their myths. Left undecorated and without the doorway, the Castle is a wonderful storage bin for yarns, needlework supplies or toys.

Materials

- 2 yards natural canvas, 48 inches wide
- 3 yards natural canvas, 30 inches wide
- Four ½-inch dowels, 15 inches long
- Four ½-inch dowels, 18 inches long
- Four 1-inch dowels, 24 inches long
- Four wooden knobs for finials (optional)
- Contact cement
- Electric or hand drill, with ½-inch bit
- Fine sandpaper
- Acrylic or fabric paints: black, red, white
- Small and medium brushes
- 6 inches Velcro

The Canvas Part   Cut out Flap A and Sides B. Cut out oval on A for entrance. The pattern is designed to save you yardage, so you will need to piece the long strip A in the middle. Merely overlap the two halves and zigzag twice. Turn under all long edges ½ inch and zigzag closely. To make tunnel for dowels, turn under short edges of Sides 2 inches and zigzag. Turn under 2 inches the straight short end of A and zigzag for tunnel. Now turn under remaining curved edge of A ¼ inch and topstitch closely to make a neat hem. Zigzag twice around oval entrance to prevent ravelling.

Painting the Totem   Mark foldlines· on canvas with pins as indicated on pattern. These will be guidelines for painting the design. Transfer the designs onto Front and Sides with pencil. Do not worry about being exact, whatever you do not like can be painted over later.

Now stretch canvas flat on a worktable or the floor. Using fabric paints or acrylics, paint in Indian designs on canvas. Allow to dry completely while you are building the superstructure from dowels.

Some Carpentry   Drill holes in the 1-inch dowels with a ½-inch drill bit. This may appear difficult if you are not confident in carpentry. Several things will make the job go smoothly even for a first timer. Mark the exact centers of the holes with a pencil. Start each hole first by drilling a small hole with a ⅛-inch bit or hammer a large nail in a short distance. This way the large drill bit will not skid sideways on the dowel. Place the dowel in a vise or hold it with C-clamps while drilling. The holes must be at right angles to each other so the Castle will be square when the ½-inch dowels are slipped through.

Now sand the dowels smooth with fine sandpaper.

Build the superstructure. Slip one short dowel out and slide tunnelled edge of A over it. Replace dowel. Slip tunnelled edges of Sides B over side dowels and replace these. The Sides will be hanging loosely in the center of the Castle. Now slip lower side dowels through holes at front and back. This snaps the floor in place tautly. *(See a).*

Finally, wrap the long piece A around the Castle and over the top of the front. Pin in place tightly to fit. Remove A and sew lengths of Velcro under each point of flap and on front. Reclose with Velcro.

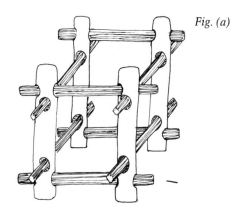

Fig. (a)

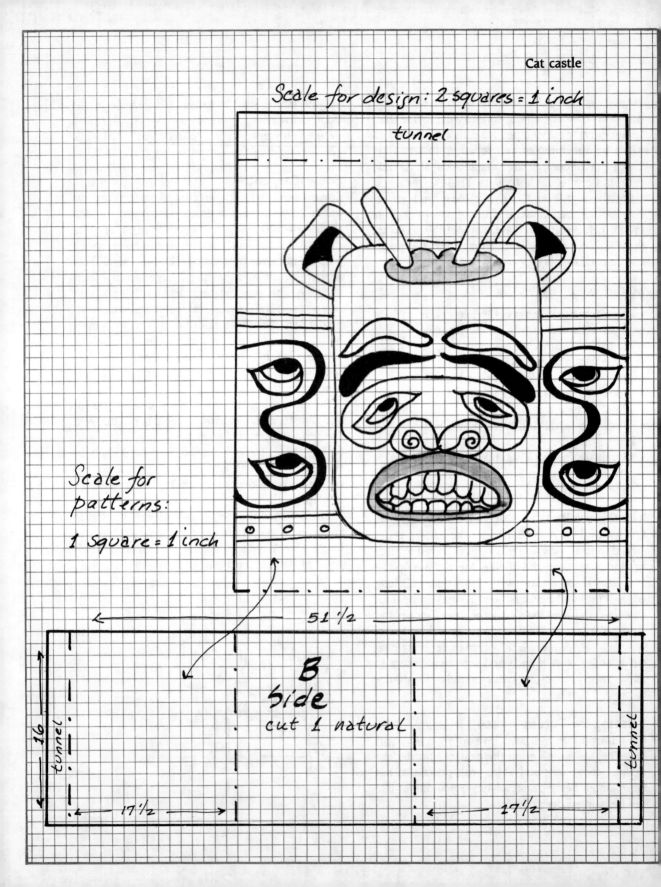

Cat castle

Scale for design: 2 squares = 1 inch

tunnel

Scale for
patterns:

1 square = 1 inch

51½

B
side
cut 1 natural

16

tunnel

tunnel

17½

17½

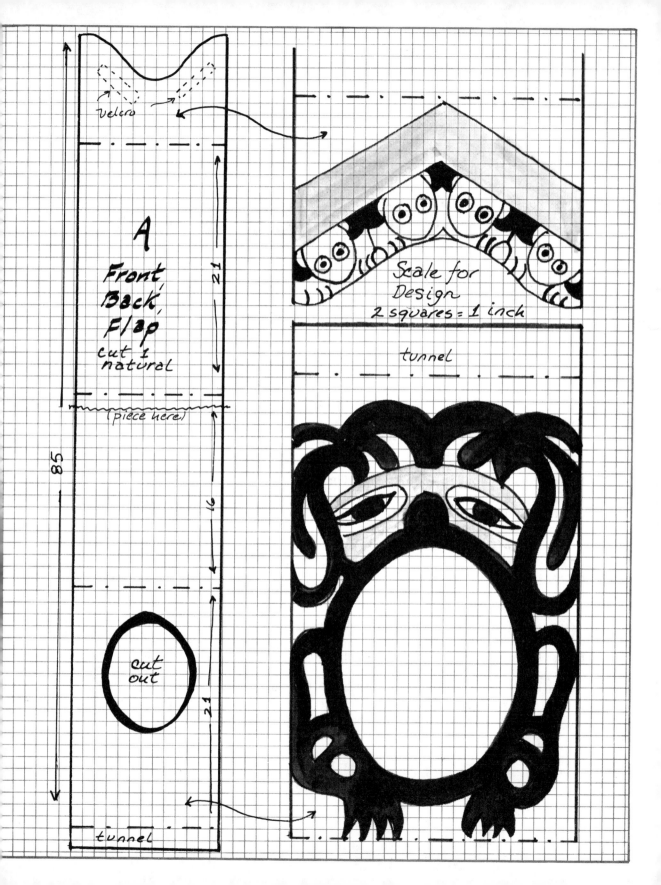

Velcro

A

*Front
Back,
Flap*

cut 1
natural

21

(piece here)

16

85

cut
out

21

tunnel

Scale for
Design
2 squares = 1 inch

tunnel

Sideshow Bunk Bed

A rainy day is a good time for small children to make hideouts of their bunk beds. Instead of using old sheets and blankets, you can provide them with canvas Tents that will entertain for hours. They are fun to make, especially if you tailor their design to the individual interests of the children who will inhabit them. Try personalizing your Tent with bits of calico, zippers, pockets, fake fur, sequins, anything in your scrap bag. This is a fine project to involve the children themselves. Their own designs are ingenuous with a spontaneous quality that an adult can never quite duplicate.

Figuring the Yardages   An average bunk bed for a child measures approximately 80 inches by 45 inches. Yardages to make a tent to accomodate this size bed would vary depending on whether you want to make it to totally enclose the bed. Depending on your room arrangement, you may only need to cover one side and one end of the bed. The Side Panels each require 2⅓ yards of canvas 48 inches wide. The End Panels each take 1 yard of canvas 48 inches wide. The Top Panel which you will tuck under the top mattress takes 2⅓ yards, but this need not be of canvas. An old sheet would do nicely for the Top Panel.

Then you need to figure the yardage it will take to decorate the Tent. The embellishments need not be elaborate, all you really need to make an entertain-ing environment is a few windows and a flap entrance. On the other hand you may want to totally applique the whole tent to transform it into an imaginative play corner.

Some Tips for Making Bunk Bed Tents

- Cut out the window holes first. You can fill these with clear vinyl to let your adventurers peek through. Cut the vinyl an inch larger than the hole and zigzag it in place with a wide stitch.

- When you are doing extensive applique, attach the small pieces to the medium size pieces first. Then applique these to the larger panels.

- Don't sew the panels of the Tent together until all the applique is done.

- When working with large panels of canvas, roll them up before slipping into your sewing machine. If you have a foot treadle you can work on the floor, with all the yards of canvas spread out around you.

Assembling the Tent   The Tent is just a rectangular box of canvas. Attach the Side and End Panels to the Top Panel with a zigzag stitch. Zigzag again for strength. Now you can turn it inside out and sew the side seams attaching the End Panels to the Sides, or leave these edges open. Again, double zigzag your seams for strength.

Sideshow bunk bed

- Escape curtain at bunk end

- vinyl windows for tossing ping pong balls, kissing, peeking out

- Booths appliqued onto side panel

30

45

25¢ FAT

SEE LADY

End Panel

Scale: 1 square = 1 inch

Getaways

Kids Backpack

This simple Pack features a double zipper closure along the top flap, making it easy to stuff last minute items into the Pack when the bell rings. Brass "O" rings make the Pack adjustable to fit any child, and a small inner pocket holds milk money or a library card.

Materials

- 1 yard canvas
- Two 9-inch zippers
- 1½ yards webbing, 1 inch wide
- Four "O" rings, 1 inch wide

Zippering the Flap   Cut out pattern pieces and zigzag edges to prevent ravelling. Turn under ½ inch all edges of Pocket D and topstitch to hold. Pin Pocket to inside of Front as shown on pattern and stitch around three sides.

Mark exact center of Flap C. Pin the two zippers face down onto Flap edge with tabs meeting in the center. With a zipper foot sew one edge of zippers to Flap edge, clipping corners as you go for ease. Place this zippered Flap face down onto Front A with zipper centers matching center of Front. Pin unsewn edge of zipper tapes to top of Front, folding up sides as you go to form a box shape. Stitch with zipper foot. Topstitch ¼ inch away from seam to keep zigzagged edges neat and away from zipper slide.

Now sew bottom corners of Front together, seam to inside. You have a boxed front of your Pack. *See (a).*

Adding the Straps and Back   To form the lower straps, cut two lengths of webbing 8 inches long. Slip one end of each strap through an "O" ring, fold over 1 inch and topstitch securely. Place the other end of each ringed strap onto edge of Back B and stitch in place.

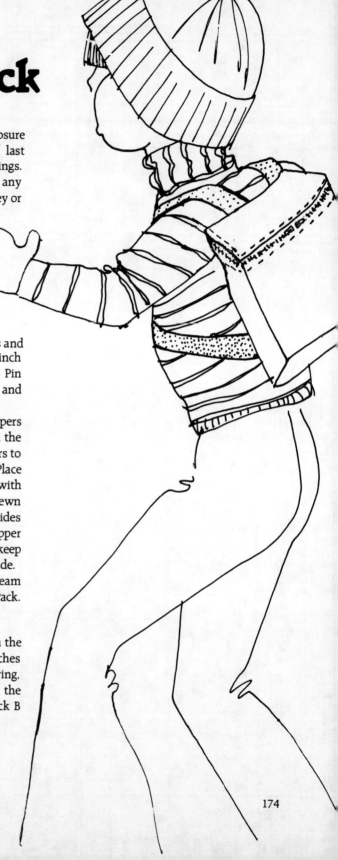

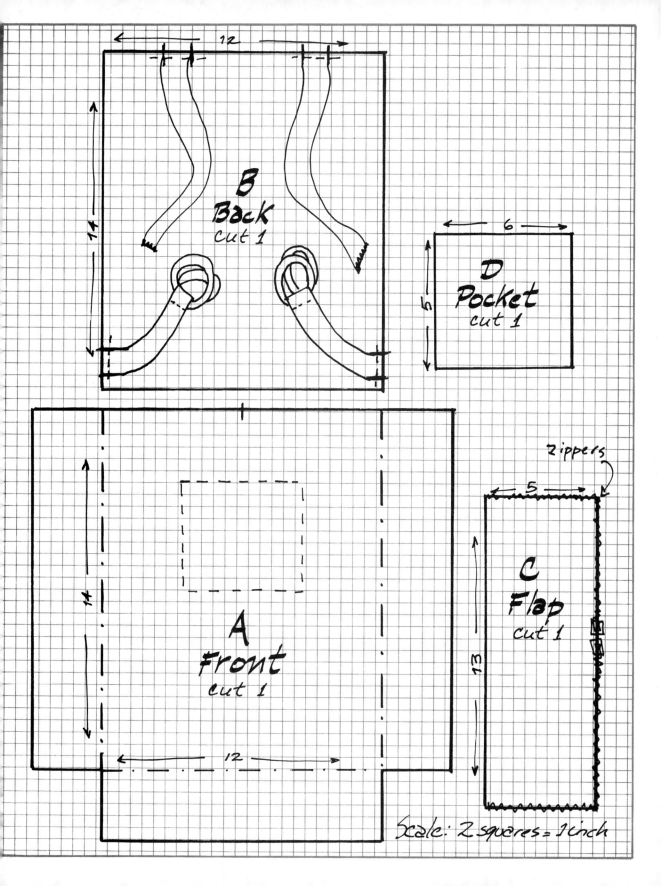

B
Back
cut 1

12

14

D
Pocket
cut 1

6

5

A
Front
cut 1

14

12

zippers

C
Flap
cut 1

5

13

Scale: 2 squares = 1 inch

Kids Backpack

Cut two more straps each 22 inches long. Place one end of each onto top edge of Back as shown on pattern. Stitch to hold. Zigzag free end to prevent ravelling. These free ends will slip through the "O" rings making the pack adjustable. *See (b).*

Now turn boxy part of Pack inside out and pin the completed Back to it, right sides together. Take care to tuck all straps to the inside, and open the zippers enough so the Pack can be turned right side out after sewing. Sew Back to Front. Turn right side out, adjust straps to fit child.

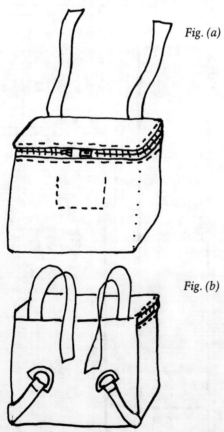

Fig. (a)

Fig. (b)

Bicycle Panniers

Biking is marvelous exercise, and a good way to keep pollution in check. But those of us used to the big personal space within the family car may feel limited on a bike. Strap on these Panniers and you can visit your favorite park with a picnic and a book. Constructed in two, zippered box-shapes, the Panniers hang over your metal book rack. Use them on your way to school, short hops to the grocery, or other errands around town. They'll make your bike more convenient, so you'll probably use it more often.

Materials

- 1⅔ yards navy canvas
- ¼ yard yellow canvas
- 1½ yards striped webbing
- Four "D" rings, 2 inches wide
- Two 18-inch oversize separating zippers, navy or yellow

Making the Panniers

Cut out all pattern pieces. Zigzag all edges to prevent ravelling. Fold one Bag Body A so that the side seams meet, leaving the Flap hanging loose. Stitch side seams, overstitch and trim. Stand pouch up on the worktable so that it forms a box shape. Pinch creases 2 inches on either side of side seam. Stitch across triangle point to form box bottom. *See (a).* The width of the side panel of the box will measure 4 inches. Trim off excess fabric. Repeat with second side. Turn pouch right side out. Pinch side creases and topstitch along edges. *See (b).* Pinch bottom edge and topstitch, too, for a clean boxy shape. Repeat process with second Pannier.

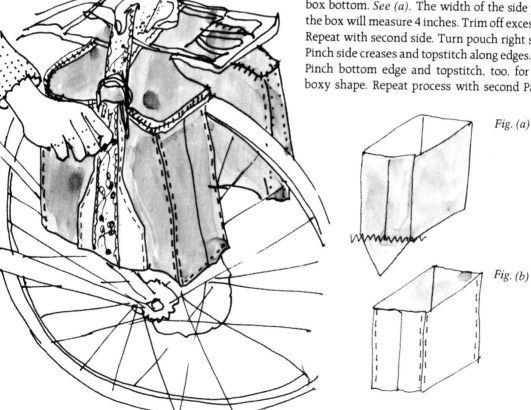

Fig. (a)

Fig. (b)

Bicycle Panniers

Zippering the Flaps   Apply separating zipper, one side at a time to top Flap and to top of Bag. This is easier if you clip the corners as you go.

Strapping Them On   Place both Center Straps together. Sew around three sides ¼ inch from edges. Turn right side out. Fold remaining raw edges towards each other and topstitch closed. Topstitch again ¼ inch from all edges with contrast stitching. Place Strap onto backs of Panniers along top edges and topstitch twice. *See (c)*. This Strap will pass under the metal snapper on your bike.

Place Lower Straps C in pairs. Stitch ¼ inch from all edges, leaving the short, straight end open. Trim, turn and press. Topstitch again with contrast color ¼ inch from edges. Pin a 15-inch length of webbing onto the center of the Strap, beginning at the short edge and ending by slipping the webbing through two "D" rings and tucking under. Stitch close to the edges of the webbing. Now, center the completed Strap with the rings onto the Pannier, beginning at the bottom back of the Pannier and bringing the strap up towards the outside of the Pannier. Stitch across bottom back twice. Repeat for second Pannier. *See (d)*.

Cut a 20-inch length of webbing. Turn under both ends ¼ inch and zigzag to keep from ravelling. Center this webbing on the Overstrap. Sew in place onto the Overstrap. Slip ends of webbing through "D" rings to cinch Panniers when they are filled and heavy.

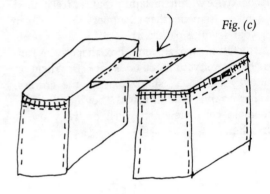

Fig. (c)

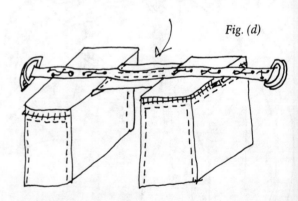

Fig. (d)

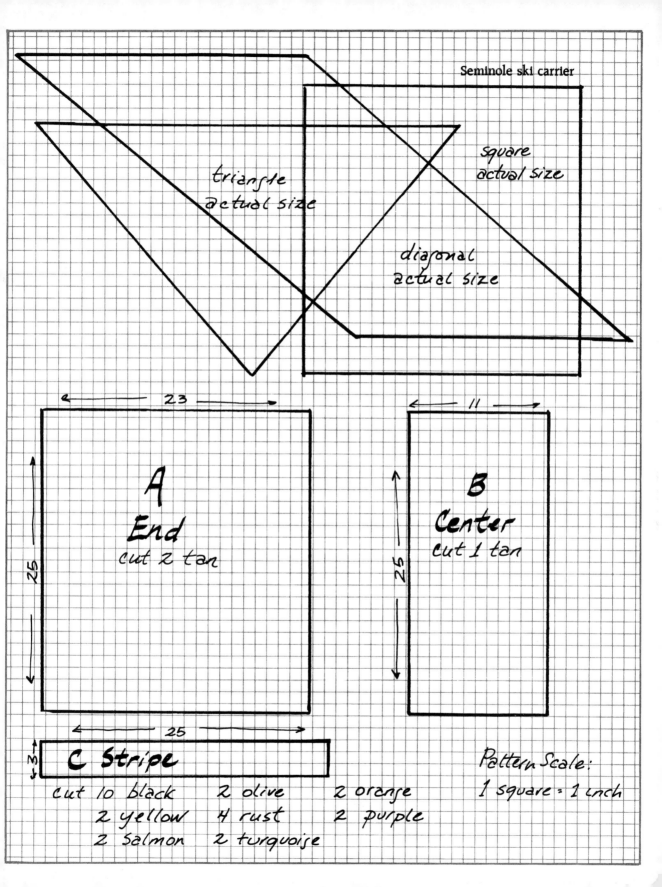

Seminole ski carrier

triangle
actual size

square
actual size

diagonal
actual size

23

A
End
cut 2 tan

25

11

B
Center
cut 1 tan

25

25

C Stripe

3

cut 10 black   2 olive   2 orange
2 yellow   4 rust   2 purple
2 salmon   2 turquoise

Pattern Scale:
1 square = 1 inch

Seminole Ski Carrier

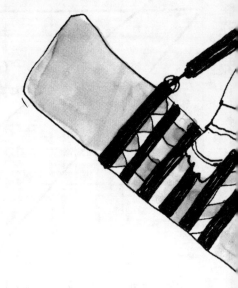

The Ski Carrier is a boon to weekenders who must make several airport hops before they reach their favorite mountain. Two pairs of skis may be carried in the tote if they are joined by elastic straps, and the canvas is tough enough to withstand most airline handling. Be sure to waterproof the Carrier before you leave, though.

The Ski Tote is brightly banded with Seminole patchwork, a technique used extensively by the Indians in Florida. Here the scale is much larger than usual. Masterful colorists, the Seminoles cut and stitch tiny geometric patches, arranging them in bands of brilliant colors and designs. These bands are used to decorate skirts, shirts and even handbags. Here the canvas patches are much larger and less intricate, but the primitive flavor is retained by the juxtaposition of unexpected colors.

Materials

- 1⅔ yards tan canvas
- ¾ yard black canvas
- ⅓ yard rust canvas
- ¼ yard *each* yellow, salmon, olive, turquoise, orange, purple canvas (substitute sailcloth if canvas not available)
- 1⅓ yards black webbing for handles
- 24 inches Velcro
- For shoulder strap (optional):
    Two 1-inch "D" rings
    Two brass snap-shackles
    Black webbing, 36–45 inches long

Working the Patches   Accurately cut out the three shapes—diagonal, square, and triangle—from stiff paper or cardboard. These will be your templates for the geometric shapes on the bands. Cut out long, colored canvas strips. From these, cut out 12 rust and 12 turquoise triangles. Arrange triangles on your worktable in two bands approximately 26 inches long. Sew triangles into bands, pressing seams as you go. Use ¼ inch seams. It may help to move your ironing board alongside your worktable at the same height, so you don't have to

jump up constantly and iron, but can merely reach around and press each seam as you stitch it. In all strips, try to iron seams in one direction. It will make a neater seam later.

Now cut 12 yellow and 12 salmon squares. Align in two equal strips. Stitch, using a ¼ inch seam. Press as you go.

Cut 12 rust and 12 orange diagonals. Align in strips, sew and iron.

Arrange the bands in order on your floor or table. Cut out remaining stripes and large pieces. Arrange solid stripes and patchwork bands in two equal sections. Sew strips together pressing as you work. Sew tan Ends A to end of each banded section.

The Monogram   Cut out a square of orange canvas about 6 by 6 inches. Trace a small oval for monogram onto it. With your machine set for a narrow zigzag, practice embroidering your initials on a canvas scrap until you feel confident. Then draw your initials within the orange oval and embroider them. When the monogram is complete, cut out the small, orange Oval and applique it onto a larger black Oval. Satin stitch this completed monogram onto the center of B. Sew center B and two sides together forming one long strip for the Ski Carrier.

Cut two tabs of webbing 4 inches long. Slip through "D" rings and fold. Stitch closed. These will be the loops for an optional shoulder strap which comes in very handy during a hurried ski trip. Pin these tabs face down on the front of the Carrier, facing to center 26 inches from each end. Stitch in place.

Closing the Gap   Place Carrier face down on the worktable. Fold one short end of Carrier to inside ½ inch. Pin one half of a 12-inch strip of Velcro to one folded side. Pin other half of Velcro to other half of same side. *See (b).* Sew both in place, covering raw edges of the canvas as you sew. Fold entire Carrier in half lengthwise, right sides together, keeping straps towards center and out of seamline. Pin. Beginning at the Velcro-less end, stitch all around, leaving the end with Velcro open. Turn right side out, press. Seal Velcroed ends.

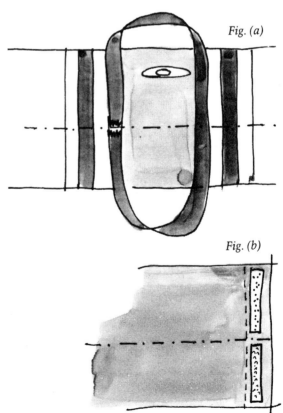

Fig. (a)

Fig. (b)

The Handles   Cut a strap of black webbing 40 inches long. Fold strap in half crosswise and mark exact center with a pin. Fold Ski Carrier in half lengthwise. Crease fold with palm of your hand. Unfold flat. Place one free end of the strap at the center fold line, next to the purple band. Place center of strap on fold line, along other purple band. The handles should now be exactly the same length. *See (a).* Pin strap and stitch close to all edges, ending 1 inch before the raw edges of the canvas.

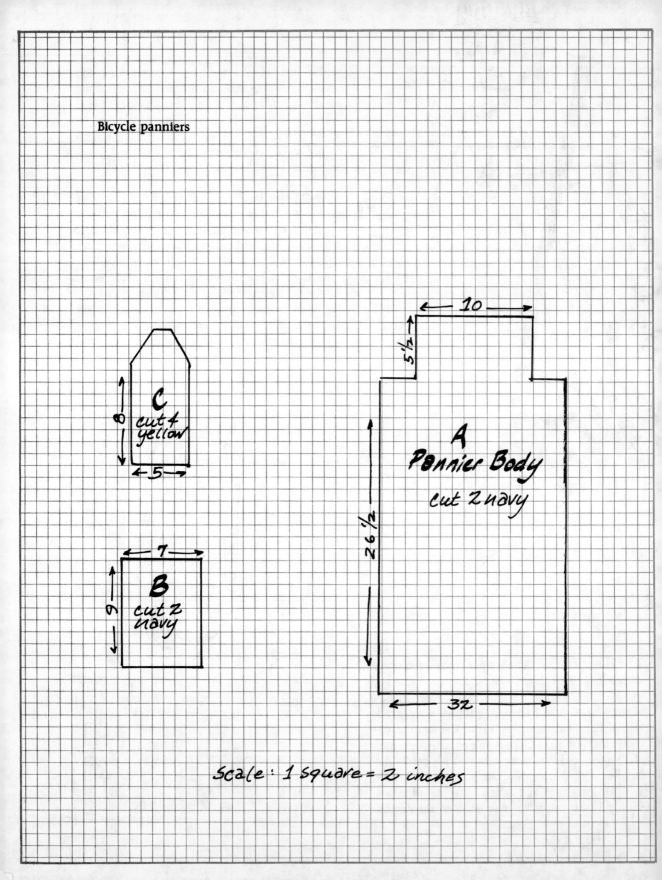

Bicycle panniers

C
cut 4
yellow
8
5

B
cut 2
navy
7
9

A
Pannier Body
cut 2 navy
10
5½
26½
32

Scale: 1 square = 2 inches

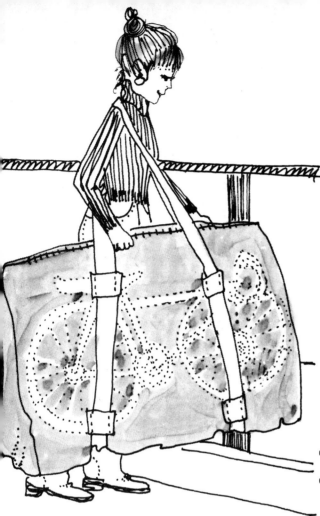

Ghostly Bicycle Carrier

Travelling with a bicycle is often awkward, especially when you are going by air. A large bike tote makes it possible to check your bicycle with a minimum of hassle. You will need, however, to dismantle your 10-speed bicycle first, removing the front wheel, pedals and handlebars. These parts will fit, along with the frame, into this canvas Carrier. And the Carrier itself can be slung over your shoulder for hauling across the airport parking lot.

The Carrier is blueprinted on its side with a ghostly image of the bicycle within. Blueprinting on fabric is an exciting technique. Unlike painting or batiking, blueprinting is an almost instant process, requiring only exposure to the sun's ultra-violet rays to create an image. The areas shielded from the sun don't print, remaining white against the background blue. Huge areas may be printed in the same amount

of time it takes to print small ones. This process, therefore, is well suited for bedspreads, wall hangings, curtains, and even tents. The only requirements are 100% cotton or Viscose rayon fabric, sun, water, and two photographic chemicals.

Directions are given here for an amount of solution large enough to saturate the canvas for the Carrier. Should there be any solution left over, it will be good for approximately six hours if not exposed to light. Have additional pieces of fabric ready to experiment with. Use interestingly shaped objects to create an image on fabric; experiment with such things as scissors, half-filled glass jars, toys, balls and blocks, strings, tools, straw, macaroni, or even photographic negatives. Drawings made on acetate with Tusche crayon (an opaque, soft black artist's pencil) can also be laid onto the fabric and blueprinted.

Materials

- For Carrier:

  5 yards natural canvas, 10 ounce weight

  5½ yards heavy natural webbing, 3 inches wide

  50-inch heavy duty separating zipper

- For Blueprinting:

  Potassium Ferricyanide, 75 grams (a Kodak product available at photographic supply stores, it is POISONOUS)

  Ferric Ammonium Citrate, 100 grams (available at Bryant Labs, 880 Jones Street, Berkeley, CA)

  Bathtub or large plastic wash tub

  Heavy rubber gloves

  Water

  Electric fan (to speed drying of sensitized canvas)

  Bicycle

  Clothespins and drying lines

  Rinse tub with running water

  Darkened room

  Gram scale

Blueprinting the Canvas

Cut out all canvas pattern pieces except the Strap Holders D. Zigzag edges to prevent ravelling. Wash canvas pieces in Sal-soda and hot water to remove any sizing. Pieces may remain damp.

The blueprinting process is not complicated. However you will be working with chemicals that are both POISONOUS and extremely sensitive to ultra-violet light. *Any* light, even a door left ajar for a few moments, will start the blueprinting process. Therefore, you will want to set aside a place where you can work undisturbed. Since you will be exposing the canvas to develop the image, it would help if your workspace were accessible to a lawn or driveway outdoors. Choose a sunny day and work between 11 a.m. and 2 p.m. The brighter the sunshine, the faster the exposure time.

The blueprinting process can be divided into three parts: sensitizing the fabric with emulsion, exposing the fabric to light, and rinsing the chemicals out.

Whatever you place on the top of the sensitized fabric will print white when exposed to light. Shadows print light blue, contact points print white. In this project you will use a bicycle, which will cast shadows on the sensitized canvas where the sun can not pass through. The bicycle image will emerge in a ghostly, three-dimensional way on the sides of the Carrier.

Sensitizing the Canvas

Prepare a darkened room in which to work. Mix the blueprint emulsions, using *exact* quantities of powdered chemicals and water. First dissolve 75 grams of Potassium Ferricyanide in 500 cc. of water. Then set it aside. Dissolve 100 grams of Ferric Ammonium Citrate in 500 cc. water. Wear rubber gloves as you work and avoid splashing these chemicals or breathing their fumes. Mix the two solutions together in a large tub.

Immerse canvas pattern pieces, trying to saturate as evenly as possible. Do not wrinkle canvas unnecessarily. When saturated, the canvas will appear a light yellowish color. Hang canvas pieces on a clothesline *in a darkened room*, and allow to dry. You may wish to use an electric fan set to "cool" to speed the drying process. When the sensitized canvas is damp-dry you are ready for the next step. ONCE DAMP-DRY, THE FABRIC MUST BE EXPOSED IMMEDIATELY.

Printing the Bicycle

You are now going to expose canvas pieces to the ultra-violet light of the sun. Have your bike ready to place onto the Sides A. Place sensitized pattern pieces onto a flat surface outdoors. Lay bikes on Sides A. A child's bike will fit within the dimensions of the Carrier Side, a 10-speed will not. But some nice effects can be gained by using only the top or bottom half of the 10-speed, or even by placing it diagonally on the cloth.

Move quickly. The emulsion begins working the moment any ambient light strikes it. Watch the canvas as it develops. It will begin turning a light greenish-grey. While your canvas is developing, prepare a large tub with a source of running water to

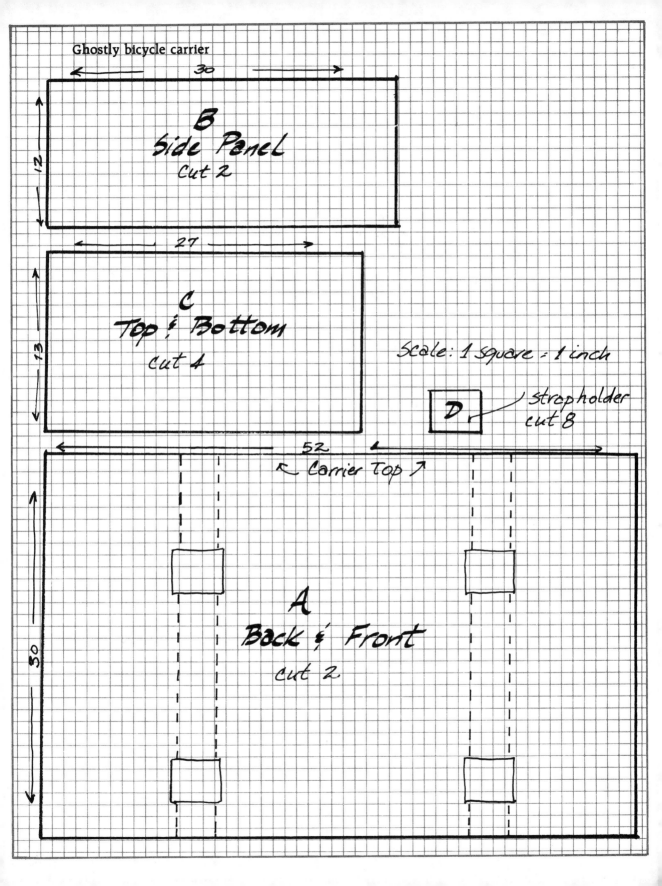

Ghostly bicycle carrier

B
Side Panel
Cut 2

30

12

C
Top & Bottom
cut 4

27

13

Scale: 1 square = 1 inch

D ⟵ strapholder
cut 8

52

⟵ Carrier Top ⟶

A
Back & Front
cut 2

30

Ghostly Bicycle Carrier

rinse the exposed fabric. A tub and hose on the shady side of the house are fine. The exposure time will vary depending upon the weather and the time of day. If you are working at noon, it should take around 5 to 15 minutes. Watch the color of the canvas. When it turns a light, crusty grey-blue it is ready to be rinsed. WORK QUICKLY NOW . . .

Rinsing the Fabric   Remove the bikes and rush the canvas pieces to the tub filled with clear water. Rinse, rinse, rinse. Most importantly, rinse the pieces with the bicycle image carefully. All the yellowish emulsion must be washed out of the white areas or they will eventually fill in, you will lose the bicycle print. You may need to rinse the canvas for as long as 30 minutes, with the water running all the time. Agitate the canvas every few minutes.

Dry the canvas pieces on a clothesline away from bright sunlight. Smooth any wrinkles from the damp canvas as you hang it to dry. The fabric *cannot* be ironed without fading the blueprint.

The Strap Holders   Cut out Strap Holders. Make a ¼-inch hem on the 3½-inch sides of each Strap Holder. Place these Strap Holders onto Sides A as shown on pattern. Stitch down close to edges to form tunnels through which the webbing will pass.

Adding the Zipper   Stitch two Bag Tops C together on short ends to form one strip 52 inches long. Trim seam closely. Now cut this strip down the middle lengthwise. Fold two long edges under ½ inch and press. Insert zipper between these folded edges and topstitch in place. Zigzag across opened ends to close seam.

Making the Bottom   Sew two remaining pieces C together to form long strip. Trim long raw edges on each side ½ inch so that strip measures 52 by 12 inches.

Boxing It In   Sew one Side Panel B to each side of Bottom. Sew zippered Top to edges of Sides forming a long circle 12 inches wide. Pin this circle onto Sides of Carrier, right sides together, with zipper at top of blueprinted bicycle image. Adjust at corners, clipping for ease. Carefully sew Circle-Side to Carrier Body. Zigzag over this seam and trim. Open zippered top halfway. Pin remaining Side A to other edge of Side section. Sew twice to hold. This is slow, awkward work. Turn Carrier right side out. Insert 3-inch webbing through Strap Holders forming two shoulder straps for carrying. Overlap webbing at bottom of one side and zigzag firmly to close straps.

Second Skin: Clothing

Chef's Tabard Apron

Nothing is simpler, more practical, and easier to make than a tabard apron. It has a multitude of uses, fits everyone, and is a delightful garment for experimenting with different methods of embellishment: applique, stencil, block printing, handpainting, or Polish cutouts. The ties at the side are optional, you may wish to omit them if you make the bib-length version for rib-eaters and barbecuers. These tabards are easy to make in multiples, and serve as splendid housewarming gifts or personalized wedding presents.

Materials (all fabric allowances make two aprons)

- Bib-length: ¾ yard canvas
- Mid-Length: 1⅓ yards canvas
- Ankle-length: 2¼ yards canvas
- Compass
- Embellishment materials according to choice: felt tipped pens, silkscreen materials, fabric paints, potatoes or lino blocks and inks, stencils, contrast canvas for pockets or applique, etc.

Instructions

Cut out pattern pieces and zig-zag all edges to prevent ravelling. Use a compass to draw round hole for head. Turn under side edges ¼ inch and stitch. Fold under ¼ inch again and restitch. Make tiny clips in neck edge, then turn under ¼ inch and stitch. Topstitch again for neatness. Try on your tabard and determine correct length for you. Turn under front and back hems 1 inch and handstitch or machine stitch.

Cut out four ties, 2½ by 16 inches. Fold ties in half lengthwise. Fold again. Topstitch along all edges. Sew ties to apron sides at correct height for you. Slightly above the waist is a flattering height for most women.

Now . . . you are ready to embellish your apron with any technique that appeals to you. The small sketches are a suggestion of the kinds of designs that can be worked onto this simple apron. Enjoy your work.

188

Chef's tabard apron

 A

 B

CHEF
CHEF
CHEF
CHEF
EF

CHEF
CHEF
CHEF
HEF

 C

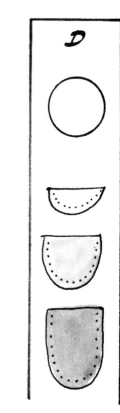 D

 E

parsley

A. Stencil Vegetables

B. Chef logo

C. Stripe giant pocket

D. multi-pockets

E. herb-painted

F. block print

G. Polish cutouts

 F

 G

Mamasan Baby-Bathing Apron

This practical bath apron has a soft, removable terrycloth collar — a perfect spot to hold a wet, squiggling child for a quick drying. Two large terry cloth pockets receive pins, cotton swabs, powder, diapers, baby clothes — everything baby needs for a smoothly engineered, enjoyable bath. The apron is trimmed with calico bias tape which may be purchased or made from scraps of your favorite print.

Materials

- 2 yards light blue canvas
- 1½ yards thick terry cloth
- 4 yards calico bias tape
- 10 inches Velcro

The Softness Part   Cut out all the pattern pieces. Zigzag edges to prevent ravelling. Bind off raw edges of terry cloth Collar D and Pockets C with calico bias tape. Do not bind off sides of Pockets, they will be hidden in the seams. On wrong side of Collar shoulders, stitch 4-inch strips of one side of Velcro. Remaining Velcro strips will be sewn to shoulders of canvas Apron. Position Pockets onto front of Apron and pin. Stitch close to edge of seam binding leaving top curved edge free for hands. Position Collar onto Front A and sew remaining Velcro strips onto shoulder ¾ inches below shoulder seam.

Making the Apron   Stitch Front to Backs at shoulder seams, be careful not to catch Velcro in seam. Try Apron on. Pin side seams. Sew side seams and restitch with a zigzag. Trim closely to prevent ravelling. Turn under all remaining edges of canvas ¼ inch. Hem neatly with a narrow zigzag. Go over again with contrast thread, topstitching for a tailored effect. Cut two ties out of canvas scraps, each 2½ by 18 inches. Fold lengthwise, press. Fold again lengthwise. Topstitch. Sew to back of neck on either side.

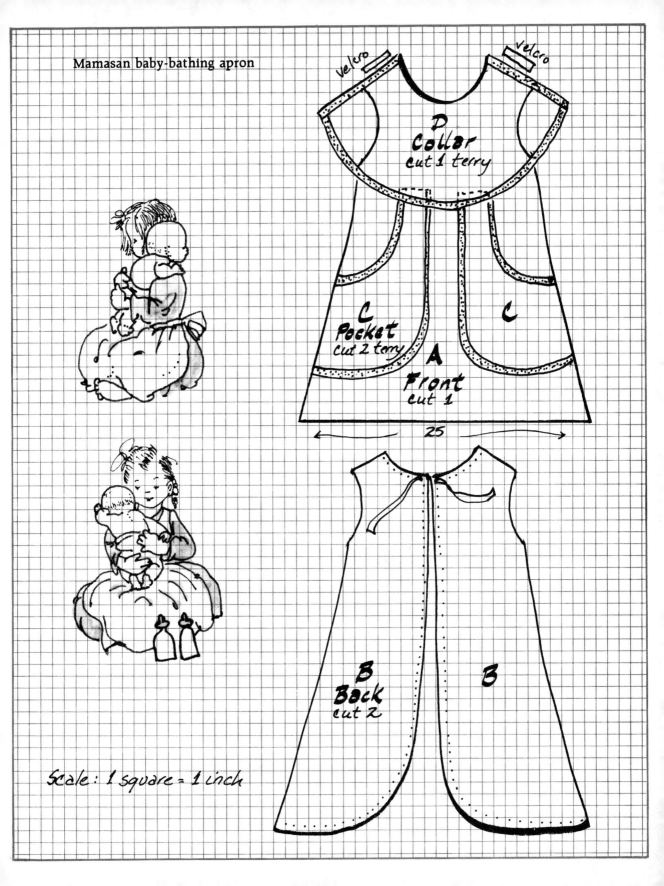

Mamasan baby-bathing apron

D
Collar
cut 1 terry

Velcro   Velcro

C
Pocket
cut 2 terry

C

A
Front
cut 1

25

B
Back
cut 2

B

Scale: 1 square = 1 inch

Chinese Art Aprons

The original mirror-image Duckling Apron was carried out of China in the 1920s by my Aunt Jill as she and her surgeon husband fled to India. The Chinese version is a delicate cotton lawn, but it works well in sturdy canvas. The Duckling has a small, crescent shaped pocket on his chest, while he, himself, forms a larger pocket at either side. The Koala Bear, inspired by the Duckling, is appliqued in one piece, the smaller pocket being topstitched on later. His tongue and claws hang playfully free.

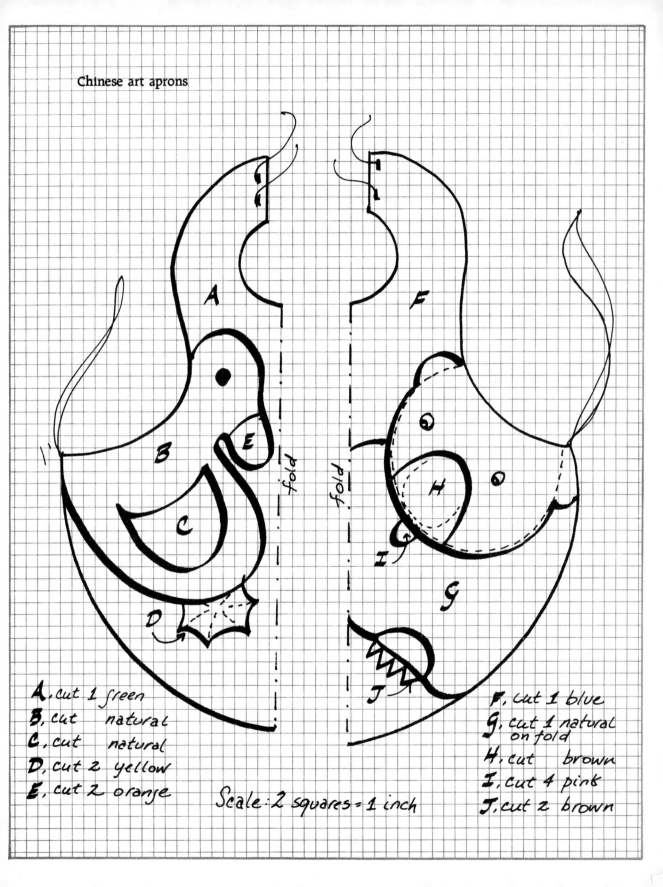

Chinese art aprons

A

F

B

E

C

D

fold

fold

H

G

I

J

A, cut 1 green
B, cut   natural
C, cut   natural
D, cut 2 yellow
E, cut 2 orange

Scale: 2 squares = 1 inch

F, cut 1 blue
G, cut 1 natural
   on fold
H, cut   brown
I, cut 4 pink
J, cut 2 brown

Chinese Art Aprons

Materials

- Duck Smock:
    - ½ yard green canvas
    - ¼ yard natural canvas
    - Scraps of yellow, orange canvas
    - Narrow ribbon for ties, approx. 1½ yards

- Koala Bear Smock:
    - ½ yard natural canvas
    - ½ yard blue canvas
    - ¼ yard brown canvas
    - Scraps of pink for tongue
    - Narrow ribbon for ties, approx. 1½ yards

Duckling Apron

Cut out all pattern pieces. Zigzag all edges to prevent ravelling. Turn under all edges of Apron A ¼ inch and topstitch twice for neat edge.

Zigzag upper curved edge of Pockets C. Place Pockets onto Bodies of Ducklings B. Sew in place with zigzag stitch, leaving top edge free. Zigzag Beaks E onto B. Place Ducklings onto front of Green Apron A and zigzag around curve, leaving curve open where Pocket matches outer edge of Smock. Sew ribbon ties at neck and back.

Koala Bear Apron

Cut out all pattern pieces. Turn under all edges of Apron Body F ¼ inch and topstitch twice to hold. Lay Koala Bear G flat on worktable. Zigzag top curved edges to form pocket openings. Make two small pink Tongues I by placing tongue sections together, stitching around curved edges, and turning right side out. Place Noses H onto Bears, tucking Tongues under bottom edge. Applique Noses to Bear. Topstitch Nose detailing.

Place Bear onto Apron and pin to hold. Tuck claws under paws. Applique entire Bear to Apron, leaving side edges open as pockets. Topstitch around Bear's head to form smaller pockets. Sew ribbon ties at neck and back.

Fly Fisherman's Vest

There are as many versions of the fly fisherman's vest as there are fishermen—or fish. They range from fancy, waterproof, lightweight, thousand-pocketed versions that do everything except tie your flies and eat your lunch, to the simplest, olive-drab, flea market versions left over from the assault on Iwo Jima. This particular canvas vest has the advantage of being light, warm, and air-conditioned at the same time. It has just enough quilting to cut the chill winds of early evening that always come up when the Browns *really* start to bite. A hand warmer pocket on the tummy comes in handy should the snow begin to fly (not unusual even in August on western rivers), and the addition of a Velcro patch makes carrying extra flies a snap.

Fly Fisherman's Vest

Materials

- 1¾ yards natural, lightweight canvas
- 1¾ yards lining fabric
- 10 inches Velcro
- 3-inch square of Velcro
- Polyester fiberfill batting
- Ruler

Quilting the Vest   Cut out all pattern pieces. Before you cut, measure your own body length and width so you can adjust pattern to fit. Remember, the side ties allow for some adjustment later. Cut out lining for all pattern pieces. Cut out fiberfill batting for all pieces. Sew batting pieces to canvas Front and Back at shoulder seams and around neck edge. You will handle the canvas and batting as one piece. Sew Front and Back together at shoulder seams, right sides together. Trim seam allowances.

Sew lining Front and Back together at shoulder seams. Place lining Vest and canvas Vest right sides together. Pin. Sew around neck edge. Trim. Turn right side out. Press gently. Turn remaining raw edges towards each other. Pin. Topstitch ¼ inch from outside edge all around.

Now mark off increments of 2 inches across Vest as shown on pattern. With matching or contrasting thread, quilt across entire vest horizontally. Topstitch around neck edge last.

Adding the Pockets   Place Large Pocket C and lining right sides together. Stitch around three sides, leaving the fourth open for turning. Turn right side out. Insert fiberfill batting between the canvas and lining. Turn raw edges of remaining side in towards each other. Topstitch closed. Mark off vertical lines 2 inches apart on Large Pocket and quilt along these lines through all layers.

Place Small Pocket B and lining right sides together. Stitch around three sides. Turn right side out. Insert layer of batting. Fold remaining raw edges towards each other. Topstitch. Now quilt this Pocket *horizontally* with lines 2 inches apart. On lining side of Small Pocket, sew two strips of Velcro. Lay small Pocket onto Large Pocket and pin remaining Velcro halves in place on Large Pocket. Sew down. Now sew Small Pocket to Large Pocket along top and bottom edges.

When the entire pocket section is assembled, lay it onto Front of Vest and sew along both sides and across bottom. Make another line of stitching vertically where Small Pocket joins Large Pocket, thus forming two generous pockets on the front of the Vest to hold spools of line, scissors, muscaline, and pipe tobacco.

The Ties   Cut four strips of canvas 2½ by 8 inches. Fold lengthwise, press, and fold again to form narrow ties. Topstitch these ties. Position on sides of Vest at a comfortable height. Sew to Vest on the lining side. You may prefer to omit the ties and add a small canvas tab which would attach with Velcro to the inside of the Vest.

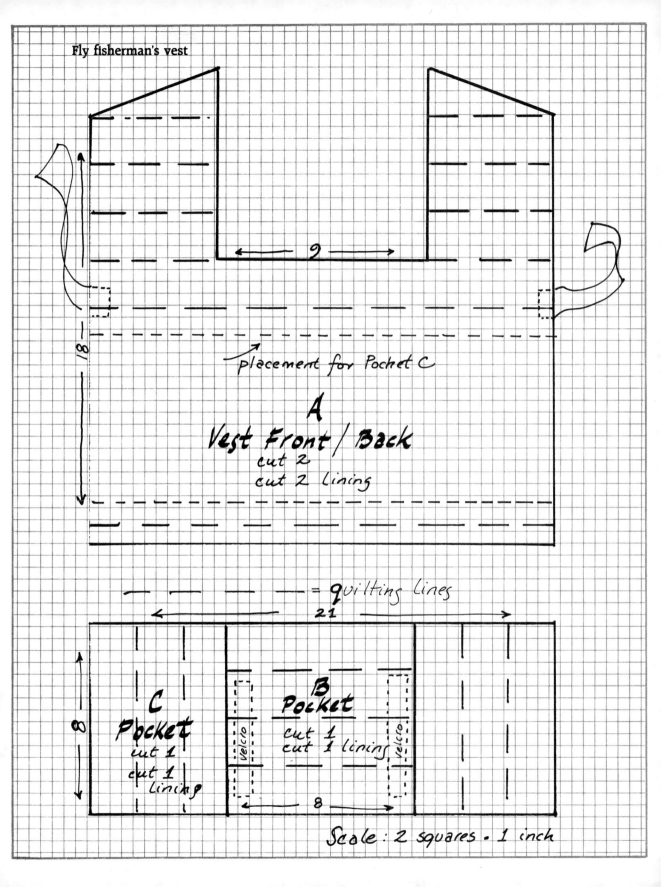

Fly fisherman's vest

9

18

placement for Pocket C

A
Vest Front / Back
cut 2
cut 2 lining

– – – = quilting lines

21

C
Pocket
cut 1
cut 1
lining

8

B
Pocket
cut 1
cut 1 lining

velcro

velcro

8

Scale: 2 squares = 1 inch

Huichol Needlepoint Work Apron

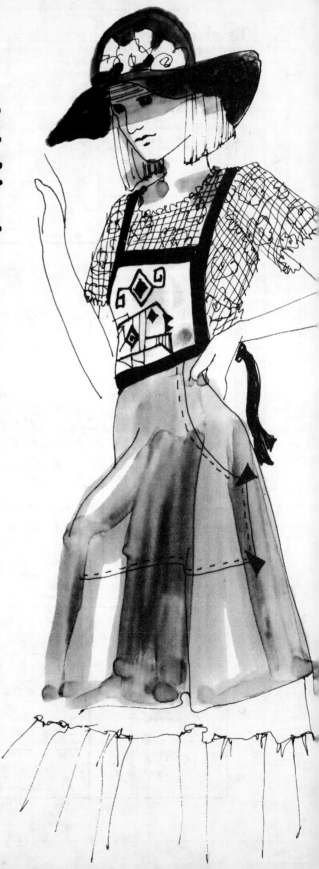

This workmanlike apron with its huge central pocket is tabbed and banded in soft, artificial suede. A needlepointed Huichol Indian design in glowing Persian wool enriches the bodice and turns an everyday garment into a celebration of your needle-working art. Huichol designs are executed by the highlands Indians of Mexico in wool yarns which are pressed into warm beeswax. The artist begins at the center of the design and works outwards in radiating bands of brilliant colored wools, outlining motifs of animals, birds, and plants. While you will not be able to exactly achieve the undulating lines of the original motifs, owing to the restrictions of working within a needlepoint grid, you will discover that the motifs nonetheless retain a primitive ingenuousness and their own particular charm. The needlepoint is worked after the apron is completed so be sure to shorten or lengthen the bodice to fit before you sew the apron.

Materials

- 1½ yards orange canvas
- 15-inch square of needlepoint mesh, 10 squares to the inch
- Persian needlepoint yarns:

    scarlet, magenta, deep orange, chrome yellow, olive, cerulean blue, black, hot pink

- ¼ yard Ultrasuede, deep rust
- Permanent black marking pens
- Colored felt tipped pens
- Crewel needle
- Push pens

Huichol needlepoint work apron

Transferring the Design Enlarge the needlepoint design on graph paper. Draw the outline of the design on the paper with a bold, black line using a permanent marking pen. Fill in color areas with felt markers. Place this drawing underneath the needlepoint canvas. Tack the canvas down with push pins to hold in place. Your design should be showing through enough to enable you to trace the outlines onto the mesh above. You may paint the colored areas onto the mesh itself using waterproof inks. However, this is not really necessary if you use your original as a color key.

Making the Apron Cut out all pattern pieces, including the four Ultrasuede tabs. When you are sure that the bodice of the Apron will fit you, cut the needlepoint mesh to fit it. Zigzag all edges to prevent ravelling.

Turn under all edges of Great Pocket B ½ inch and topstitch. Place Pocket onto front of Apron A as shown and topstitch again, leaving curved edges free for hands. The top edge of the Pocket will be hidden by the needlepoint. Place four Ultrasuede tabs onto corners of Pocket and topstitch in place.

Turn under straight edges of Apron sides ½ inch and topstitch twice to prevent ravelling. Cut two strips of canvas 2½ by 18 inches for ties. Fold in half lengthwise. Fold again. Topstitch. Sew ties securely to Apron corners at waistline.

Adding the Bodice Lay the mesh onto the front of the Apron. Stitch around all edges and across waistline ¼ inch from edge. Cut a length of Ultrasuede ¾ inch by 15 inches. Lay this banding across the Apron at the waist, covering the joint of the mesh and canvas. Topstitch banding close to both edges.

Cut another length of Ultrasuede 1½ by 7 inches. Fold in half over top edge of Apron bodice covering mesh and canvas. Topstitch. Cut two lengths of Ultrasuede 1½ by 20 inches for binding off side edges. Apply as before.

Measure the length strap you will need for your neck. Cut a strip of canvas that length by 2½ inches wide. Make a strap as you did ties and handstitch one side of it to back of Apron at neck edges. Attach second end with large snap. Zigzag bottom hem edge of Apron. Turn to back ½ inch and topstitch hem.

Needlepointing Work the design in Persian wools according to the graphed colors. The design may be executed entirely in the Tent stitch, [See (a)] or you may use Bargello for the background.

Fig. (a)

199

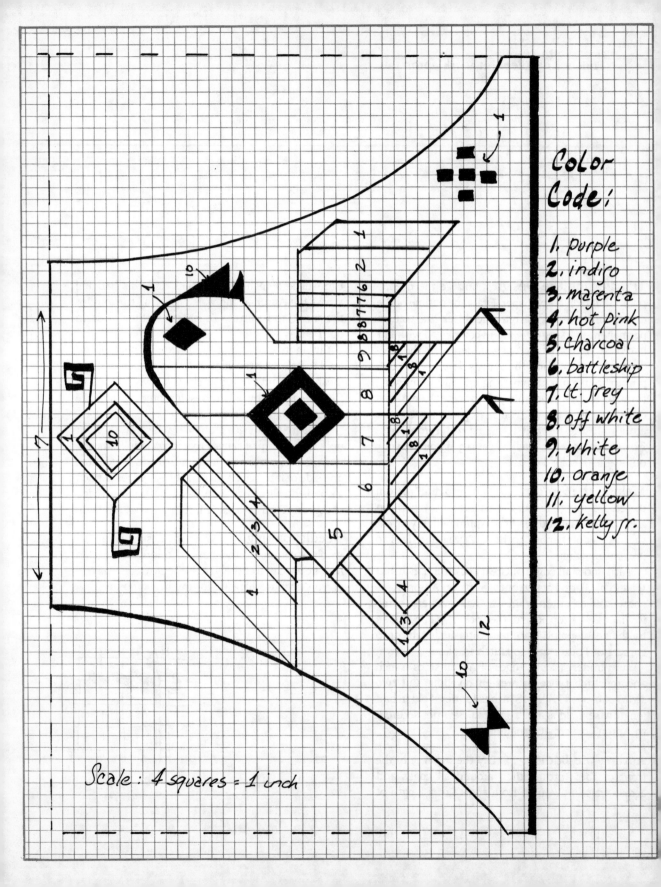

Color
Code:

1. purple
2. indigo
3. magenta
4. hot pink
5. charcoal
6. battleship
7. lt. grey
8. off white
9. white
10. orange
11. yellow
12. kelly gr.

Scale: 4 squares = 1 inch

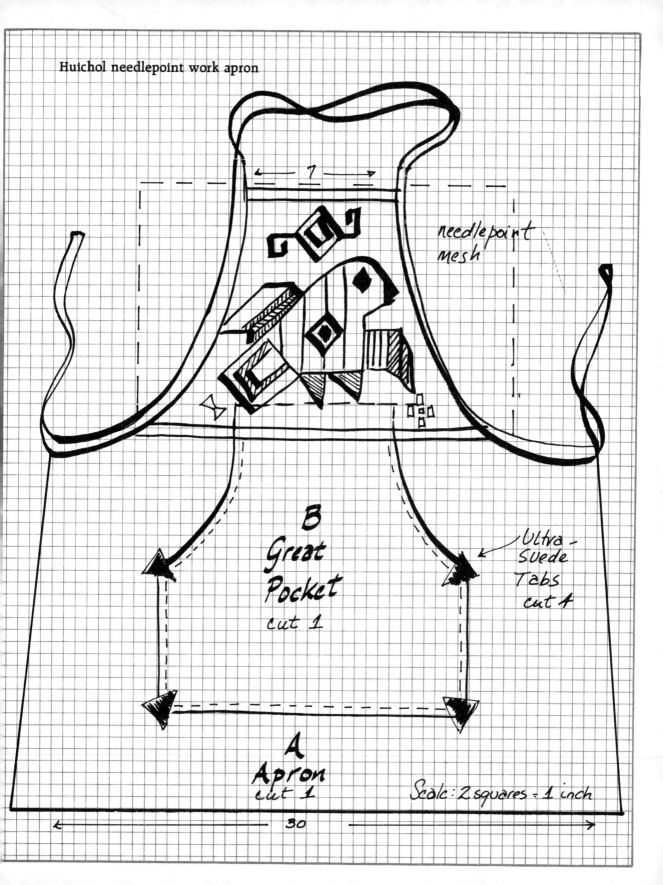

Huichol needlepoint work apron

needlepoint mesh

B
Great
Pocket
cut 1

Ultra-
Suede
Tabs
cut 4

A
Apron
cut 1

Scale: 2 squares = 1 inch

30

Switchback Apron

In Scandinavia, aprons exist in a wide variety of styles and fabrics, and are worn as fashionable fragments of clothing, even for business or streetwear. Although this layering of clothing is necessary in countries where winters are severe and prolonged, even in summer one sees apron-like garments sported by women as well as men. The Switchback Apron is a favorite style in Denmark, worn by clerks in shops as well as green-grocers outdoors. The pattern is suitable for a medium sized man, you will want to try yours before hemming the sides. Adjust the shoulders and length to fit. The large, scooped pocket is handy for craftsmen as well as cooks, although you might want to delete the central pocket in favor of two side pockets. These can be made from the fabric cut out from the curved armholes. As with all flat-surfaced canvas items, this apron fairly begs for some design to enliven its austere curves and instructions are included for stencilling a plum design.

Materials

- 1½ yards canvas
- Two buttons
- Roll of adhesive-backed contact paper
- X-acto knife, with #11 blade
- Stencil brush
- Straight pins or push pins
- Fabric paints, or Dr. Martin's Watercolor inks in purple, magenta, and deep green
- Permanent black marking pen

The Apron   Cut out Apron and Pocket. Turn under all edges of Pocket ½ inch and topstitch. Try on the Apron and check for fit. Adjust, if necessary. Turn under all raw edges of the Apron and top-stitch also.

Stencilling the Plums   Enlarge the plum design and transfer to shelf paper. Since the Apron is curved, you will be able to stencil only two plums and leaves at a time before moving the stencil around the long curve. Therefore, your entire stencil

should measure approximately 6 by 8 inches.

Lay the Apron flat on a large table or the floor. Pad underneath with newspapers. Beginning at the center bottom, stencil the plum design with full strength paint or dyes. Make sure the edges of the contact paper are stuck down tightly onto the canvas so no paint will creep under and ruin the sharp edge of the design. It will go faster if you have a brush for each color paint. Work with your brush upright, remembering to pounce excess paint or dye on an old towel each time you charge your brush with new color. Be very careful when you unstick and move the stencil. Don't smudge the design you have just completed. Haste and stencilling do not mix. If you work with Versatex paints, however, you can dry each plum with a hand-held hair dryer very quickly, and move to the next easily. Check underneath the stencil each time you move it to make sure that no paint has crept under to mar your new edges.

In this same manner, stencil plums across top of Pocket edge. Allow Apron to dry thoroughly. Press with hot iron to set color. With a pencil eraser tipped in dark ink, paint or dye, mark off spots on plums at random.

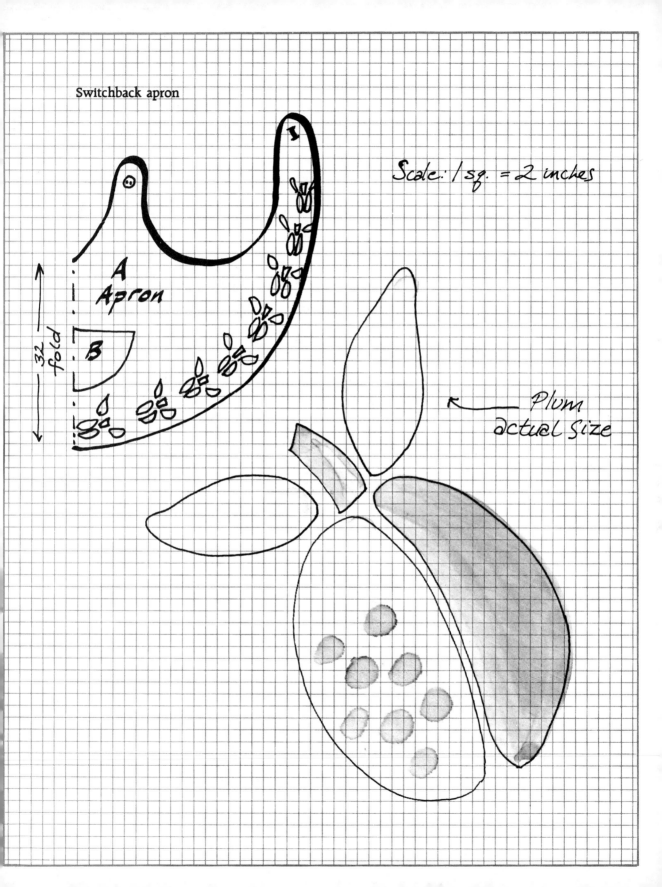

Switchback apron

Scale: 1 sq. = 2 inches

A
Apron

B

32
fold

Plum
actual size

Roasty Toasty Boot

Tuck two frozen feet into this capacious fur-lined Boot and while away a snowy day. The Boot fits all pairs of feet, and is especially popular with skiers exhausted from conquering the mountain and content to snooze in front of a roaring blaze. It is made as two separate boots, one canvas and one fur. Then the fur boot is turned inside out and stuffed into the canvas one, the deep cuff folded over and hand-stitched invisibly.

Materials

- 1 yard canvas
- ½ yard fake fur

The Canvas Boot Cut out all pattern pieces. Stitch one Side A to Center B. Clip curves and trim. Stitch second Side A to Center, clipping curves as well. Trim ankle edges evenly and zigzag.

The Fur Boot Sew Fur C's to Fur Side A's. Sew Fur D's to Fur Center B. Stitch Sides to Center as with canvas boot. Turn fur boot inside out and insert into the canvas boot. Fold cuff over and blindstitch to canvas boot.

To adjust Boot to children's sizes, alter the Side dimensions and narrow the Center strip.

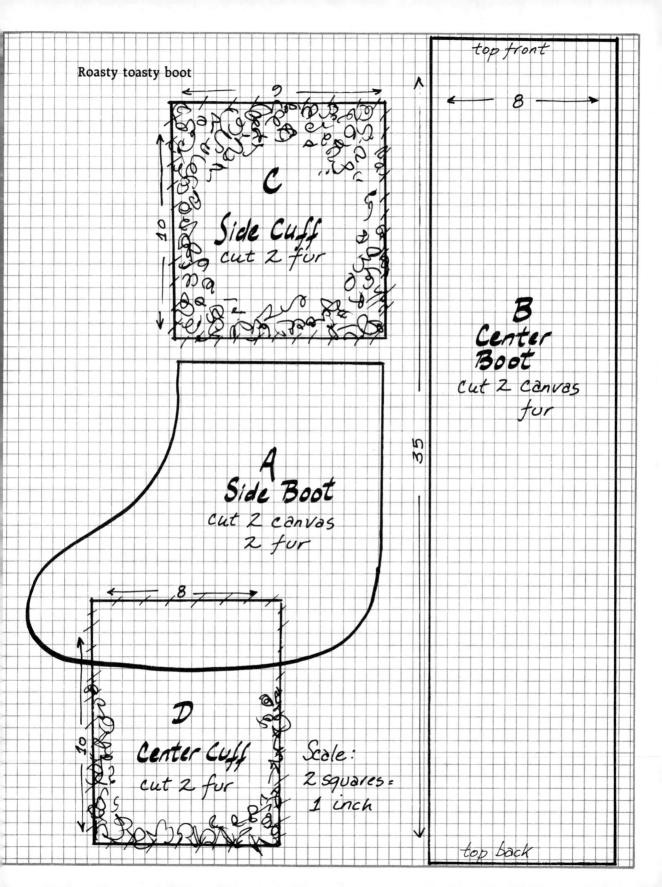

Roasty toasty boot

C
Side Cuff
cut 2 fur

A
Side Boot
cut 2 canvas
2 fur

D
Center Cuff
cut 2 fur

Scale:
2 squares =
1 inch

top front

B
Center Boot
cut 2 canvas
fur

top back

8

35

10

8

10

These felt-lined boots are a delight to snuggle into after a day skiing. They are embellished with designs constructed from folded paper cutouts, a Polish folk art. You will enjoy experimenting with color and shapes as you plan your applique designs. Children, especially, love this project. They fold and cut with abandon, designing boots to wear with their pajamas or their play clothes. You can let them measure their legs, trace their own feet and cut out their own designs. After you have made your first pair you will be able to make others with very little trouble. It is helpful to complete each step for both boots simultaneously. That way you don't have to change thread color constantly or start over from scratch on the second boot, a boring prospect at best.

Materials

- 1½ yards solid canvas
- ½ yard contrasting color canvas
- Assorted color scraps for applique
- 2 yards polyester fiberfill batting
- 2 yards 45-inch felt
- ½ yard fur trim.

Measuring   Measure your feet and legs carefully. Alter the basic pattern pieces to fit your body. You can always *reduce* the boot slightly by taking in the back seam, but you cannot increase it. Better to err by making them too large.

Cutting   Cut out all pattern pieces, including lining and fiberfill. To cut the Sole, trace your foot on a piece of paper, adding ¾ inch all around. Cut out four canvas Soles, four fiberfill Soles, and four felt Soles. Cut out Sole Band according to the circumference of your foot, adding ¾ inch for back seam. Lay out all your pieces — Foot, Leg, Soles, and Sole Band — as sandwiches with felt on the bottom followed by fiberfill and canvas. Zigzag ¼ inch from edge of all sandwiches to hold in place. You will sew *two* Sole sandwiches together for each boot. Trim all sandwiches neatly.

Paper Cutouts   Use scraps of canvas or colored construction paper, fold pieces in half and begin cutting out free-form designs to fit the Leg and Foot. Experiment with wild colors and shapes, geometric designs, paisleys, spots, hearts, diamonds, flowers, rainbows. Place the shapes one on top of the other on your boot sections until you are pleased. Remember, the front seams will obscure some of the design, so either make allowances for them, or better, use the seam itself as part of the design. When you have devised your happiest combinations, cut

Polish After-

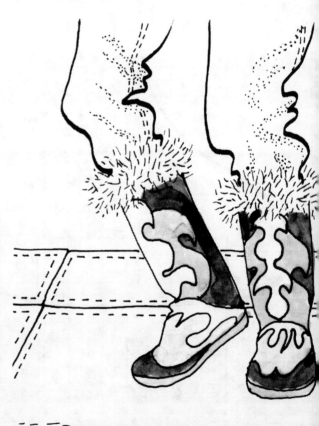

206

the shapes out of canvas scraps. Pin the designs and begin appliqueing the boots. You may want to use a satin or zigzag stitch for polished edges. Or, if you sew a straight stitch ¼ inch in from the edges, you will get a frayed edge, similar to Pakistani folk art. Begin appliqueing with the smallest, topmost pieces. Add the bigger pieces next. This is in contrast to the usual applique, in which you build up from the bottom, leaving the top piece until last. When you quilt through several layers at once, it works better to begin at the center and work towards the edges, smoothing as you go.

Ski Boots

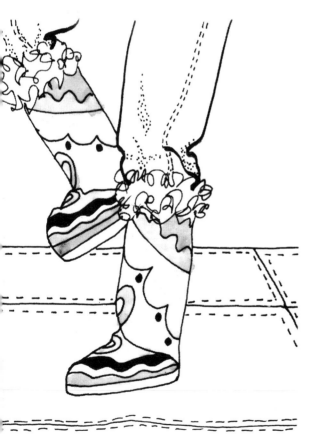

Fur Cuffs   Place a strip of fake or real fur, *right* side against lining, at the top edge of each Leg. When the boot is right side out the fur will flip over to the outside and form a cuff which then can be tacked down.

Sewing   With right sides together, sew Leg to Foot. Sew carefully, turning at center top of Foot. Trim. Now sew the Sole Band around the entire bottom edge of the Foot section. *See (a).* This will form a Lapland-style border to which you will attach the Sole.

Fit   Place boot, right side next to leg, around your leg and pin along back seam. The boot should fit comfortably and be fairly snug along the knee and upper calf in order to stay up. Allow for your idiosyncrasies in dress. Will you tuck jeans into them, or wear heavy knee socks? Or will you go barefoot inside? Now stitch up the back seams and zigzag the seam allowance for firmness.

Soles   Turn boots wrong side out. Place each Sole sandwich into the boots with canvas side to inside. Pin all around. If the Sole seems slightly large, cut down and re-pin. Stitch securely and zigzag in the seam allowance for strength. Trim. Turn boots right side out, flip fur cuff and tack down to outside.

Fig. (a)

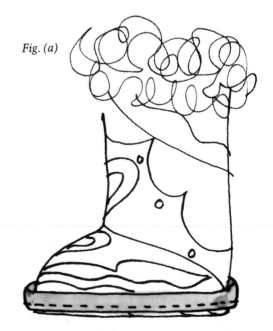

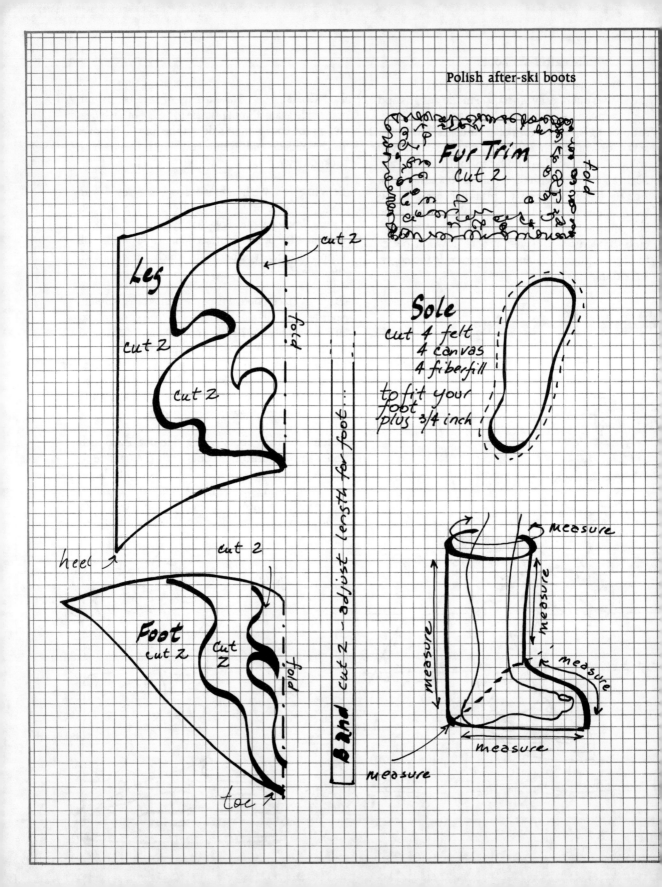

Fur Trim
cut 2
fold

Leg
cut 2
cut 2
cut 2
fold

heel →

Sole
cut 4 felt
4 canvas
4 fiberfill
to fit your
foot
plus 3/4 inch

cut 2

Foot
cut 2
cut 2
fold

Band cut 2 — adjust length for foot...
measure

toe →

measure
measure
measure
measure
measure
measure

Headgear

Seaman's Hat

This sturdy hat is a classic style favored by yachtsmen. Generally made of heavy, natural colored canvas, it looks equally well in bright colors. With the brim widened, it makes a stunning sun hat. By adjusting the measurements of the three pieces you can create hats to fit anyone from your toddler to a bushy haired mountaineer. The rope zigzagged to the underside of the brim enables you to adjust the floppiness as much as you wish.

Materials

- 1 yard natural canvas
- Seven #1 or #2 grommets, and setter
- 8 feet nylon mason line, size 4½

Before Beginning

Cut out all pattern pieces, and zigzag edges to prevent ravelling. Measure the largest circumference of your head. Adjust each pattern piece to fit your measurements. The pattern given fits a medium head. If you change the pattern, make sure you adjust each pattern piece by the same increment. Install grommets as shown on pattern, according to instructions on the package.

Making the Hat   Join Band B along short edges to form a circle. Zigzag. Sew Crown C to Band B. Keep the Crown on top of the band as you sew, working the circle slowly and turning the Crown under your presser foot.

Make darts in underside of Brim as shown on pattern. Do not cut darts, but press them to one side. Sew Crown and Band section to Brim. Zigzag this edge to prevent ravelling. Trim closely. Turn this seamed edge *up* to inside of hat and topstitch to Band $1/8$ inch away from seam. This makes a neat inner edge to the hat.

The Rope Trim   Turn under outer edge of hat Brim ¼ inch and zigzag. When you reach darts, clip bottom up ½ inch to reduce thickness of layers. *See (a).* Now lay a 48-inch length of mason line on top of this zigzagged edge. Using the widest zigzag and a medium length stitch, sew top to underside of Brim. This makes a tidy and malleable edge for the hat.

With the remaining rope, braid or macrame a hatband. Insert through grommets on the Brim and tie off.

Fig. (a)

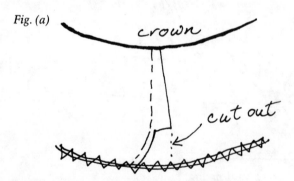

Canvas Sun Visor

Sun visors are eminently practical hats, used for tennis, fishing, backpacking, boating, all outdoor activities. They can be embellished in numerous ways, from delicate silk embroidery to silkscreened logos. They make fine gifts for groups or children's parties, and once you have made your first, you will find that you can cut and sew them in multiples with ease.

Materials

- ½ yard canvas
- ¼ yard wide cotton bias tape, to match canvas
- 3 inches Velcro
- ¼ yard interfacing
- 30 inches lightweight cardboard
- X-acto knife

Instructions   Cut out all pattern pieces. If you are going to embellish the Visor or Band, do it now before sewing. Place Visor sections A together and stitch around long curved edge. Trim, notching outer curve. Turn right side out and press.

Place interfacing on one side of Band B. Stitch in place $3/8$ inch from outer edges. Trim away excess interfacing. Place Bands B right sides together and stitch along long curved upper edge. Trim seam and turn right side out. Machine baste lower edges of Band to hold.

Attaching the Visor   Fold both Visor and Band in half, pressing with your hand to mark exact centers. Pin machine basted edge of Band to one side of Visor matching at centers. *See (a).* Leave the other edge of the Visor free for turning under later. Cut out one cardboard for Visor, cutting ½ inch inside canvas pattern to allow for seams. Insert this cardboard between the canvas sections, making sure that the cardboard fits into the Visor without stretching the seams. Fold wide bias tape over long raw edge where Band joins Visor and sew with zipper foot to hold. *See (b).* Tuck ends of Band to inside and sew across neatly. Hold Visor on your head and pin to size. Sew Velcro to both sides of Band so Visor fits. Three inches of Velcro should allow an adequate range of adjustments to fit everyone in your family.

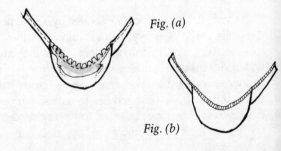

Fig. (a)

Fig. (b)

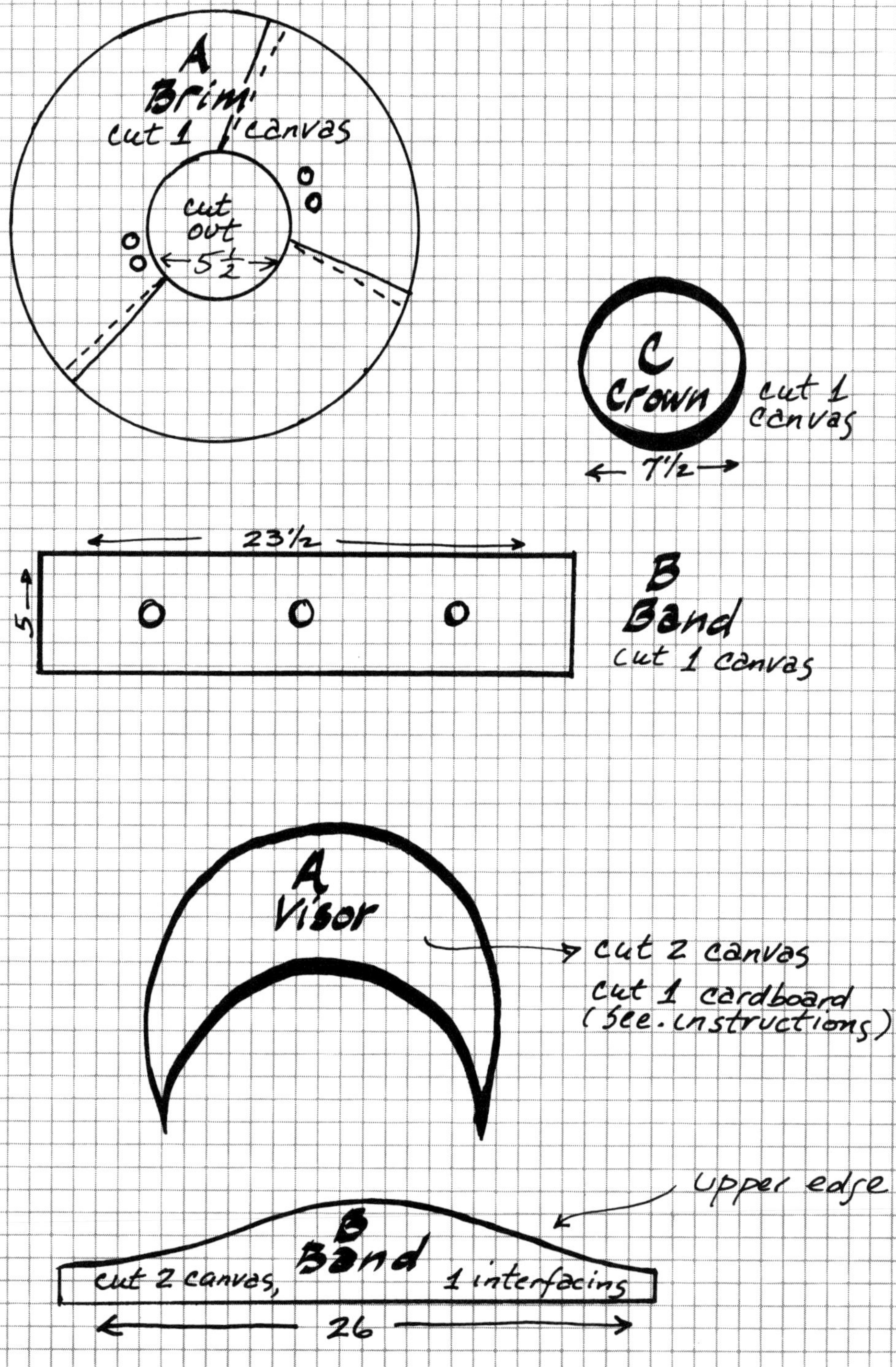

Headgear

A
Brim
cut 1 canvas

cut
out
5½

C
Crown
cut 1
canvas

← 7½ →

← 23½ →

5

○   ○   ○

B
Band
cut 1 canvas

A
Visor

cut 2 canvas

cut 1 cardboard
(see instructions)

upper edge

B
Band

cut 2 canvas,   1 interfacing

← 26 →

Toys, Games and Fantasies

Nesting

These Nesting Bubbis are peculiar little Granny-people who lack only a steaming bowl of chicken soup to have just stepped out of a shtetl in Eastern Poland. They are seven, hollow dolls, each nesting within the other in a canvas lineage of ancestral Grannies. Each doll is a different color, and they are arranged in a rainbow beginning with the Great Red Bubbi on top and ending with the Tiny Black One. Feeling sorry for her witchiness, I gave her a gold petticoat to compensate.

The faces are a delight to work on. Although the overall mien of my Bubbis' faces is one of long-suffering acceptance, you may wish to recall other qualities as you create your own Bubbis. I used free machine embroidery to stitch the features, and wasn't too careful. The resultant wiggly lines create unpredictable characterizations and give the faces their wry homeliness.

Children love to help dress the Bubbis. A scrap bag of colorful fabrics and sparkling trims will keep a gaggle of girls occupied all afternoon as they bedeck the ladies in fantasy costumes. Beware, you may find the dinner grown cold as you add another bit of lace here, a satin ribbon there.

214

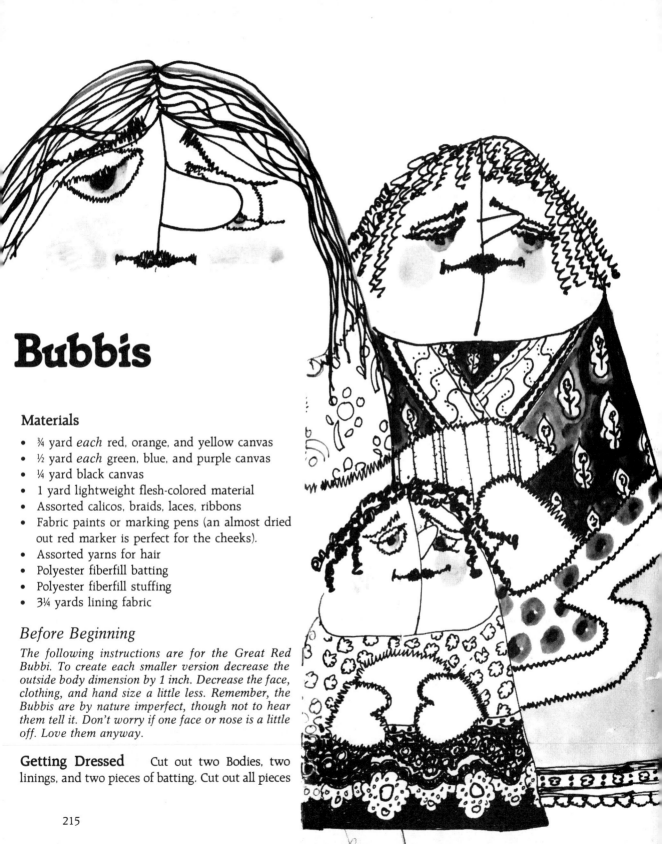

Bubbis

Materials

- ¾ yard *each* red, orange, and yellow canvas
- ½ yard *each* green, blue, and purple canvas
- ¼ yard black canvas
- 1 yard lightweight flesh-colored material
- Assorted calicos, braids, laces, ribbons
- Fabric paints or marking pens (an almost dried out red marker is perfect for the cheeks).
- Assorted yarns for hair
- Polyester fiberfill batting
- Polyester fiberfill stuffing
- 3¼ yards lining fabric

Before Beginning

The following instructions are for the Great Red Bubbi. To create each smaller version decrease the outside body dimension by 1 inch. Decrease the face, clothing, and hand size a little less. Remember, the Bubbis are by nature imperfect, though not to hear them tell it. Don't worry if one face or nose is a little off. Love them anyway.

Getting Dressed Cut out two Bodies, two linings, and two pieces of batting. Cut out all pieces

Nesting Bubbis

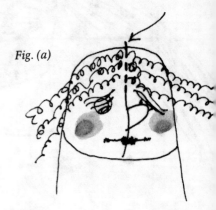

Fig. (a)

to be appliqued onto Body. For this first doll, the sequence of application is as follows:

1. Skirt G
2. Skirt H
3. Lace and ribbon trim
4. Blouse D
5. Apron F
6. Hands E

You will notice the Blouse has a slit in the arms to enable you to slide the Apron up underneath it. The Hands should be puffed with a wad of soft fiberfill stuffing as they are sewn on.

Making the Faces

Cut out two faces B and two Noses C. Stitch Noses together leaving short end open. Turn right side out. Stuff gently with fiberfill stuffing, being careful to not break through the seams. Place two Faces on table, right sides together. Insert Nose between the Faces at correct height and angle. Pin, check. Stitch along center seam, enclosing Nose as you go. Fold outwards and press. Cut a piece of fiberfill batting a little smaller than the Face. Pin Face, with batting underneath, onto Body and zigzag around Face.

Now lightly draw in Bubbi's features with a pencil. With black thread, machine (or hand) stitch the eyes. If you use your machine, vary the stitch *width* as you sew around the eyes and eyebrows. Change to red thread and sew in her rosebud mouth. If you are not used to free embroidering on your machine, make several test samples on scraps of fabric. Be loose, your mistakes will amaze you with their primitive charm and ingenuousness. Play with your sewing machine as you practice on the Bubbi's face. You will enjoy watching her personality emerge. When you feel sure of your skill, embroider the facial features. Then with a very dry red marking pen, a brush barely loaded with fabric paint, or a Q-tip saturated with red paint, gently rouge the Bubbi's cheeks. Using the same process, sadden her eyes with brown or ochre.

Completing the Doll

When the Bubbi's face has dried completely, make a sandwich of Body, batting, and lining. Stay stitch around long curved edge. Leave bottom edge open. Make a similar sandwich of Back, batting, and lining. Stay stitch also.

Now apply her hair to the Front section. Cut a bunch of yarn about 18 inches long, 50 strands in width (this will depend on the loft of the yarn). Spread yarn to a width of about 2 inches and stitch down on her face with a straight stitch forming a part. Spread yarn and arrange alongside the Bubbi's face. Tack in place with small hand stitches. *See (a).* Make sure the hair does not overlap the seam line around the face so that it will not be caught when the Back is sewn onto the doll.

Place Body Front and Body Back right sides together. Stitch around long curve, starting and stopping ½ inch above bottom. Turn right side out. Press. Hem bottom edge by hand or machine, turning canvas and lining in towards each other as you go.

The Other Six

The remaining Bubbis are made exactly as the Great Red One, only 1 inch smaller each time. If you have made a paper pattern of the first one, you should have no trouble reducing the size as they get smaller. Cut the clothing pieces approximately ½ to ¾ inch smaller each time. The exact dimensions are not critical. Also you may wish to change the order of application of the dress pieces to alter the dolls' couture.

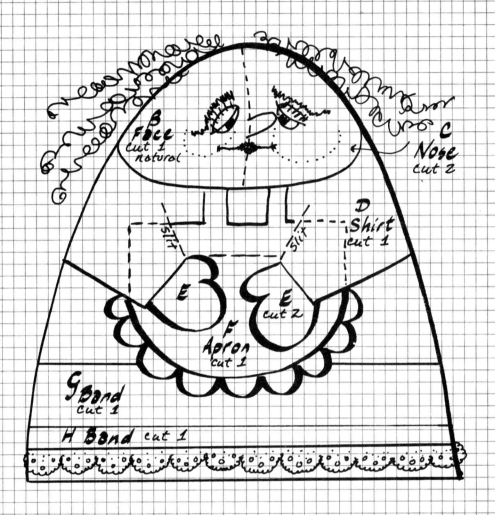

B Face
cut 1
natural

C Nose
cut 2

D Shirt
cut 1

slit

slit

E

E cut 2

F Apron
cut 1

G Band
cut 1

H Band cut 1

A Body: cut 2 entire outlines, 2 linings

Scale: This Bubbi is exactly ½ as large
as the tiniest doll, which measures
9 x 9 inches. Increase ½ to 1 inch
for each successive Bubbi.

Black Hole Bean Toss

Rainy day blues: kids home with nothing to do and too much energy. Everybody going crazy . . .

The Black Hole Bean Toss game is a marvelous energy releaser for a rainy day. Merely unroll it, slip a spring-loaded curtain rod through the top loop, hang it in a doorway, and let the kids go. The appliqued design is an interstellar variation on the ancient bean toss game. The sizes of the holes vary, so you may assign points according to the degree of difficulty. Included in the pattern is a Rocket bean bag which is stuffed with lentils. Pinto beans are too heavy, and turn the Rocket into a dangerous projectile. Stopping by for a couple of free throws on the way from the laundry room one stormy afternoon, I discovered that tightly rolled socks are a satisfactory substitute for the Rocket. They are lighter (better for small children), and there are usually lots of them so that you can stand with a full basket and not have to run after your "spaceships" so often.

It should be added that this game is by no means only for children. One can hurl rolled socks at the firmament with enormous strength and rage, and yet no one gets hurt, nothing gets broken. The therapeutic effects of the game are as yet uncharted. But best of all, it is SILENT.

Materials

- 1½ yards black canvas
- ¾ yard yellow canvas
- Scraps of white, red canvas
- One spring-loaded curtain rod, 31 inches long
- One bag lentils, or split peas

Appliqueing the Planets   Cut out all yellow and white shapes and place onto black Background as shown in pattern. One by one, applique these stars and planets in place with a close zigzag or satin stitch. Then zigzag around what will become the edges of the holes. Do not cut out holes until you are completely finished appliqueing. Go around the edges of the inner holes twice to insure that they will not unravel. If you roll up the excess background fabric as you sew, it will be much easier

to slip under the arm of your sewing machine. When all the planets are sewn down, only then cut out the central holes with very sharp scissors. Cut carefully in good light so that you do not cut into the satin stitches. If you do make a mistake, go over the edges again. These holes take quite a beating, so err on the side of too much sturdiness rather than too little.

Finishing Details   Form fringe out of the bottom of the Background. Cut slits 6 inches up from the bottom edge. Cut them every ½ inch or so. Sew a line of straight stitching at the top of fringe to hold it. Fold over the topmost edge of the Background about 1½ inches to form a tunnel for the curtain rod. Stitch in place. Slip spring-loaded rod into tunnel. Hang up in an open doorway.

Making the Rocket   Cut out Rocket pieces. With fabric paint or permanent marking pens, draw appropriate outer space symbols onto Rocket Body. These may be stars, planets, numbers, lightning, or whatever suits your child's fancy. When these are dry, lay red Fringe on top of Body A and zigzag onto Body 1 inch from end. With right side to inside, roll Body into a tube and sew together. Leave open the center 3 inches of this seam for inserting beans later. Be careful not to catch the red Fringe in the seam. Now pin round End D into fringed end of Rocket Body and sew in place, easing gathers if necessary.

Place black Noses B together and stitch along short edges to form a point. With Rocket Body still wrong side out, pin black Nose to remaining open end of tube. Sew in place. This is a tricky stitching job, and will work best if you stuff the point of the nose back down into the tube before you sew. If you have a free arm on your machine, you can slide the end over it and stitch this seam more easily. Turn Rocket right side out and fill with lentils. If it seems too heavy, stuff Body with fiberfill and fill only the black Nose with beans. Handstitch belly opening of Rocket closed.

218

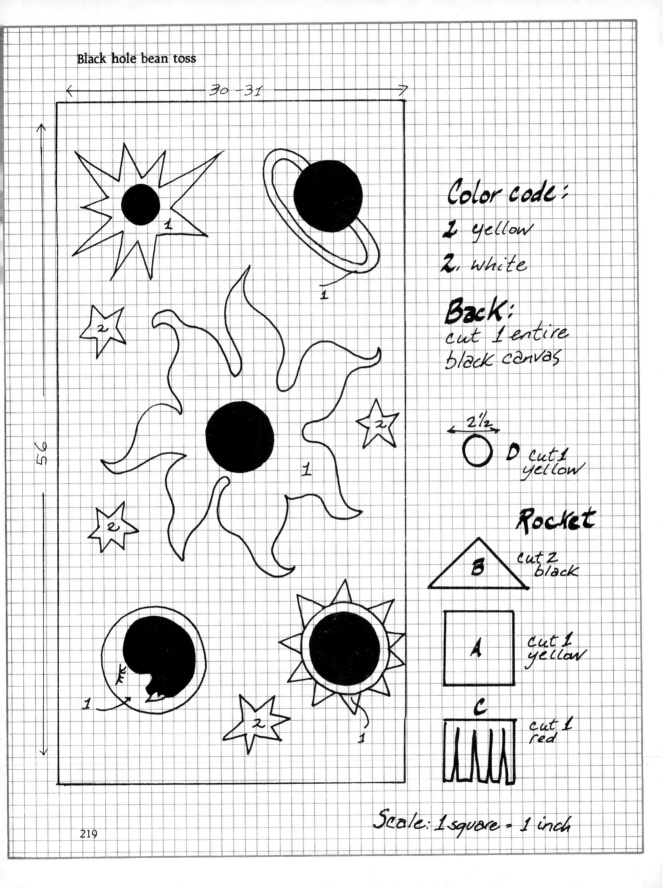

Black hole bean toss

30 - 31

56

Color code:
2. yellow
2. white

Back:
cut 1 entire
black canvas

2½

D cut 1
yellow

Rocket

B cut 2
black

A cut 1
yellow

C cut 1
red

Scale: 1 square = 1 inch

219

Draft Doggy

In our adult hugeness we don't realize that the floor is an Antarctica for toddlers and creeping babies, with drafts blowing around every corner and under every door. The Draft Doggy was created as a non-prescription antidote to the runny noses and earaches that children can catch while wandering through those drafts. As well as acting as a doorstop, he receives hugs and can withstand cowboys riding on his back. He is stuffed with soft fiberfill, except for the bottom of his belly, which is loaded with sand purloined from a neighborhood sandbox. Placed in front of a creaky door, he weighs enough, and is long enough, to effectively cut off most of the cold draft and to keep the door shut too. Kids love to ride him and he has room enough to accomodate two creepers on his long haunches. The legs are assembled separately and stitched on by hand, and his spots are potato prints stamped with fabric paint.

Materials

- 1¾ yards natural canvas
- ½ yard black canvas
- Scraps of pink and red canvas
- Eight pipe cleaners
- Two bags polyester fiberfill stuffing, or shredded foam
- ¼ yard finely woven fabric or canvas scrap
- Sand, gravel, birdseed, or beans for weighting
- Two potatoes, one large and one small
- Black fabric paint or indelible ink
- Black indelible marking pen
- Quilting needle, thimble

Decorating His Body   Cut out pattern pieces. Applique pink Nose G to each side Body A with close zigzag. Lay both Bodies A on table with their outer sides towards you. With a black indelible marking pen, draw in eyes and mouth. Make sure they are at the same level on both halves of face, so that when he is assembled, he won't be cross-eyed. Cut potatoes in half with a clean, sharp knife. Allow to bleed by placing onto a paper towel face down for a few minutes. Paint flat potato ends with black fabric paint or dip into black ink. Stamp different sized spots at random onto the Doggy's Body to create a Dalmatian pattern. Allow to dry completely. It is usually best to keep the painted canvas out of the direct sun, although it may not seem expedient at the time. Canvas is all cotton, and the painted part of the fabric sometimes shrinks while it dries, causing wrinkles and bumps that are impossible to iron smooth. It is best not to rush it, and to let the canvas dry naturally.

Creating the Appendages   Stitch together two sections of black Tail D. Clip curves, turn right side out. Press. Stuff very firmly, and set aside.

Place pink Ear section F onto two black Ears E. Applique with zigzag stitch. Now place these Ears face down onto remaining solid black Ears. Pin. Stitch around long curve, leaving short end open. Turn right side out. Using pipe cleaners, or two 10-inch lengths of light wire, form ear shape and insert into completed Ears. This will help the Ears retain their shape.

Draft doggy

Sew two sections of pink Tongue I together, turn right side out. Press.

Applique black Footpads H to each of the eight sections of Legs B and C. If you do these in pairs for each leg, you will find it easier to match them up later. Place legs together, right sides matching. Stitch around legs leaving an opening where indicated on pattern. Turn right side out. This may be difficult if you are using a heavyweight canvas. Try pushing the foot out with the eraser end of a pencil.

Attaching the Appendages   Place the completed (but unstuffed) Legs B and C onto Bodies A. Using a quilting needle, a thimble, two strands of polyester thread or buttonhole twist, handstitch the Legs to the Bodies. This may tax your patience, but take it slowly. *See (a).* Be sure and stop sewing at least 1½ inches before you reach the raw edge of the Body itself. This will allow easy machine sewing when you put the two sides of the Body together. Now, pin the Tongue and the Tail on one side of Body A facing inwards. Stitch down.

Cut a slit about 2 inches long into each side of Body A at the appropriate spot for attaching the ears. Fold each Ear in center with a tuck and slip the Ear into the slit. Stitch Ear onto Body from the inside, pinching the slits together as you sew. *See (b).* Place black Bellies J along bottom of Bodies A, right sides together. Sew one Belly to each side of the Dog's Body.

Completing the Body   Pin all loose appendages towards center outside of both Bodies. This will keep them from being caught in the seamline when you join the Bodies together. Place both sides of Body together, right sides facing. Stitch around entire edge, leaving only center section of black Belly open for stuffing. Turn entire Doggy right side out and press. Stuff with fiberfill or shredded foam, beginning with the nose and working along top of back. Pack the stuffing hard, for the Doggy will get knocked around if there are small children riding on him. Stop when the Dog is almost filled. Make a bag of canvas scrap of tightly woven cloth, 5 by 15 inches. Fill this bag with pea gravel, sand, birdseed, beans—whatever you have handy. Stitch open end closed. Stuff bag into Doggy's Belly at the last. Handstitch Belly opening closed. Now stuff each Leg and handstitch closed.

Fig. (a)

Fig. (b)

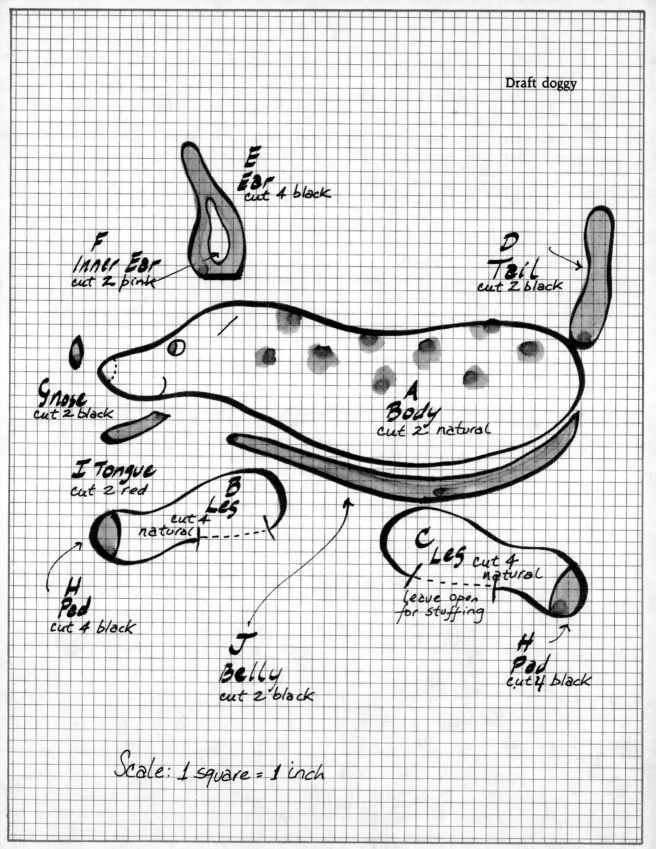

E
Ear
cut 4 black

F
Inner Ear
cut 2 pink

D
Tail
cut 2 black

G Nose
cut 2 black

A
Body
cut 2 natural

I Tongue
cut 2 red

B
Leg
cut 4
natural

C
Leg cut 4
natural

leave open
for stuffing

H
Pad
cut 4 black

J
Belly
cut 2 black

H
Pad
cut 4 black

Scale: 1 square = 1 inch

Viennese Puppet Stage

"All the world's a stage . . . "
And so it will be. Let your imagination take wing and create an ornate, foldable puppet stage worthy of the great Grimalkin. This one, emblazoned with gold braid trim and the initials of the players, is made to be hung from a spring-loaded curtain rod in the center of an open doorway or hall. The height can be quickly altered to accommodate any size thespian, from a two-year old to a grandfather with a bent for the dramatic. The stage utilizes the entire width of standard 10 ounce canvas (about 31 inches). A dowel slips through a tunnel across the bottom of the stage opening to give support where a puppeteer's hand reaches through. The stage can be made in a morning's work, especially if you have cut out the applique pieces the night before.

You have but to sew . . . and then watch the players strut.

Materials

- 1⅓ yards red canvas
- ½ yard green canvas
- 1 yard bold black and white stripe canvas
- ½ yard pink canvas
- Scraps of yellow canvas
- 1½ yards assorted gold braids and trims
- 1 yard gold fringe
- One ½-inch dowel, 36 inches long
- One spring-loaded curtain rod that extends to 36 inches

Viennese Puppet Stage

Preparing the Escutcheon   Cut out Awning and all pieces relating to the applique on it. Cut out initials or name of the puppeteers. Small children delight in owning their own stage, but then perhaps we would all like our name in lights. Place initials onto pink Oval E and satin stitch in place. Pin ornate braid onto inside edge of Oval E and sew down. Make sure to tuck under raw edges of braid before you sew. If you have chosen a rough, raised type of braiding you may have to use a loose zigzag stitch along both edges. If necessary, use transparent nylon thread on the top bobbin so that no stitches will show, or use yellow thread.

Making the Applique   With a pencil, trace the Oval in center of striped Awning A. You will be sewing the other applique pieces under the Oval, so this will provide an indication of where it will lie when completed. Pin Crown H onto Awning, its lower edge inside the penciled oval. With close zigzag stitch or satin stitch, sew Crown onto Awning. Now position yellow Swords G and Curtains F onto Awning and pin. Refer to pattern for correct placement. Zigzag yellow Swords onto the Background. Make small tucks in the Curtains to give the illusion of real swags. Zigzag Curtains onto Awning, leaving bottom edges *free.*

You have completed everything except the Escutcheon itself. Place your Oval onto the Swords-Crown-Curtain applique. It should fit in the pencil marks covering all raw edges except the flying Swag Curtains. With a long stitch, machine baste Oval onto Awning. Pin wide, ornate gold braid around outer edge of Oval. It should cover stitching line as well as the raw edge of the Oval itself. Sew down carefully.

The Curtain   Turn under ¼ inch all edges of Stage Curtains C and topstitch close to edge. Apply ornate braids, rick-racks, gold fringe to the bottom of the curtains. Go all out here, the more rococo the better. This is a chance to buy snips and snaps of outrageously expensive trims that you always drool over, but pass by at the fabric store. Cut out red Stage Bottom B. Turn under edges of Stage opening. Topstitch to prevent fraying. Lay red Stage onto worktable face up. Center completed Curtains over stage opening, making sure that they match exactly in the middle. Pin securely to red Stage. They should overlap the sides by about 1 inch on either side, and hang down slightly below opening. Baste Curtains to Stage at upper outside corner, by hand or machine. Whipstitch the curtains together by hand at the top center to hold evenly.

Place Awning on top of completed red Stage so that the scalloped edge overlaps the Stage and tops of the Curtains, and no raw edges show anywhere. Pin in place along scalloped edges. It is important that the Awning be pinned very securely prior to the final zigzagging which will join it to the Stage. Otherwise, as you feed the heavy Stage through the arm of your machine it may pull crooked. When you make a mistake, zigzagging is not fun to remove and it leaves holes in canvas too.

Working slowly, zigzag Awning to Stage along scallops. Check your progress as you go.

Finishing   Flip Stage Curtains up onto Awning and pin out of the way. With Stage face up on the table, fold it *upwards into itself,* on inside, just below the Stage opening so that a long tunnel ¾ inch wide is formed. This tunnel will accomodate a ½-inch dowel. Stitch tunnel along both edges. Insert dowel.

Fold topmost edge of Awning to back forming a 1-inch wide tunnel. Topstitch. Insert curtain rod for hanging.

If you like, a strip of striped fabric can be added along the bottom edge of your completed stage to finish it in style.

Viennese puppet stage

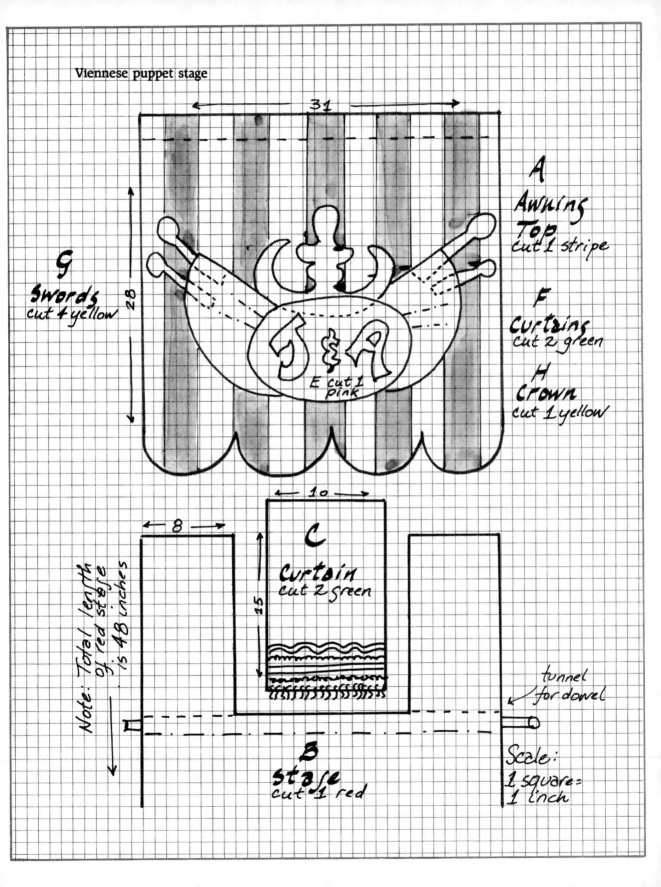

31

A
Awning
Top
cut 1 stripe

G
Swords
cut 4 yellow

28

F
Curtains
cut 2 green

H
Crown
cut 1 yellow

E cut 1
pink

10

C
Curtain
cut 2 green

8

15

Note: Total length
of red stage
is 48 inches

tunnel
for dowel

B
Stage
cut 1 red

Scale:
1 square=
1 inch

Soft Name Book

Soft name book

Scratchy, furry, sandy, shiny, sticky . . .

A baby's first word associations are almost invariably linked to her tactile explorations. She wants, needs, to find out everything about the world. She must grab it, sit on it, stuff it in her mouth, lick it, rip it, roll in it and jump on top of it. A child's inventiveness as explorer-scientist taxes our patience and challenges our own perceptions. We try to stay one jump ahead of our midget barbarians, while they wreak doom and destruction through the house.

Created to withstand such onslaughts, the Soft Name Book is virtually indestructible, and FUN. Each page is fashioned of two layers of canvas, with a layer of fiberfill between. A large alphabet letter is appliqued onto each page, together with an appropriate picture of a word beginning with that letter. The whole book spells out your child's name. Each page provides a different tactile, visual, auditory, or olfactory experience. For instance, a clear vinyl window to peek through can represent "W," a glossy photo of father for "D"addy, a fake fur tail on the rabbit for "R," an actual sandpaper desert for "S." The list is as limitless and entertaining as your imagination itself. The final page contains a small mirror appliqued with colored braids, which announces the most important person alive . . . ME.

Materials

- ⅓ yard natural canvas per page
- Three 1-inch grommets per page, and grommet setter
- Polyester fiberfill batting
- Three 3-inch brass rings, *not* welded together
- One pair of pliers
- Scraps of canvas, fur, satin, vinyl, calico, leather, velour, velvet, lace, etc.
- Small mirror
- Embroidered braid trims, gold lace, fringe, buttons, jewels, bits of old jewelry, family photographs, baby pictures, any trinkets that can be appliqued or hand stitched onto pages, bits of handkerchiefs dipped in cologne, cotton balls, zippers, buckles . . .

The Basic Page   Although this is a very simple project, and an entertaining one to work on, it will prove frustrating if you do not cut out all page pieces exactly the same size. Too, you have to maintain the same seam allowance for all. It will help to cut a pattern piece from paper to use as a template, rather than merely stacking one canvas page on top of another as a cutting guideline.

Cut out two squares of canvas and one of fiberfill batting. Place batting between the two squares. Pin, stitch around three edges, ³/₈ inch in from the edge. Leave fourth edge open. Turn right side out. Tuck open ends to inside. Pin, topstitch ¼ inch from outer edge to close. Continue topstitching around two more sides. Leave one side without topstitching, this will be the side into which you will insert grommets.

Depending upon your child's name, applique the pages as suits your fancy. The alphabet letters should be at least 3 inches square. Don't hesitate to let the letter overlap your picture. A crowded page is appealing to a child, and graphically more exciting. It is also easier to design and applique larger shapes. The bolder the shape the stronger the statement. Young children respond readily to shapes themselves, so abstract an object as freely as you like.

Hanging It All Together   When you have completed your book, mark placement of grommets on top page. Apply grommets according to instructions in your kit. You will probably be more successful if you use tiny, very sharp embroidery scissors to cut the holes through the layers of canvas instead of the punch provided in the kit. Do not worry if you cut holes that are slightly larger than necessary. The brass grommets will cover the raw edges. Trim excess fabric around holes before tapping grommets in place. It will look neater if you insert the grommets *down* through the pages, hammering from the backside, rather than the front.

After completing the grommets in the first page, lay it on top of the second. Mark the center of the holes on the page below with a pencil. Continue to grommet all pages this way. When the book is complete, bend the brass rings with pliers and slip through grommet holes. Re-pinch rings to close.

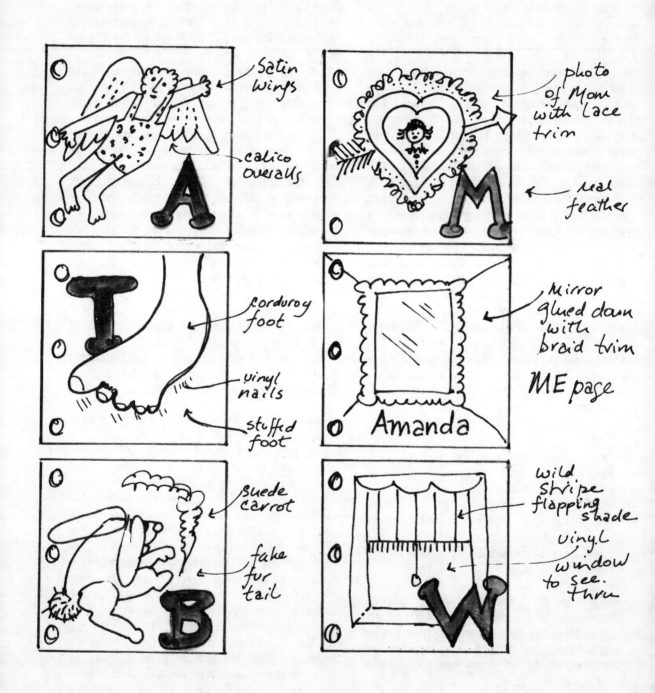

satin wings

calico overalls

photo of Mom with lace trim

real feather

corduroy foot

vinyl nails

stuffed foot

Mirror glued down with braid trim

ME page

Amanda

suede carrot

fake fur tail

wild stripe flapping shade

vinyl window to see thru

First Family

The First Family is designed as a learning and play experience, one that will help your child satisfy the need to know where babies come from. The Family is a teaching tool parents can use when explaining a most basic, and joyful, part of life. Children often have strange notions about birth, but these can be set straight if facts are discussed in a non-threatening situation. With the canvas Family, children can participate in the play-birth of Baby Boy without fear or confusion. Of all the projects in this book, the Family has most delighted and entertained the children in this neighborhood. Left alone, the children demonstrated astounding scientific accuracy as they explained "how it all happened." All children want to be the doctor, of course, and delight in hanging Baby Boy upside down and spanking him into life. You may want to demonstrate LeBoyer's gentler methods by lowering the lights and playing soft music as the infant is delivered. Listening to the children play with the Family will give you insights into many related areas of their lives, such as sibling rivalry. What begins as a specific teaching toy can become a valuable tool for opening up family communication.

Before Beginning

All members of the First Family are assembled in a like manner. That is, their Front Bodies are sewn, embellished and appliqued. The Legs and Arms are then stitched onto these Fronts. The Back Bodies are stitched on last and the torsos are stuffed to complete.

The Father

Materials
- 1½ yards natural canvas
- 2 bags polyester fiberfill stuffing
- Scrap of red canvas
- Buttons for eyes

Making His Extremities   Cut out Arms and Legs. Place fronts and backs together in sets and stitch around outside, leaving the short ends open for turning.

It is difficult to turn long, thin tubes of canvas right side out. But if you have sewn a piece of string inside it is easier. Cut the string longer than the canvas pieces to be sewn together. Place it inside the pieces so one end is in the seam at the bottom of the tube—in this case in the hand or the foot—and so the other end sticks out of the canvas. *See (a)*. When you join the two pieces of canvas, stitch right across the string. Then, when you have finished sewing, tug the loose end of the string and the tube—Arm or Leg—will turn right side out with no trouble. Afterwards, clip the string off on the outside.

After turning right side out, press the Arms and Legs. With the help of a yardstick, gently insert stuffing in both Arms and Legs. These People are designed to be more flat than round, so don't fill too firmly with stuffing. Beginning at the opened ends, topstitch ¼ inch in from outside edges. When you come to the toes and fingers, gently delineate them as in the pattern. Stitch all around each Arm and Leg. Stitch across the Legs at the knee and ankle, stitch across the arms at the elbow. Set aside.

Making His Necessities   Cut out Father's Genitals. Place fronts and backs together in sets and stitch. Turn right side out and gently stuff. Sew together at top as shown in pattern.

Making Father's Torso   Cut out Body Front and Back, and Ears. Place two sets of Ears together, stitch around curve. Leave straight edge open. Turn right side out. Stuff gently. Topstitch ¼ inch from outside edge. Make a tuck in the middle of each Ear and stitch across straight edge to hold.

Cut out red Heart and applique onto Father's chest with a satin or zigzag stitch. Sew buttons onto face for eyes.

On Body Front, the one with the red Heart, pin Ears at correct height. Pin, top sides facing, with curved edges facing inwards. Sew to face. Now pin Arms onto Body Front, again facing inwards. They must be ½ inch below the shoulders to allow for shoulder seam. Sew Arms to Body, making sure the hands are pointing the right direction in relation to the torso. Now place Genitals onto Body Front, upside down and facing towards center of Body. Stitch in place. *See (b)*. Lastly, place Father's Legs onto his Body, again facing inwards. They will meet in the middle on top of his Genitals. *See (c)*. Stitch across.

Completing the Father   Pin remaining Body Back on top of Father's completed torso, his Arms and Ears still facing inwards. Begin at one shoulder and stitch around head and down across other shoulder. Trim and clip curved head seam. Sew neck seam again for Father will be subject to rough handling by children. The neck is always vulnerable in any stuffed creature.

Re-pin torso if necessary. Stitch side seams, going slowly over arms. Leave bottom edge open. Turn right side out. Stuff with fiberfill.

If you like the head to stay precisely upright, place a piece of very stiff cardboard or a length of dowelling inside before you stuff. Without an armature, the neck will bend, rather tenderly, towards his wife and new son.

On Father's Back, tuck open edge under and handstitch closed.

Fig. (a)

Fig. (b)   Fig. (c)

230

The Mother

Materials

- 1½ yards natural canvas
- 2 bags polyester fiberfill stuffing
- One 7-inch beige zipper
- Three large snaps
- Buttons for eyes
- Scrap of red canvas
- ½ yard silky red material
- ⅔ yard soft upholstery cording
- Scrap of soft, light blue material

Making Her Extremities Cut out Mother's Arms and Legs. Place fronts and backs together in sets and complete exactly as in instructions for Father. Set aside.

Making Her a Mother Cut out Mother's Front and Back Body. The Front Body is noted on the pattern by a dotted line and is cut larger in order to accomodate Baby Boy inside. Cut out her Ears and her Breasts.

Cut a slit on the Breasts as indicated on pattern. Overlap these cut edges towards each other to form a cone shape. Zigzag edge closed to form a softly rounded breast. Place Mother's Breasts on her chest as indicated and zigzag in place. Stuff with fiberfill as you sew. The object is to indicate, in an abstract way, Mother's nursing ability. Sew the male sections of a snap onto each Breast. Cut out a red Heart and applique it to Mother's chest, slightly overlapping the left Breast.

Cut a slit in Mother's tummy as indicated on pattern. Fold side of cut under ¼ inch and press to hold. Insert zipper and sew in place. Zipper should open from *bottom*. You will need to make two small snips at the top of the cut in order to go around the top of the zipper neatly. *See (a).*

Cut out Plackets. Fold Plackets in half lengthwise and press. Place Plackets so that the folded edges meet on Mother's tummy discreetly covering her zippered opening. Applique them in place with a satin or close zigzag stitch. *See (b).* Start appliqueing at the bottom edge, sew up one side, across top and down other side.

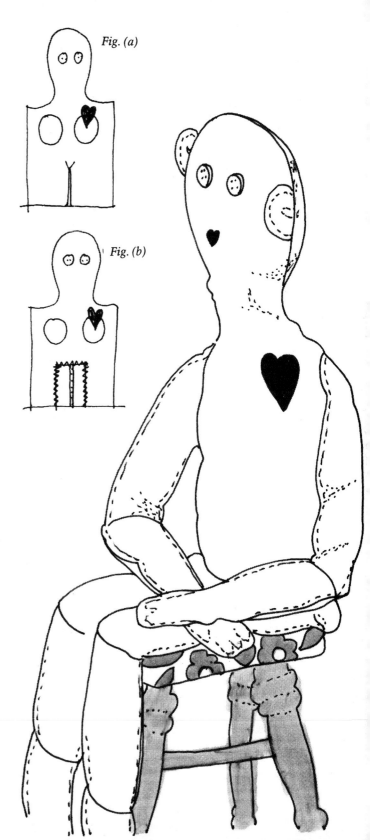

Fig. (a)

Fig. (b)

231

First Family

Completing Mother's Body   Place Mother's Arms onto her Body Front ½ inch below shoulder seams. Have the Arms facing inwards towards Body. Sew in place.

Cut out and make Mother's Ears as in instructions for Father. Sew Ears to Mother's head, facing inwards. Sew buttons on face for eyes.

Lay Mother's completed torso onto her Body Back. Using the dimensions of Body Back as guide, make two deep tucks in Mother's tummy on either side of the zipper, bringing the Front Body in to match the Body Back. Tucks should be facing towards the side seams. Stitch tucks close to edge to hold. Now place completed Legs onto tucked edge of Mother's tummy, facing inwards. Sew in place.

Place Body Back on *top* of Mother's completed Front Body and pin in place. Beginning with one shoulder, sew around head and across other shoulder. Stitch neck twice. Bundle Mother's Arms to center of Body and sew side seams. Turn right side out. Press. Stuff Mother's torso halfway *only*, you need to allow room for Baby Boy. On Back, tuck open edge under and handstitch closed.

Baby Boy

Materials

- ½ yard natural canvas
- Scrap red canvas
- Two large snaps
- Buttons for eyes
- ¼ bag polyester fiberfill stuffing

Making the Baby   Cut out all pieces and make exactly like Father. Owing to his small size, you may wish to simplify the topstitching on his hands and feet. Sew a female snap onto his face for a mouth. Now he can be snapped to Mother to "nurse." Sew a female snap onto his tummy as an umbilicus. Sew buttons onto face for eyes.

Important Authenticities   Fold one edge of red silk under 1 inch and hem. Fold silk in half and sew along three sides to form pouch. This simulates the placenta, a part of every human birth.

With a scrap of blue fabric, wrap the upholstery cording and handstitch to cover. This will be the umbilical cord. Sew a male snap to one end. This will snap onto Baby's belly button.

Fold Baby Boy into a neat bundle and stuff him in the pouch, snapping the umbilical cord to his little tummy first. Insert this silky pouch into Mother's belly. It is a tight squeeze. But then, that's something to learn too. No birth is without some effort.

First family

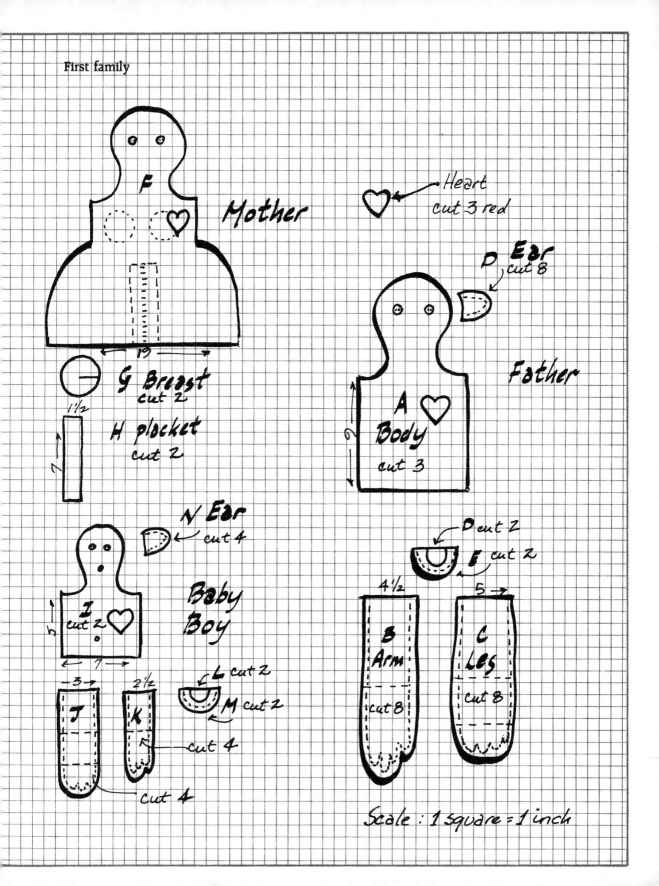

Mother

Heart
cut 3 red

D Ear
cut 8

Father

A
Body
cut 3

G Breast
cut 2

H placket
cut 2

1½

7

N Ear
cut 4

Baby
Boy

D cut 2
E cut 2

4½   5

I
cut 2

B
Arm

C
Leg

cut 8   cut 8

5

7

J   K   L cut 2
                 M cut 2

3   2½

cut 4

cut 4

Scale : 1 square = 1 inch

Interiors

Dowel Sling Lounger

The old-fashioned porch swing brings back memories of lazy summer afternoons in small towns where grass grows lush and green and freshly baked apple pies stand in open windows to cool. The Sling Lounger will not guarantee a nostalgic voyage into the past, but it will enliven a front porch. Or you can hang it from a sturdy oak branch in a shady backyard. It seats three, each with his own adjustable pillow. The abstract sunset design is painted on first, while the canvas is wet. A driveway or patio is a good place to work, providing the family dog doesn't decide to chase the cat while you are sloshing on the colors. You'll need a few woodworking tools to complete this project, but they are common ones and should be readily borrowable from neighbors.

Materials

- 6 yards natural canvas
- Twelve #3 grommets, and grommet setter
- 1½ bags polyester fiberfill stuffing for pillows
- Two 2-inch dowels, 80 inches long each
- Electric drill with ⁵/₁₆-inch bit
- Two 2 × 4's of pine or fir, 54 inches long each
- Four eyebolts, ⁵/₁₆ by 4 inch. Two washers and one nut for each eyebolt
- 4 yards ¼-inch or ³/₈-inch soft rope for pillows
- Four ¼-inch quick-links (or other snap-type fastener to link chain to eyebolt)
- 1½-inch chain long enough to hang lounger
- Red, blue, yellow acrylic paints, fabric paints or fabric dyes in quantity to cover three slings
- Wide brushes, buckets for mixing paints

Dowel sling lounger

Painting the Graphics   Cut three lengths of natural canvas, each 65 inches long. Zigzag all edges to prevent ravelling. Turn under canvas 3 inches on each long edge and zigzag to form deep hems. Make 3½-inch hems at the top and bottom edges of the sling seats. Stitch twice for sturdiness. Insert #3 grommets at the edge of each seat just under the hem as shown on pattern. Cut out six pieces of canvas, 12 by 30 inches each, for Pillows. Set aside three Pillow pieces which will be the Backs.

Fill a large sink or bathtub with cool water and put the Sling backs and the Pillow Fronts to soak. If the canvas seems *very* stiff, you may have to wash it first in Sal-soda and warm water to remove the sizing so the fabric will absorb the paint. If you do not wash, agitate it in your tub, or better still trample on it to make sure all the fibers are wet. If wrinkles bother you, fold the canvas neatly before soaking, then trample it.

Using acrylic paint, fabric paint, or fabric dyes mix up a fairly large quantity of each color, using the pattern as guide. Make the colors quite thin, almost transparent. You will need a jar or bucket wide enough to dip your brush into for each color. Now lay your wet canvas onto the driveway, sidewalk or patio. Position canvas Slings side by side, next to each other so you can paint the stripes on all of them at once. Place Pillow Fronts next to Slings at the same height they will be when lounger is completed. Now you can paint all the pieces of canvas at once. Beginning at the bottom, slosh the colors onto the canvas one at a time, working towards the top. If you feel unsure of this technique, practice first on a scrap of wet canvas, tipping it at various angles and exploring how one color bleeds into another. Strive for a delicate sunset effect. Allow to dry slowly, preferably not in the direct sun, as this might cause the canvas to shrink unevenly.

Pillowing   Place Fronts and Backs of the three Pillows right sides together and stitch around three sides. Turn right side out, leaving the fourth side open for stuffing. With a grommet setter, insert a #3 grommet in each upper corner of the Pillows, approximately 2 inches from the edges. Stuff Pillows with shredded foam, fiberfill, or kapok and blindstitch open edge.

Slinging the Seats   Round the ends of the 2 × 4's and drill 1½-inch holes in each end. This can be achieved in various ways. You can take the 2 × 4's to a cabinet shop and have the ends curved and the holes drilled by a carpenter. Or, using a surform plane (a small plane with a rasp-like bottom blade) or a rasp, you can round off the ends by hand. This is not difficult, and is only slightly time consuming. To drill the holes through which you will insert the dowels, use a special drill bit called a speed-bore. This bit looks like a razor blade set on edge, and will fit any regular hand-held electric drill. Position the drill bit in the center of the 2 × 4, 3 inches from the end and begin routing out the hole. Work slowly without forcing the speed-bore, nursing it in and out, and allowing it to kick out the excess shavings. Repeat, drilling holes in all four ends. Sand holes smooth.

Hanging It Up   With a ⁵/₁₆-inch drill bit, drill holes through each dowel 2 inches from the ends. Make sure the holes are positioned at the same angle so when the bolts pass through the eyes will be upright. Now slip the canvas Slings onto the dowels.

Insert the dowels through the holes in the 2 × 4's. Screw the eyebolts through the dowels. Place a washer next to the eye as at the protruding end before the nut. This will protect the wooden dowel from wear. Snap one end of each length of chain onto the eyebolts with a quick-link. *See (a).* You will have to adjust the length of chain according to your particular porch setting.

Finishing   Place Pillows at correct height against back of Slings so that your painted design matches. Cut six lengths of rope long enough to allow it to be knotted in back of Sling, pass through grommet in chair back, through grommet in Pillow, and be knotted again. *See (b).* Attach Pillows to Sling backs and relax.

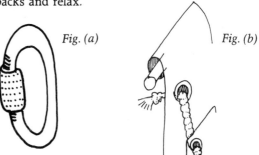

Fig. (a)   *Fig. (b)*

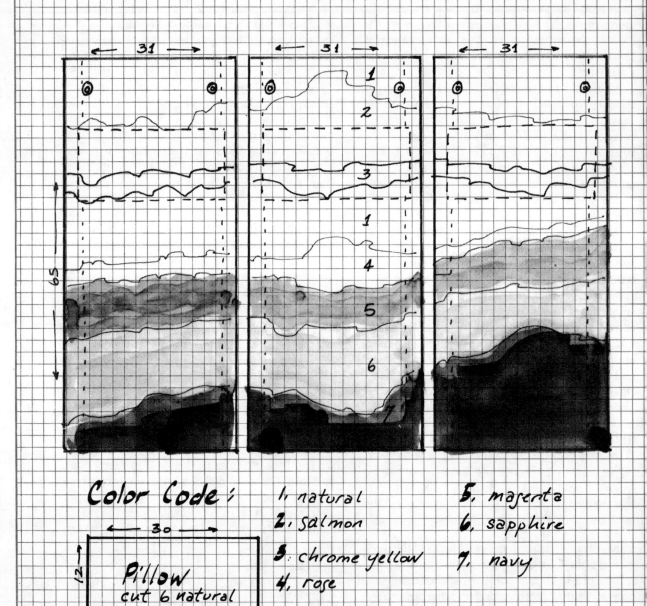

Dowel sling lounger

31   31   31

1
2
3
1
4
5
6
7

65

Color Code:

1, natural
2, salmon
3, chrome yellow
4, rose

5, magenta
6, sapphire
7, navy

30

12

Pillow
cut 6 natural

Scale: 1 square = 2 inches

Hippo Hammock

While the Hippo quietly chews, you can drowse away a lazy afternoon. Simply constructed, this hand-painted hammock is suspended between two aluminum pipes and hung beneath your favorite tree by either ropes or chains. After enlarging the Hippo and his Nile flowers, you paint him onto the canvas with acrylic paints and broad strokes. Then bask away the long day in Oriental comfort, swayed only by an errant summer breeze.

Materials

- 2⅔ yards natural canvas, 48 inches wide
- Two lengths ¾-inch hollow aluminum pipe, 44 inches long each
- Electric drill with ¼-inch metal bit
- Four ¼-inch eyebolts with washers and nuts
- Four "S" hooks
- ⅛-inch coil chain, or ³/₈-inch rope, enough to suspend hammock.

- Artist's acrylic paints:
  1 tube *each* of hot pink, maroon, green, scarlet, deep turquoise, light turquoise, chrome yellow. 2 tubes of orange.
- Buckets or jars to mix paints
- Narrow, medium and wide brushes.

The Hammock   Cut out all pattern pieces. Zigzag all edges to prevent ravelling. Sew Side Bands B onto each side of Hammock A. Lay Hammock on flat surface with raw edges of seams facing you, press seam toward Side Bands. Now fold raw outside edges of Seam bands inwards ½ inch. Press. Fold Side Bands again so that the pressed edges just cover the seams you have sewn. Pin. Stitch close to edge. These 2-inch Bands will strengthen the side edges of the Hammock and provide a finished look. Turn under the remaining short ends of the Hammock 3 inches and topstitch *three* times for strength.

239

Hippo Hammock

Painting the Hippo   Lay the Hammock on a flat surface and mark off a grid with straight pins. Each square section on the pattern equals 2 inches. The pins are merely a guide to help you transfer the design to the canvas. With a light pencil, draw the hippos's nose section and his tail section. With these two ends as a guide, fill in the rest of his body. Then fill in details of the body and the water-hyacinths he munches so contentedly. Finally, pencil in the stylized flowers at either end of the Hammock. One flower fills approximately 9 inches so you may wish to re-grid the ends with pins to aid you.

Mix the paints according to the color chart on the pattern. You have to experiment to see how much water will thin the colors to a workable consistency. Mix more paint than you think you will need so there will be enough to complete the design. It is important with acrylics, particularly if they are thinned, to experiment first on a scrap of canvas. Acrylics are brilliant colors and do not fade as you paint, but they will *bleed* at the edges of your design. By testing, you will be able to determine how great the bleed is, and can paint your design inside the outline accordingly. You may wish to add a bordering dark line around every edge to give sharp definition. Do this last, after the colors have dried, with a narrow brush.

Hanging It Up   With drill and a ¼-inch metal drill bit, drill holes through aluminum tubing 2 inches from each end. Slip tubing through the casings at either end of the Hammock. Insert washers and an eyebolt through each hole and tighten nut. Make sure you have a washer next to the aluminum pipe on either side. Slip "S" hooks through eyebolts and hook through chain to hang. *See (a)*.

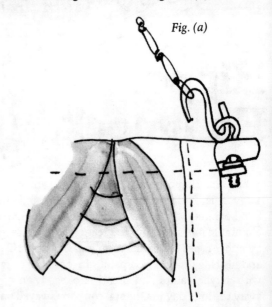

Fig. (a)

Hippo hammock

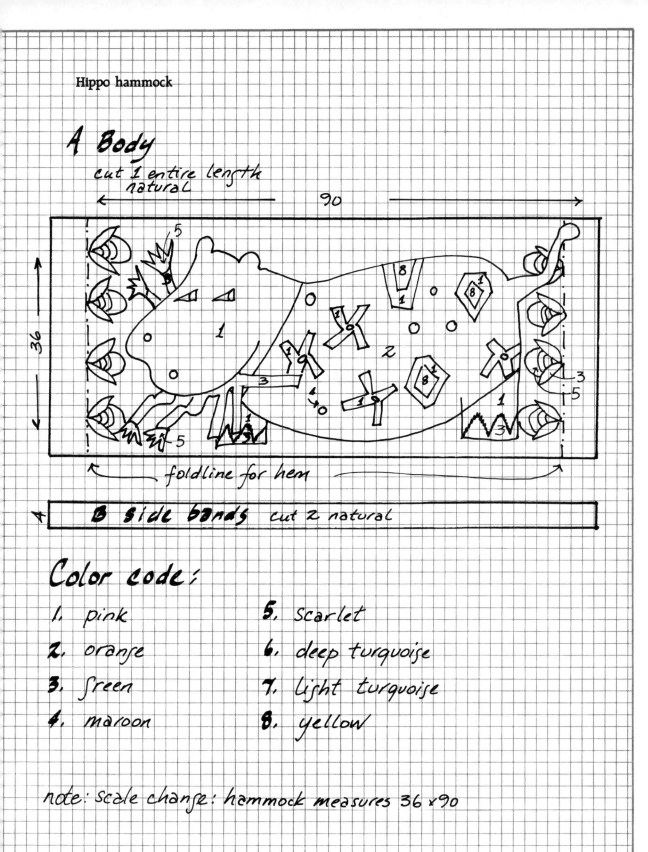

A Body

cut 1 entire length
natural

← 90 →

36

foldline for hem

B side bands cut 2 natural

Color code:

1. pink   5. scarlet
2. orange   6. deep turquoise
3. green   7. light turquoise
4. maroon   8. yellow

note: scale change: hammock measures 36 x 90

Caterpillar Lounger

It's no fun to climb cold and shivery from a swimming pool only to flop down on hard cement. You will find children much more agreeable about leaving the pool if they have a humorous Caterpillar to lounge on. This silly, striped bug bumps along your patio, his antennae quivering and his feet creeping. The Caterpillar is sewn in cushioned sections and stuffed with a squashy mixture of shredded foam and plastic pellets.

Materials

- 1½ yards green canvas
- 1½ yards yellow canvas
- 3½ yards black canvas
- Scraps of natural canvas for eyes
- Lightweight wire
- 3 cubic feet shredded foam
- 3 cubic feet polyurethane pellets (used for bean bag furniture)
- Tailor's chalk
- White glue

Striping the Body   Cut out pattern pieces. In order to get 84-inch lengths, you will have to piece the canvas for the stripes. The widths of the stripes are indicated on the pattern. Cut out one black Back 30 by 84 inches.

Sew stripes together lengthwise to form front of the Caterpillar. Sew them together in a pattern of green-black-yellow-black-green. Cut out two Straps each 4 by 6 inches. Fold in half lengthwise. Fold again. Topstitch to form Strap. Baste short edges of Straps along top edge of Caterpillar front.

The Feet   Make feet by placing 28 black Feet together in 14 sets. Closely zigzag around edges of Feet. Pin Feet towards center front of Caterpillar along long edges. Space Feet at intervals as shown in pattern. Machine baste to hold. *See (a).*

Looking Ahead   Cut out two black Eyeballs and zigzag onto two natural Eyes. Place these Eye Fronts onto Eye Backs right sides together, and stitch close to edges. Leave straight edge open. Turn right side out. Stuff gently with a wisp of fiberfill or pellets. Stitch Eyes closed. Place Eyes onto one black Head, face down facing towards center. Machine baste in place.

Cut two lengths of black canvas 1½ by 8 inches. Fold in half lengthwise, fold again and topstitch. Cut two 8-inch lengths of wire and insert into these slender tubes to form Antennae. Cut four circles of black canvas about the size of a nickel. Glue two of these together at the ends of each Antennae as shown on pattern. Pin these Antennae onto Head between Eyes, facing towards the center. Machine baste with small stitches to hold. Place back of Head on top of Head and stitch around curved edge. Trim. Turn right side out carefully. Stuff with combination of foam and pellets. Stitch across opening to hold. Next place Head onto striped Caterpillar face *down* and facing towards the center of body. Stitch.

Caterpillar lounger

Note: cut 1
entire black
Back 30 × 84.

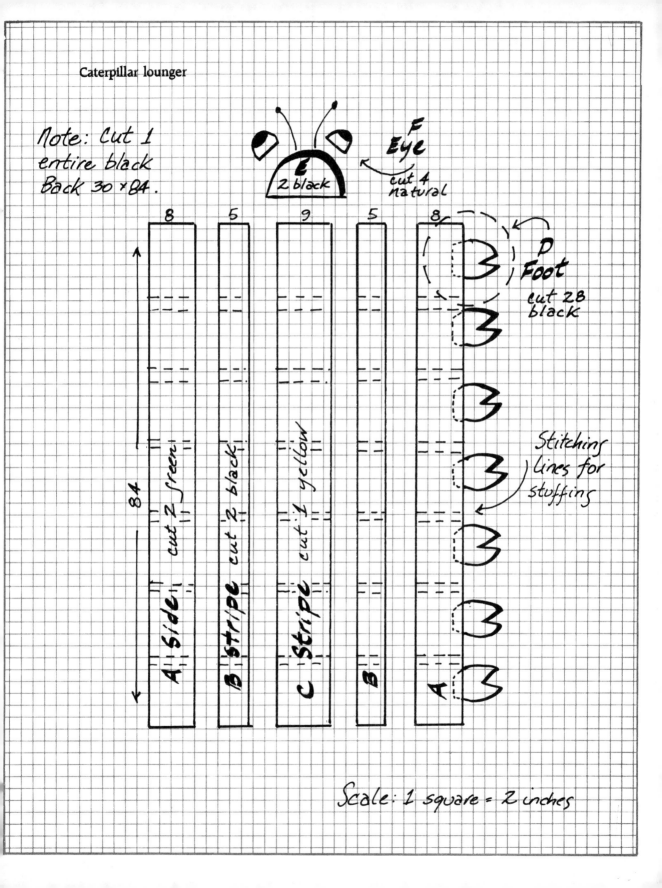

E
2 black

E
Eye
cut 4
natural

D
Foot
cut 28
black

Stitching
lines for
stuffing

8   5   9   5   8

84

A Side   cut 2 green
B Stripe   cut 2 black
C Stripe   cut 1 yellow
B
A

Scale: 1 square = 2 inches

Caterpillar Lounger

Adding Softness   Pin black Back onto completed striped Front of Caterpillar, making sure that the Straps and all appendages are facing inwards. Begin stitching along one long side, across top with Head, and down opposite side. Leave bottom end open. Trim, clip corners, turn right side out and press. Using a yardstick and tailor's chalk, mark off seven 12-inch cushion sections. The cushion sections will be 10 inches wide, with 2-inch flat divider spaces between. Therefore, you will need to mark off 1 inch above and 1 inch below each 12-inch line. These will be your actual stitching lines.

In a *large* box, make a mix of shredded foam and polyurethane pellets. This is messy work. You may want to move your sewing machine to the garage while you do the stuffing and stitching. Beginning at the top of the body, near the Caterpillar's Head, start stuffing the first cushion section. As you near the stitching line, stop and pin the lounger closed. Stitch across. Move down 2 inches and stitch second seam of this first divider. Leave the divider strip *unstuffed*.

Fill second cushion and repeat along entire length of Caterpillar's body until all seven cushions are filled. Turn final raw end edges inwards and topstitch.

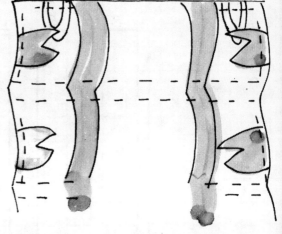

Fig. (a)

Ark Wallhanging

This dimensional wallhanging of gently puffed figures gliding peacefully under a canvas rainbow is perfect for a young child's room. The Ark and its inhabitants are guided along by a pair of doves carrying an olive branch. The pieces of the Ark are assembled separately, then stitched together with a satin stitch. Mount the wallhanging in your children's playroom as a cheerful example of peaceful co-existence.

Materials

- ¾ yard green canvas
- ½ yard *each* red, blue canvas
- 1 yard *each* orange, yellow, and pink canvas
- Scraps of natural or white, and black canvas
- 3 yards lining
- Polyester fiberfill batting
- Five buttons for eyes
- Two small brass rings
- Threads in colors to match canvas

Instructions   There will be NO seam allowances on the Ark. It is constructed piece by piece, and then assembled like a collage. In every case your method will be the same. Place a piece of lining fabric roughly the same shape as your pattern piece face *down* on the worktable. Then place a piece of batting on top, and on top of that your specific canvas shape. Pin all three layers together in a fabric sandwich. With a straight stitch baste sandwich together close to outside edges. Do not worry about extra fabric hanging out, this will be trimmed off later. With a satin stitch or close zigzag, sew around outer edge. Trim closely but not so close as to cut into satin stitching. Inevitably, this does happen, and your piece will look better if you zigzag around a second time for a firm edge. After all the pieces are made they are then assembled into a unit.

The Rainbow   Cut out one lining and one layer of batting slightly larger than the entire Rainbow. Cut out the pink, orange, and yellow canvas Rainbow Arcs. Lay upper edge of yellow Arc C so that it overlaps the lower edge of orange Arc B. Zigzag together closely. Now place upper edge of Arc B overlapping lower edge of pink Arc A. Zigzag together. Zigzag the two remaining outer edges of the Rainbow. With scraps of green and black, cut out branch and leaf shapes. Applique Olive Branch onto Rainbow with black zigzag.

The Ark   Cut out one green Ark D and one lining and batting slightly larger than the Ark. Make a sandwich and baste around outer edge. With black thread and a long machine stitch, trace outlines of boards in Ark. You may wish to draw the lines in slightly with a pencil first. However, I think it is easier to do machine embroidery with no prior plan, merely guiding the fabric gently under the presser foot and letting the irregularities become a part of the charm of the piece. When you have completed outlining the boards, zigzag around outer edge twice. Set Ark aside.

The Lion, Elephant, and Whole Troop

Cut out red Elephant. Cut out lining and batting approximately the size of the Elephant. Sandwich lining, batting and red canvas together by zigzagging around the outer edges. Accentuate curves of ears with zigzagging as shown on pattern. Starting with a medium width zigzag stitch, dimishing to very narrow, embroider his mouth. Add two buttons for eyes.

Cut out basic sandwich pieces for the blue Giraffe. Do *not* zigzag outer edges until last. Cut out Giraffe's spots from yellow canvas and zigzag onto his Body. Make his two yellow Ears M separately as Ear

Interiors

Ark wallhanging

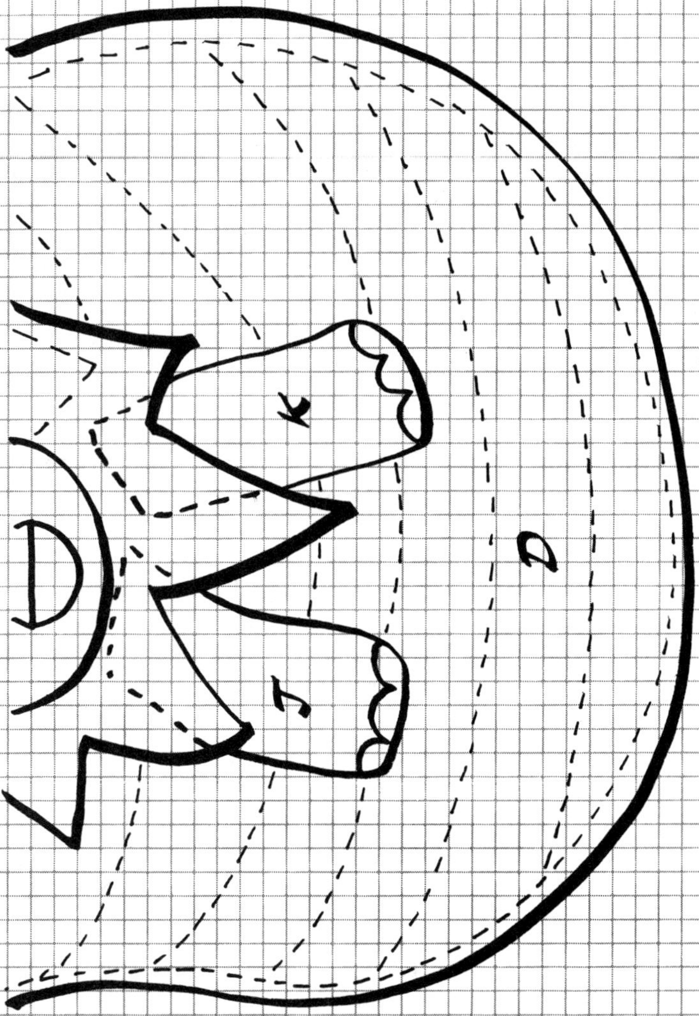

Color code:

A. pink
B. orange
C. yellow
D. green
E. red
F. orange
G. pink
H. blue
I. blue
J. orange
K. orange
L. blue
M. yellow
N. yellow
O. natural

WWW: overcast zigzag

Scale: 1 square = 2 inches

Ark Wallhanging

sandwiches. Zigzag these onto his head. Now go around entire Giraffe shape with wide zigzagging to finish, including the antlers. Embroider a smiling mouth and sew on eyes.

Cut out lining, batting and canvas for entire orange Lion's Ruff F. Complete this sandwich, including zigzagging the outer edge. Place pink Face G onto the orange Ruff and zigzag in place, tucking blue Ears H under *as you sew*. Zigzag the tops of the Ears with blue thread. Now add his blue Nose, continuing the wide zigzag down and embroidering his mouth at the same time. Complete his orange Legs J and K as you have the other pieces, adding his black toes from scraps. Sew on his eyes.

Make the Doves from natural canvas. They are one piece, but when you zigzag the outer edge, continue to curve down with a seam to delineate their bodies. Machine embroider in black their pointy beaks and small eyes.

Assembling   Lay all completed parts and animals on worktable and arrange as shown. Study the arrangement carefully, noting on the pattern page that the pieces are joined wherever marked. You may find sewing the parts of the Ark together an exasperating task. Try to arrange your workspace so you have a wide table extending to the left and to

the back of your sewing machine. This will help prevent "Ark-fall," which occurs when the weight of the hanging pulls it out from under your presser foot just as you are getting ready to begin sewing. After you complete each seam, lay the Ark flat on your worktable and re-pin the remaining pieces. This will help you keep the animals straight, and your temper cool.

Begin by sewing the Elephant to the Rainbow, then sew the Giraffe to the Rainbow. Note that the Giraffe is NOT sewn all around his head, the Ear section and Nose are left free to stand out. Use the same width satin or zigzag stitch and the same black thread that you have used already, going over the existing seams carefully.

Reposition the remaining pieces, and sew Ark to Elephant and Ark to Giraffe. Lay Lion's Head in place, slip his legs under him at correct angle, then remove Head. Sew Legs to Ark at top ends only, allowing them to hang down free. Now zigzag the top of the Lion's Head to the other piece. Everything is complete except . . .

The Doves   Handstitch the tops of the Doves' heads to the Rainbow above the Olive Branch, let their bodies float free against the bright arcs of color. Sew two small brass rings to the top of the Rainbow, for hanging.

Three Astonished People

Whimsy is a quality not ordinarily associated with sturdy canvas, yet it is the very essence of the Three Astonished People. The People are flat, skinny and brightly dressed. They peer around as if wondering what in the world they are doing hung up in such bewildering positions. They may be used in many ways: as space or room dividers, hung across lintels in place of awkward doors, or as wall hangings in your favorite room. But their main function is to amuse, to tickle the fancy. A noble function, too, in these times.

Materials

- Two round wooden drawer-pulls
- One ¾-inch dowel, 36 inches long
- Fine sandpaper
- Contact cement
- Woman in Orange Apron:

  2⅓ yards natural canvas
  ⅓ yard orange canvas
  ⅓ yard purple cotton
  ⅔ yard yellow canvas
  ¼ yard green canvas
  ⅓ yard rust canvas
  1 yard lace trim
  3 inches Velcro
  Two small buttons for eyes
  Polyester fiberfill batting
  Black thread

- Soccer Boy:

  2⅓ yards natural canvas
  ½ yard blue canvas
  ⅓ yard green canvas
  ⅓ yard white canvas or cotton
  Scraps of red canvas
  3 inches Velcro
  Two small buttons for eyes
  Six unmatched colored buttons for shirt
  Polyester fiberfill batting
  Black thread

- Woman in Turquoise Apron:

  2⅓ yards natural canvas
  ⅓ yard tan canvas
  ⅓ yard turquoise canvas
  ¼ yard black canvas
  Scraps of orange, green, purple, pink, lilac
  Two overall buckles with buttons
  3 inches Velcro
  Two small buttons for eyes
  ⅓ yard eyelet trim
  Polyester fiberfill batting
  Black thread

Before Beginning

The People are completely flat, except for their heads which are lightly stuffed with batting. The arms are made separately from the bodies, and sewn on last. The bodies of the People are appliqued first. Then front and backs are sewn together by turning the long edges in towards each other and topstitching. This eliminates the laborious process of turning them inside out.

Cutting Out   Cut out six main Bodies with Heads. The only difference between these Bodies will be the feet. Cut out twelve identical Arms. Match these backs and fronts into sets of three People. Remember that the thumbs of the hands are towards the center of the Body.

The Woman in the Orange Apron   Cut out all pieces of clothing. Place these clothes onto the main Body and adjust for overlap. Applique clothing in the following order:

1. Boots
2. Green skirt
3. Yellow dress
4. Purple under-apron
5. Orange apron
6. Purple upper-apron
7. Heart
8. Lace trim

Completing the Woman   When all clothing has been appliqued, place Back Body on top of Front Body, right sides together. Pin so edges match.

Three astonished people

With a straight stitch, sew around entire Head section, including shoulder seams. Smooth Bodies down to feet with your hand, making sure that they are pinned together without any lumps. Stitch around Boots where indicated by ---- in pattern. Trim closely. Now turn Woman in Orange Apron right side out. Press feet and head. Cut pieces of batting slightly smaller than head. Insert batting into head. Pin.

With a pencil, draw in features of face. Using a medium zigzag, embroider around eyes. With a narrow zigzag, make line for nose and with a satin stitch indicate bottom of nose. With a very narrow zigzag, make astonished mouth. Roll up the long Body while you work. Sew on eyes.

Lay Body flat on your worktable. Fold remaining raw edges towards each other. Pin and press to hold. Working slowly, topstitch remainder of Body together.

Adding the Arms   Cut out yellow Sleeves and lace trim. Stitch onto two Arms close to outside edges. Place these two Front Arms onto their matching Back Arms, right sides together. Stitch around hand sections only as indicated by ---- in pattern. Turn these Arms right side out. Press. Turn remaining open edges of each side of the arms toward each other. Pin and press. Topstitch around Arm with black thread. Topstitch design of hand. The hands will flip over the dowel from back to front, so be sure your black topstitching is on the *back* side of the Arm. Now lay the completed Arms underneath the completed Woman. Match lengths. Pin in place. With a straight stitch, sew Arms to Body along shoulder seam. Turn Woman over to backside. Tuck excess Arm under and blindstitch by hand. *See (a).*

The Soccer Boy   Cut out all applique pieces, including green stripes for Shirt. Applique pieces to Boy's Body in this order:

1. Socks
2. Shoes
3. Red stripes on socks
4. Blue shorts
5. Stripes on shorts
6. White collar

Sew buttons on Shirt. Complete Boy's Body exactly like Woman in Orange Apron.

Cut out stripes for Sleeves and place onto two Arms at appropriate angles. Make sure thumbs will be centered when Arms are sewn onto Body. Applique stripes onto Front Arms with zigzag. Place striped Front Arms and Back Arms right sides together and stitch around hands as indicated by ---- in pattern. Turn Arms right side out. Turn remaining raw edges towards each other. Pin and press. Topstitch Arms. With black thread, topstitch again in hand pattern so that when hands are flipped over the dowel the fingers will show.

Add Arms as you did for Woman in Orange Apron.

Fig. (a)

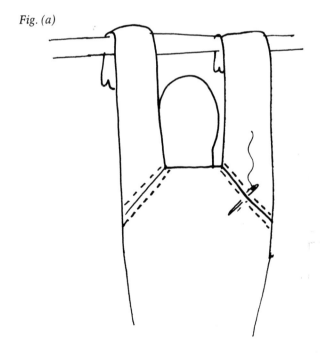

251

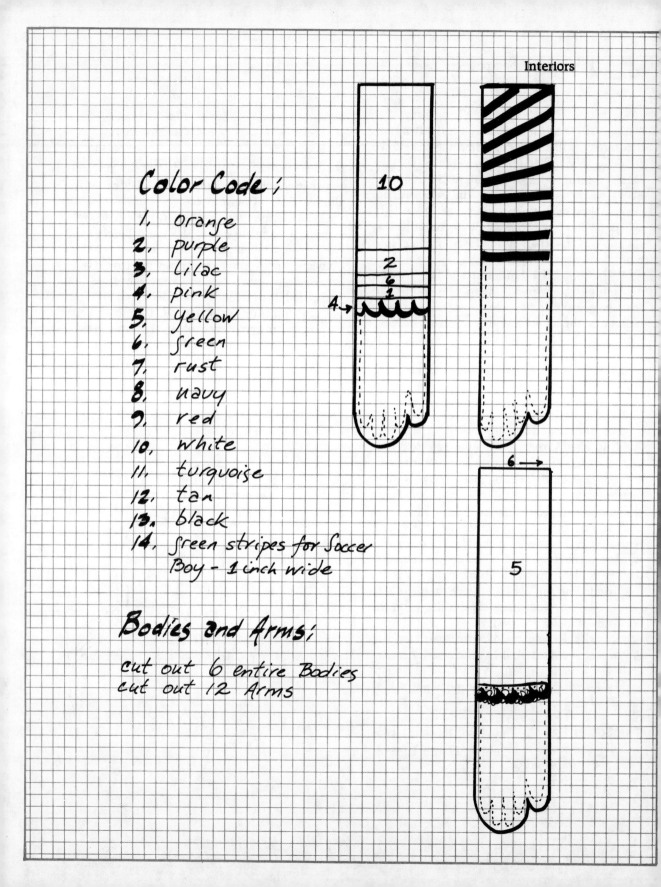

Color Code:

1. orange
2. purple
3. lilac
4. pink
5. yellow
6. green
7. rust
8. navy
9. red
10. white
11. turquoise
12. tan
13. black
14. green stripes for Soccer
    Boy - 1 inch wide

Bodies and Arms:

cut out 6 entire Bodies
cut out 12 Arms

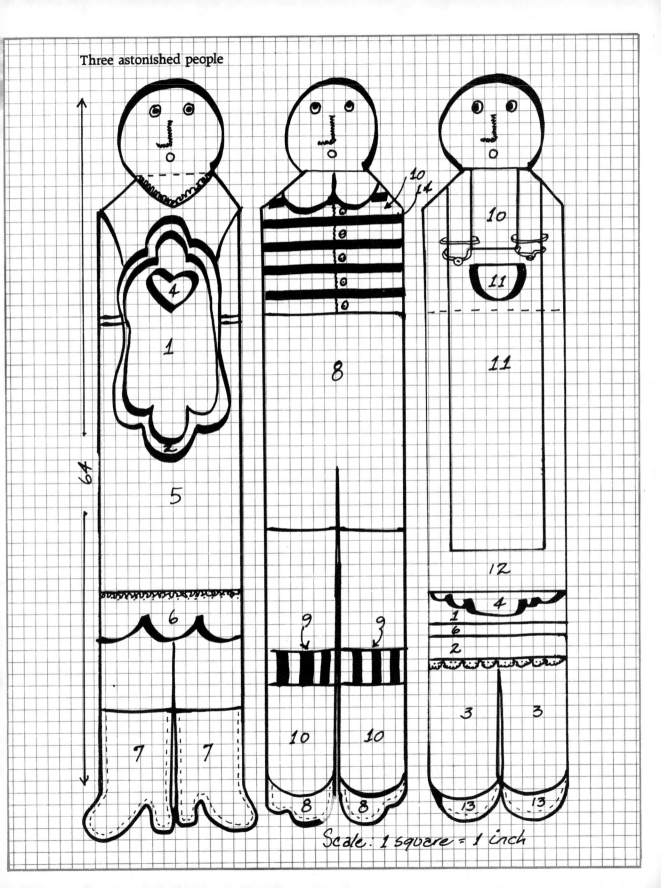

Three astonished people

Scale: 1 square = 1 inch

Three Astonished People

The Woman in Turquoise Apron   Cut out all applique pieces. Turn under upper edge of Apron Pocket ¼ inch and topstitch. Zigzag Pocket onto turquoise Apron. Turn under edges of Apron Straps and top Bodice ¼ inch and topstitch. Slip overall buckles into Straps. Sew overall button in place, and fasten buckle. Applique pieces of clothing onto Woman in this order:

1. Lilac stockings
2. Black shoes
3. Black shoe straps
4. Eyelet trim
5. Orange band
6. Green band
7. Purple band
8. Pink scallop
9. Tan skirt
10. Turquoise apron

Complete this woman exactly as you did the Woman in Orange Apron and the Soccer Boy.

Cut out white Sleeves and Bands for Arms. Pin onto front of each Arm as indicated on pattern. Applique in place. Place Front Arms and Back Arms right sides together and stitch around hands as indicated by ---- on pattern. Turn Arms right side out. Turn remaining raw edges of Arms in towards each other. Pin and press. Topstitch around entire Arm. With black thread, topstitch again the design of hand so that when hands are flipped over dowel, the stitching will show. Sew Arms to Body as with the first two figures.

Hanging Them Up   Cut six strips of Velcro, 1½ inches each. To determine placement, fold hands over dowel to obtain desired grip. Now sew Velcro on each hand and on the corresponding spot on the Arms so their grip can be fastened closed. Sew the Velcro by hand.

Sand the dowel, sand flat end of decorative drawer-pulls. Apply contact cement to dowel ends and to knobs. Wait fifteen minutes until glue becomes tacky. Glue dowel and pulls to each other. Slip dowel through all hands and hang as desired.

A Canvas Garden

The ultimate in an easy-care garden . . . a canvas cactus, grape ivy or philodendron. No more worrying about who'll water when you're on vacation, no more spider mites or mildew to contend with. Just simple, natural, eternal plants to amuse guests and delight house-sitters. All three of these plants are constructed from off-white canvas, and their abstract shapes make no attempt to be literal about their origins. Any indoor plant is a good subject for a canvas garden. By using lightweight wire armatures and stuffing firmly, you can create shadowy schifflerias, rampant Creeping Charlies, or whole groves of bamboo for an entryway. Look around your garden and choose a favorite plant or flower to translate into your own version of a fabric garden.

Split Leaf Philodendron

Materials

- 3½ yards natural canvas
- Polyester fiberfill batting
- 10 feet #12 gauge galvanized wire
- Large clay pot
- Gravel or river rock to fill pot (You may wish to embed your leaves permanently in plaster or cement. If so, purchase this from hardware store and follow directions on package.)
- Wire cutters

Making the Leaves   Cut out as many leaves as you will need, depending upon the size of your pot. Do NOT cut out splits in leaves yet. From three to five leaves look suitably imposing in a large terracotta pot. Cut out three layers of fiberfill batting for each leaf. Make a sandwich of batting, canvas and canvas for each leaf and stitch around edge, ½ inch from outer edge. Leave an opening for turning as indicated on the pattern. Trim. Turn leaves right side out. Press. Slipstitch opening closed. Now cut splits in leaves, cutting through all three layers. Turn canvas edges of splits under towards each other to hide raw edges. Pin. You will find that the point of each split is tricky to turn under. Topstitch ³/₈ inch from the outside edges of each leaf. When you get to the split, stitch closer to the edge to hold the canvas firmly.

Adding the Stems   From the remaining canvas, cut out strips for stems 1¼-inch wide and approximately 4 or 5 feet long. The length will depend on how tall you want your plant to be. You will cut two stem strips for each leaf, one will be a leaf-length longer than the other.

Fold the long edges of each stem strip inwards toward the center of the strip and press firmly to hold. Pin one strip along the center of each leaf in a slightly undulating line. Tuck the tip of the stem strip under at the top of the leaf. Stitch along both sides of the strip to form a casing for wire. You now have a leaf with one raw stem dangling from it. Make another strip and tuck it under so it joins the first stem neatly. Pin two stems together so that a long casing is formed. *See (a).* Continue stitching stem halves together to complete stem. Repeat for all leaves.

Now topstitch the veins of the leaves, beginning at the outside of each leaf and curving towards the center stem. Delineate each vein with two rows of stitching ³/₈-inch apart as shown on pattern. Sew freely with easy curves.

Assembling   Insert wire through stems and up into tips of leaves. If you are using a heavyweight canvas, you will need to insert two wires for each leaf.

When all leaves are wired, wrap their lower stems together and place into a pot. It helps to have another pair of hands for this, one person can hold the bouquet upright while you fill the container with gravel or river rock. You may find that bending the bottom ends of the wired stems at right angles will give the plant more stability. If you are using cement or plaster, brace your plant in the position you want. Then fill the pot. Sprinkle a layer of gravel or vermiculite on the surface to hide the plaster.

Grape Ivy

Materials

- 1 yard natural canvas
- 12 feet #16 gauge galvanized wire
- One roll brown double-faced florists masking tape
- Hanging pot
- Gravel or river rock
- Wire cutters

Stems   Cut out an assortment of leaves. Forty or fifty leaves makes an abundant hanging plant. With wire cutters, snip 20 to 25 lengths of wire from 8 to 10 inches long each. Cut also 6 to 10 lengths of wire ranging from 36 to 48 inches in length. These longer lengths of wire will depend upon the size pot you choose, as well as the space you intend to fill.

Wrap each length of wire with the brown masking tape. This can be done by pinching the top of the wire and the end of the tape together. Twirl them together while pulling them downwards towards your lap. The tape stretches and you can pull it along

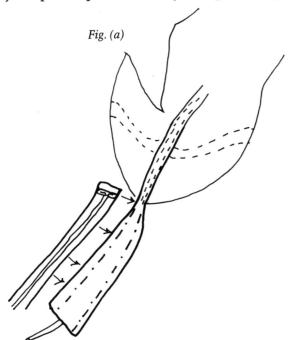

Fig. (a)

the length of wire at quite an acute angle, all the while wrapping it tightly around the wire. Practice with the short lengths of wire first. Once you get the knack of it, it goes quickly.

Attaching the Leaves   You will sew a leaf on both ends of the short lengths of wire. Using a close zigzag stitch, sew over the wire and through the canvas. Adjust your stitch width to fit the width of the wire stem so the leaf is held firmly. Complete all short wire lengths.

You will sew a leaf on only one end of the long pieces of wire. Complete all long pieces of wire. Now lay a long piece of wire on your worktable. Starting 4 to 6 inches in from the leaf end, wrap the middle of a short wire around the long stem. Continue twisting the short stems around the long stem at 3 to 5-inch intervals until the ivy branch reaches the desired length. Vary the size leaves you use. Make as many of these draping branches as you need.

Filling the Pot   Grasp the raw ends of your completed stems in one hand and twist together to hold. Roll these stems into a small circle and place at the bottom of a hanging pot. Fill the pot with gravel or rocks. Adjust the leaves. Make very sure that the cord with which you hang your plant is strong enough to support the weight. Check also to make sure the hook on which you hang the pot is securely screwed to the ceiling.

Chollo Cactus

Materials

- 3 yards natural canvas
- One ball of natural string. (Kite string sometimes matches the canvas very well. Or you can find handspun cotton string at weaving supply stores.)
- Hay, straw or shredded foam
- Two thin boards or sticks, 48 inches long
- Very sharp embroidery scissors or leather punch
- Bodkin

A Canvas Garden

Soft Thorns   Cut out all pattern pieces. On the outsides, make tucks 3 inches apart along the entire length of all the pieces. These tucks should be at least 3/8-inch deep so holes can be punched through them. When all tucks are completed, lay all pieces for Trunk and Branches flat on your worktable. With sharply pointed scissors, or a leather punch, poke holes through the tucks at approximately 4-inch intervals. Alternate and vary the holes so the effect is natural.

Thread a doubled string, 3 feet long, through the eye of the bodkin. With the bodkin pass the doubled string through each hole in the tucks. Let the string dangle about 3 inches on each side of the tuck. Snip off string and knot twice. Go on to next thorn. This is a somewhat tedious task which seems to go faster with good music or conversation. Also, if you do all the stringing first, then follow up with all the knotting you will have the illusion of speed, even if it isn't really so.

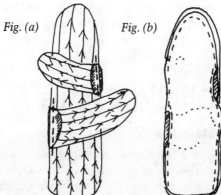

Fig. (a)   Fig. (b)

Making the Branches   Place front and back of thorned Branches right sides together. Pin, making sure that the strings are not caught in the seams. Stitch around curved edges, leaving short ends open. Turn right side out. Stuff firmly with straw or foam. You may use fiberfill, of course, but this cactus is a large piece and becomes expensive to stuff with polyester, or even kapok.

Place one side of the Trunk on the worktable, thorned side up. Pin stuffed Branches onto Trunk, facing *inwards* to center. Stitch each Branch onto Trunk along one side of Branch. *See (b).*

Place remaining thorned Trunk on top of first, right sides together, and pin in place. Beginning at the top of one Branch, sew Trunk sections together stopping at top of second Branch. *See (c).* Turn Cactus over. Tuck Branches inside Trunk as best you can. Stitch remaining side of each Branch to Trunk and continue down to bottom each side. Turn Cactus right side out.

Stuff Trunk with straw, hay or shredded foam, making sure to stuff firmly at the point where each Branch joins the Trunk. Insert one slender stick or board up inside Trunk on either side as an armature. Cut piece of canvas slightly larger than the round bottom, and a piece of stiff cardboard slightly smaller. Insert the cardboard first, then handstitch canvas over it, tucking raw edges under as you go.

258

A canvas garden

Ivy

Cactus

C
Trunk
cut 2

A
Branch
cut 2

tuck
tuck
tuck
tuck

B
Branch
cut 2

tuck
tuck
tuck

52

tuck
tuck
tuck
tuck

Philodendron

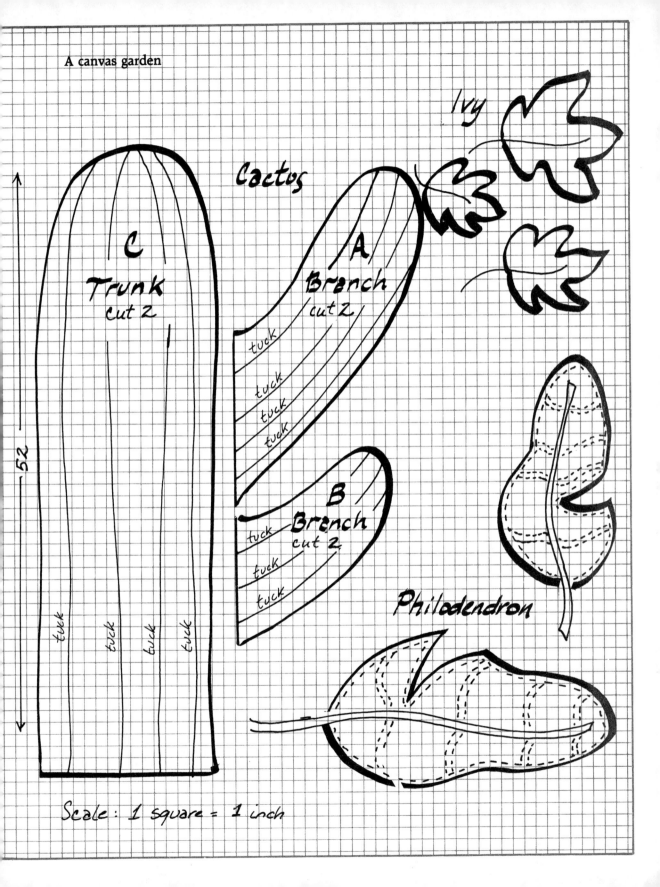

Scale: 1 square = 1 inch

Cloud Cradle

A new baby in the family is always an event, and what better way to get ready than making your own hanging Cradle. Canvas, cheerfully printed and shaped by dowels, makes a wonderful environment for baby's first few months. The carpentry involved in constructing the Cradle is simple even for a beginner, and the silkscreening is a good introduction to this intriguing art. The product, swinging gently to rock baby asleep, should please mother and child alike.

Materials

- For Cradle:

    4 yards natural canvas
    2 yards lining
    polyester fiberfill batting

    Foam rubber, 3 inches deep, 15 by 24 inches
    Buttonhole twist, sky blue

Cloud cradle

- For Silkscreening:

    Silkscreen(s), 18 by 24 inches. More than one screen greatly speeds the process.
    Water-base silkscreen inks: yellow, pink, and sky blue
    Liquid Tusche
    Iron oxide
    Squeegee, 16 inches wide
    Used toothbrush
    Small, medium paintbrushes
    Drawing pencils
    Lots of old newspapers
    Turpentine
    Masking tape
    Lacquer Thinner for cleanup

- For Construction:

    Four ¾-inch wooden dowels, 36 inches long
    Eight wooden finials for ends of dowels
    Drill with ³/₁₆-inch bit
    Narrow rope or mason line, 36 inches
    Contact cement
    Masonite or plywood, 15 by 24 inches
    Macrame cord, chain, or rope to hang cradle

Before Beginning

The Cradle is silkscreened using the wax-resist method. By painting on the screen with a waxy substance you create a positive blockout; wherever the wax is drawn or painted your design will print. The Cloud Cradle needs three successive screenings to achieve the final four-color print. These may be three separate screens, or you can print, clean and reuse one.

Transferring the Design   Enlarge the Cloud Cradle design onto a fairly large sheet of paper; one repeat of the design measures 17 by 18 inches. Now use carbon paper and transfer the outline of design A from your completed sketch to another piece of paper. This design will be the first printing. Place your silkscreen face down onto design A and lightly trace the Sky with a pencil onto the mesh. Turn screen over and paint the entire Sky with Liquid Tusche. Check the screen by holding it up to the light, look carefully for pinholes. Whatever is painted will print blue.

Adhering the Blockout   Work on a table covered with several layers of newspapers. Tilt the silkscreen and pour a ribbon of iron oxide into one short end. This is a blockout solution which resists ink. With a squeegee, make one swipe across the screen with a gentle, even pressure. Keep the squeegee at a 45° angle. This is critical since the iron oxide must block the screen completely. Let the screen dry, and repeat the process.

Dissolving the Wax   When the screen is completely dry, remove the Tusche wax by scrubbing with turpentine and an old toothbrush. Scrub carefully and gently, melting the wax with solvent. Wherever the wax was, ink will pass through the screen. You're now ready to print.

Printing the Canvas Sky   Pad your worktable with a fresh set of clean newspapers. Now spread your canvas out and tape it to hold. Lay your silkscreen with the cloud design onto the canvas and mark the correct positions for each repeat of the design with masking tape. The Cradle design is printed twice on each side and once on each end. The design requires correct registration for the printing, so that the clouds join at the center of each repeat. When you work, don't print each connecting design in succession, let the inks dry first. Then go back and print the middle designs when the first prints are dry. Allow yourself extra yardage to print. You can always use the additional printed fabric for tote bags or pillows.

On a separate sheet of newspaper, make your first strikeoff. A strikeoff is a sample printing which will help you determine how many pulls of ink across the canvas will be needed for a clear print. Place the screen face down on the paper. Pour blue ink across one short edge of the screen in a thick puddle. Weight screen with bricks if necessary. Holding your squeegee perpendicular to the screen pull the ink all the way across. Push the ink back and pull again for a second pass. Use steady, even pressure and a flowing motion. Feel strong yet graceful. Remember that you do not need to bear down to make a clear print.

When you are finished printing, lift the screen straight up off the paper. Do it quickly so you don't smudge the print. If you are satisfied with the inking, move to the canvas and print every other repeat. Let the prints dry and ink the alternate repeats. *See (a), (b), (c).*

Cleaning the Screen

If you are using only one screen, you will have to clean it between printings. Fill a tub with an inch of VERY hot water. Soak the screen. Scrub the screen with an old brush. Scrub and rinse until the screen is completely clear of blockout solution. If any iron oxide adheres still, clean with laquer thinner and a soft brush.

The Rest of the Printing

After the Sky has dried, you are ready to continue printing. Place clean screen over design B, the Stork, and trace design onto the screen. Turn over and paint Stork with Tusche as before. Complete printing process as with Sky. You will notice that the Stork's Beak is printed yellow. This will change to orange when overprinted with pink.

The last screen will be used to print the pink Baby and the Stork's Beak. Place design C under your clean screen and proceed as before. Let the fabric dry.

Assembling the Fabric Sides

When the fabric is absolutely dry, cut apart the design sections. You need two repeats for each side, and one design for each end. Cut linings to match each of these four sections. Lay all Cradle Sides and Ends face up on worktable.

Cut out 16 Ties and 12 Tabs from natural canvas. Zigzag all edges to prevent ravelling. Position Ties on side edges, 3 inches from top and bottom. Pin towards center. Fold Tabs in half and pin raw edges on top of Sides and Ends. Now place lining fabric face down on these pieces and pin around sides and top. It helps if the lining fabric is lightweight so you can see through to the silkscreen design. Stitch lining to canvas around sides and top. Trim excess fabric and turn all pieces right side out. Press.

Fig. (a)

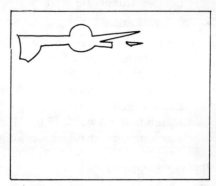

Fig. (b)

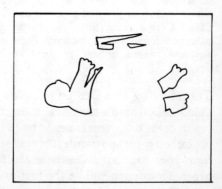

Fig. (c)

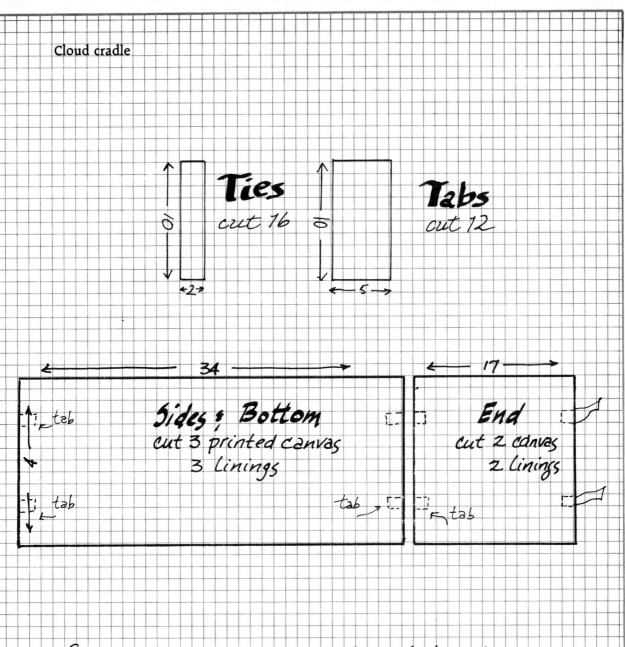

Ties cut 16

Tabs cut 12

Sides & Bottom
cut 3 printed canvas
3 linings

End
cut 2 canvas
2 linings

Scale of pattern:
1 square = 1 inch

Scale of Stork design:
2 squares = 1 inch
One module: 17 × 14 inches

Cloud Cradle

Quilting the Design   Thread the top needles of your machine with buttonhole twist. Cut four pieces of batting, double thickness, just slightly smaller than the dimensions of the Sides and Ends. Insert these between canvas and lining of each section. Smooth away lumps and tuck batting into corners. Pin closed at bottom edge. Quilt with a long stitch around clouds and laundry bag. Check underneath to make sure the lining is smooth. Now change to polyester thread and sew across bottom with a straight stitch.

Making the Box   Cut out natural Bottom piece. Place this on worktable. Lay completed Sides and Ends around it. Stitch Sides to Bottom first, leaving an equal seam allowance at each end of the Bottom. Trim raw Bottom seam closely. Now sew Ends to Bottom, centering each End onto Bottom section evenly. Trim. You now have a box whose sides fold up and tie.

The Mattress   Cut a piece of lining large enough to cover the foam block. Lay lining on worktable and set foam rectangle on top. Wrap mattress as you would a gift, and handstitch closed. Insert masonite into Cradle as floor. Place mattress on top.

Hanging It Up   Cut two of the dowels to 21 inches. Leave the other two 36 inches long. Drill $3/16$-inch holes ½ inch from the end of each dowel. Make sure both holes on each dowel are drilled in the same direction so the cradle will hang neatly.

With contact cement glue round knobs to ends of dowels. Allow to dry. Lightly sand with fine sandpaper. Varnish or stain if desired. Insert dowels through Tabs. Cut four 6-inch lengths of narrow rope and slip through holes at each end of dowels, tying them together securely so that they do not slip inwards with the weight of the child. The End dowels should be on top. Hang cradle with macrame cords, chain, or rope.

Suggested Reading

Design Inspiration

BLAIR, Margot Carter and RYAN, Cathleen, *Banners and Flags: How to Sew a Celebration*, N.Y.: Harcourt, Brace, Jovanovich, 1977.

BOAS, Franz, *Primitive Art*, N.Y.: Dover, 1955.

"California Design", *California Design 1969, 1971, 1974, 1976*, Pasadena: California Design Publication.

CONSTANTINE, Mildred and LARSEN, Jack Lenor, *Beyond Craft: The Art Fabric*, New York: Van Nostrand Reinhold, 1973.

FRANCK, Frederick, *The Zen of Seeing*, New York: Random House, 1973.

HANSEN, H. J., *European Folk Art*, New York: McGraw-Hill Co., 1968.

LICHTEN, Frances, *Folk Art of Rural Pennsylvania*, New York: Charles Scribner's Sons, 1946.

MEILACH, Dona Z., *Creating Art From Fibers and Fabrics*, Chicago: Henry Regnery, 1972.

Museum of Contemporary Crafts, "Fabric Collage," New York: 1965; "Sewn, Stitched and Stuffed," New York, 1973—"Homage to the Bag," New York, 1975. (catalogs)

PLATH, Iona, *Decorative Arts of Sweden*, New York: Dover, 1966.

ROSSBACH, Ed, *Baskets as Textile Art*, New York: Van Nostrand Reinhold Co., 1973.

RICHARDS, M. C., *Centering*, New York: Wesleyan, 1964.

SIEBER, Roy, *African Textiles and Decorative Arts*, New York: The Museum of Modern Art, 1972.

Quilting, Applique

LAURY, Jean Ray, *Quilts and Coverlets*, New York: Van Nostrand Reinhold, 1970.

KEELER, Clyde E., *Cuna Indian Art*, New York: Exposition Press, 1969.

KREVITSKY, Nik, *Stitchery: Art and Craft*, New York: Reinhold Publishing Corp., 1967.

LAURY, Jean Ray, *Applique Stitchery*, New York: Van Nostrand Reinhold, 1966.

LILLOW, Ira, *Introducing Machine Embroidery*, New York: Watson-Guptill Publications, 1967.

McCall's Needlework and Crafts, *Needle-Art: Machine Embroidery*, New York; McCall Pattern Company, 1977.

SAFFORD, Carleton L., and BISHOP, Robert, *America's Quilts and Coverlets*, New York: E. P. Dutton & Co., Inc., 1972.

STROBL-WOHLSCHLAGER, Ilse, *Fun with Applique and Patchwork*, New York: Watson-Guptill Publications, 1969.

Surface Embellishment, Block Printing, Silkscreen

BIEGELEISEN, J. I., *The Complete Book of Silkscreen Production*, New York: Dover Publications.

FOBEL, Jim and BOLEACH, Jim, *The Stencil Book*, New York: Holt, Reinhart and Winston, 1976.

GRISWOLD, Lester and Kathleen, *The New Handicraft Processes and Projects*, New York: Van Nostrand Reinhold.

ROTHENSTIEN, Michael, *Linocuts and Woodcuts: A Complete Block Printing Handbook*, Watson-Guptill Publications, 1963.

TORBET, Laura, *How to do Everything with Markers*, New York: The Bobbs-Merrill Company, Inc. 1976.

VALENTINO, Richard and MUFSON, Phyllis, *Fabric Printing: Screen Method*, San Francisco: Bay Books, 1975.

Fabric Sculpture, Soft Objects

• HALL, Carolyn Vosburg, *Stitched and Stuffed Art*, New York: Doubleday & Company, Inc., 1974.

KINSER, Charleen, *Sewing Sculpture*, New York: M. Evans & Co., Inc. 1977.

LAURY, Jean Ray, *Doll Making*, New York: Van Nostrand Reinhold Publications, 1970.

LOCKWOOD, Gillian, *Making Soft Toys*, New York: Watson-Guptill Publications, 1976.

SOMMER, Elyse and Mike, *A New Look at Crochet*, New York: Crown, 1975.

SWIRLES, Frank Jr., *Handbook of Basic Fabrics*, Los Angeles: Swirles & Co., 1962.

Canvas Suppliers

CANADA

NORWOOD TENT AND AWNING CO. LTD.
1235 Sargent Ave.
Winnipeg, Manitoba Canada R3E 0G2
(204) 774-2444

PERC W. BRUSEY & SONS LTD.
497 Hughson St., N.
Hamilton, Ontario, L8L 4N8
(416) 522-5625

ALABAMA

CANVAS PRODUCTS CO., INC.
2601 Halls Mill Rd.
Mobile 36606
(205) 471-5308

ARIZONA

PHOENIX TENT & AWNING CO. INC.
2533 N. 16th St.
Phoenix 85006
(602) 254-4141

CALIFORNIA

CANVAS SPECIALTY
7344 E. Bandini Blvd.
Los Angeles 90040
(213) 723-8311

CANVAS WORKS
2113 National
Costa Mesa 92626

RAE'S INTERIORS
186-1 Sunnyoaks Ave.
Campbell 95008
(408) 378-7737

SULLIVAN CO.
245 S. Van Ness
San Francisco 94103
(415) 861-4572

TENT CITY SURPLUS CANVAS HOUSE
6722 N. Blackstone
Fresno 93710
(209) 439-1345

VAN NUYS AWNING CO., INC.
5661 Sepulveda
Van Nuys 91401
(213) 782-8607

COLORADO

OUT WEST AWNING CO.
1405 S. 8th St.
Colorado Springs 80906
(303) 632-0303

CONNECTICUT

ECONOMY CANVAS CO.
390 Prospect St.
East Hartford 06108
(203) 289-5281

EDDY AWNING & DECORATING CO.
231 Arch St.
New Britain 06051
(203) 229-0279

O'NEILL SAILMAKERS
193 Penn Ave.
Niantic 06357
(203) 739-5993

STATE AWNING CO.
100 Cedar St.
Hartford 06106
(203) 246-2575

FLORIDA

DOYLE'S UPHOLSTERY & CANVAS INC.
Hwy. 441 (P.O. Box 458)
Fruitland Park 32731
(904) 787-2460

MARKHAM CO., INC.
1184 Alden Rd.
Orlando 32802
(305) 898-8981

SCHMITT AWNING CO.
2612 S. Federal Hwy.
Fort Lauderdale 33316
(305) 522-6512

SUNMASTER AWNING & SHADE
3860 N. Trail
Naples 33940
(813) 261-3581

GEORGIA

BAILIE'S CANVAS SPECIALTIES
2344 Walden Dr.
Augusta 30904
(404) 733-7752

COASTAL CANVAS PRODUCTS CO. INC.
3 North Fahm St.
Savannah 31402
(912) 236-2416

MACON TENT & AWNING CO.
230 South St.Macon 31202
(912) 743-2684

IDAHO

KETCHUM CANVAS
No. 6 Trail Creek Village
Ketchum 83340
(208) 726-3555

ILLINOIS

CHESTERFIELD WINDOW SHOP
16999 Van Dam Road
South Holland 60473
(312) 596-4434

DANVILLE TENT & AWNING CO.
1706 Warrington Ave.
Danville 61832
(217) 443-0800

FOXLAKE CANVAS SHOP
119 S. Rt. 12
Foxlake 60020
(312) 587-7000

GALESBURG CANVAS PRODUCTS, INC.
187 W. Losey St.
Galesburg 61401
(309) 343-9384

INDIANA

LAFAYETTE TENT & AWNING CO., INC.
125 S. 5th St.
Lafayette 47901
(317) 742-4277

IOWA

CLEMENS CANVAS & MANUFACTURING
839 2nd Ave. SW
Cedar Rapids 52404
(319) 363-0296

CEDAR RAPIDS TENT & AWNING CO.
533-1st St. SW
Cedar Rapids 52404
(319) 366-7107

MASON CITY TENT & AWNING CO.
406-08 S. Federal Ave.
Mason City 50401
(515) 423-7745

LOUISIANA

C. BEL FOR AWNINGS
3139 Tchoupitoulas St.
New Orleans 70115
(504) 891-3768

MARYLAND

BETHESDA SHADE & AWNING SHOP, INC.
4922 Del Ray Ave.
Bethesda 20014
(301) 656-6161

CITY AWNING CO.
1311 West St.
Annapolis 21401
(301) 263-4461

NINER AWNING CO.
427 E. Franklin St.
Hagerstown 21740
(301) 739-7534

MASSACHUSETTS

PELLETIER HOME DECORATORS
65 Congress St.
Salem 01970
(617) 745-4710

WORCESTER AWNING CO., INC.
456 Park Ave.
Worcester 01610
(617) 755-8675

MICHIGAN

BATTLE CREEK TENT & AWNING CO.
128 E. Michigan Ave.
Battle Creek 49017
(616) 964-1824

BENTON HARBOR AWNING & TENT CO.
2275 M-139
Benton Harbor 49022
(616) 925-2187

MARYGROVE AWNING CO.
26000 W. 8 Mile
Southfield 48034
(313) 353-8850

MINNESOTA

DULUTH TENT & AWNING CO.
1610 W. Superior St.
Duluth 55806
(218) 722-3898

HARRIS WAREHOUSE & CANVAS SALES
501-30th Ave. SE
Minneapolis 55414
(612) 331-1829

HOIGAARD'S
3550 S. Hwy. 100
Minneapolis 55416
(612) 929-1351

KAISER MANUFACTURING CO.
9445 Brookview Rd.
Lake Elmo 55042
(612) 739-7411

MANKATO TENT & AWNING CO.
1021 Range St.
Mankato 56001

MISSOURI

COGLIZER TENT & AWNING CO.
106 Joplin (P.O. Box 165)
Joplin 64801
(417) 623-4444

SPECIALTY AWNING & CANVAS
2518 Woodson Rd.
St. Louis 63114
(314) 429-4474

WELHENER AWNING CO.
505 W. Commercial
Springfield 65803
(417) 862-3763

MONTANA

GREAT FALLS TENT & AWNING
615-611 8 Ave. N.
Great Falls 59401
(406) 453-6688

RELIABLE TENT & AWNING
116 N. 30th St.
Billings 59101
(406) 252-4689

NEW JERSEY

CALDWELL AWNING & SHADE CO.
34 Passaic Ave.
Fairfield 07006
(201) 227-1471

LAGGREN'S INC.
1414 South Ave.
Plainfield 07062
(201) 756-1948

G. E. MARSHALL INC.
810-812 S. Broad St.
Trenton 08611
(609) 392-2464

SKIPPER CRAFT INC.
666 Momtoloking Rd.
Brick Town 08723
(201) 477-2466

ED WEISS & SONS CANVAS PRODUCTS
516 Ship Ave.
Beachwood 08722
(201) 349-8708

NEW YORK

ARMOR CANVAS PRODUCTS
2194 Flatbush Ave.
Brooklyn 11234
(212) 859-1271

CANVAS WORLD
Building Q Mohawk Park
Alplaus 12008
(518) 399-2884

GENEVA AWNING & TENT WORKS INC.
96 Lewis St.
Geneva 14456
(315) 789-3151

MACMILLAN INDUSTRIES, INC.
58 Renwick St., (P.O. Box 889)
Newburgh 12550
(914) 565-3975

WEDEKIND SAIL & CANVAS CO.
101 Surf Ave.-E. Broadway
Port Jefferson 11777
(516) 928-6840

NORTH CAROLINA

CLARK ART SHOP, INC.
300 Glenwood Ave.
Raleigh 27603
(919) 832-8319

OHIO

QUEEN CITY AWNING & TENT CO.
318 E. Eighth St.
Cincinnati 45202
(513) 241-0437

ROLOSON TENT & AWNING CO.
302 S. Union St.
Lima 45801
(419) 223-1831

SOUTH AKRON AWNING CO.
763 Kenmore Blvd.
Akron 44314
(216) 762-7611

OREGON

BECKEL CANVAS PRODUCTS
7924 SE Stark
Portland 97215
(503) 252-0946

PENNSYLVANIA

GUY E. ALLEN & SONS
1139 W. 26th St.
Erie 16508
(814) 459-6388

AWNINGS BY SHUSTER
P.O. Box 570
Vandergrift 15690
(412) 567-5689

BARNETT CANVAS GOODS & BAG CO., INC.
131 Arch St.
Philadelphia 19106
(215) 627-2160

C. B. DOMBACH & SON
252 N. Prince St.
Lancaster 17603
(717) 392-0578

H. A. HARPER SONS
2800 Chichester Ave.
Boothwyn 19061
(215) 485-4776

O. K. MCCLOY AWNINGS INC.
2029 Noble St.
Pittsburgh 15235
(412) 271-4044

WEAVER CANVAS PRODUCTS
Rd. No. 2 Route 65
Beaver Falls 15010
(412) 843-8561

SOUTH CAROLINA

CARTER CANVAS CO.
1245R Newberry Ave. (P.O. Box 321)
Irmo 29063
(803) 781-2289

GREENVILLE AWNING CO.
317 Old Laurens Rd.
Mauldin 29662
(803) 288-0063

TENNESSEE

MAHAFFEY TENT CO., INC.
5625 E. Shelby Dr.
Memphis 38118
(901) 363-6511

269

MEMPHIS DELTA TENT & AWNING CO.
296 East St.
Memphis 38126
(901) 522-1238

TEXAS

AMERICAN CAMPING
5440 Willruth (P.O. Box 12564)
El Paso 79912
(915) 757-1543

AVALON CANVAS & UPHOLSTERY, INC.
4617 N. Shepherd
North of the 610 Loop
Houston 77018
(713) 697-5040 or 697-0156

CAPCO MANUFACTURING CO.
111 S. Glenwood
Tyler 75702
(214) 592-2712

CBF INDUSTRIES, INC.
10414 Harry Hines Blvd. (P.O. Box 20204)
Dallas 75220
(214) 358-3281

CLANTON'S QUALITY AWNING CO.
3111 N. Fitzhugh
Dallas 75204
(214) 521-0424

W. K. HILL AWNING & TENT CO.
1111 W. Drew St.
Houston 77006
(713) 526-1347

SOUTHWEST CANVAS MANUFACTURING CO.
37th St. & Quirt Ave.
Lubbock 79408
(806) 747-0201

UTAH

SUGAR HOUSE AWNING & CANVAS
2005 South 1100 E.
Salt Lake City 84106
(801) 486-7237

VIRGINIA

CUSTOM CRAFT TOP CO., INC.
123 Battlefield Blvd., S.
Chesapeake 23320
(804) 547-2628

SUNNYSIDE AWNING & TENT CO., INC.
621 First St., S.W. (P.O. Box 2602)
Roanoke 24010
(703) 344-7726

WASHINGTON

CAMP LEWIS TENT & AWNING CO.
1111 First Ave.
Seattle 98101
(206) 623-3411

SEATTLE TENT & FABRIC
1900 N. Northlake Way
Seattle 98103
(206) 632-6022

WISCONSIN

BARABOO TENT & AWNING
123 Second St. (P.O. Box 57)
Baraboo 53913
(608) 356-8303

DOW CANVAS PRODUCTS
2705 Calumet Ave.
Manitowoc 54220
(414) 682-7796

FOND DU LAC TENT & AWNING CO.
321 West Scott St.
Fond du Lac 54935
(414) 921-7321

IGL-WISCONSIN AWNING, TENT & TRAILER CO., INC.
8768 W. Fond du Lac Ave.
Milwaukee 53225
(414) 463-7640

OSHKOSH TENT & AWNING CO., INC.
135 High Ave.
Oshkosh 54902
(414) 235-3170

WYOMING

KISTLER TENT & AWNING
424 South Oak (Box 671)
Casper 82602
(307) 237-3020

SUSAN DWORSKI
lives in Malibu,
California with
her husband and
two children.